THE
SORTI
MACHINE

Educational Policy, Planning, and Theory
SERIES EDITOR: Don Adams, *University of Pittsburgh*

Contemporary Educational Theory
  Robert E. Mason

Educational Patterns and Cultural Configurations:
  The Anthropology of Education
  Joan I. Roberts and Sherrie K. Akinsanya

Education as Cultural Imperialism
  Martin Carnoy

Education in National Politics
  Norman C. Thomas

Schooling in a Corporate Society:
  The Political Economy of Education in America
  Martin Carnoy

Schooling in the Cultural Context:
  Anthropological Studies of Education
  Joan I. Roberts and Sherrie K. Akinsanya

Two Hundred Years of American Educational Thought
  Henry J. Perkinson

THE SORTING MACHINE

NATIONAL EDUCATIONAL POLICY SINCE 1945

JOEL SPRING
Case Western Reserve University

LONGMAN
New York and London

THE SORTING MACHINE
National Educational Policy Since 1945

Longman Inc., New York
Associated companies, branches, and representatives
throughout the world.

Manufactured in the United States of America

Printing: 10 9 8 7 6 5 4
Year: 8 7 6 5 4 3

Library of Congress Cataloging in Publication Data

Spring, Joel H
The sorting machine.

(Educational policy, planning, and theory)
Includes bibliographical references and index.
1. Education—United States—History.
2. Education and state—United States. I. Title.
LA216.S67   379.73   75–53801

ISBN 0-582-28127-X

PREFACE

This book grew out of my interest in the relationship between American education and American foreign policy in the years that followed World War II. Originally I thought the use of educational institutions and programs during the cold war added a new dimension to the social uses of schooling in American society. As my research progressed, I began to realize that foreign policy and education could not be isolated from more general economic and social trends and that American foreign policy had a significant impact on educational development within the United States. This led to a closer look at the manpower discussions, military-training debates, and national school controversies in the early 1950s. From these events I began to understand more clearly the economic and social forces that produced the National Defense Education Act and the new mathematics and science curriculums of the latter part of the decade. All these events seemed to serve the needs of a foreign policy designed to contain communism and protect the interests of American corporate expansion into foreign markets.

The one outstanding contradiction to these trends during the 1950s was the civil rights movement with its concern about inequality in schooling and its potential for organizing the poor and creating social-class conflict. I wanted to understand how the potential revolutionary nature of this movement was contained. I found this in a theory of poverty which denied class conflict and used education as an instrument for maintaining social order. This theory of poverty found expression in the Economic Opportunity Act and Elementary and Secondary Education Act of the 1960s. This led to an interest in discussions about career education and equality of opportunity during the Nixon administration and how they fit into the general trends of educational development since World War II.

I would like to thank my colleagues Eugene Bartoo, Richard Derr, and Gerald Jorgenson in the Department of Education at Case Western Reserve University for their suggestions and careful reading of parts of this manuscript. I would also like to thank Deanna Spring for major editorial work on the manuscript and important suggestions about its contents. Martha Hallberg did an excellent job of proofreading and typing the final manuscript.

CONTENTS

1 The National Battle of the Schools   *1*

2 The Channeling of Manpower in
  a Democratic Society   *52*

3 The Development of
  a National Curriculum   *93*

4 The Civil Rights Movement   *140*

5 The War on Poverty   *186*

6 Career Education and Equality
  of Educational Opportunity   *230*

7 Conclusion   *259*

  Notes   *267*

  Index   *301*

THE
SORTING
MACHINE

THE NATIONAL
BATTLE OF
THE SCHOOLS

1 Since 1945, the federal government of the United States has played an increasing role in the conduct and policies of educational institutions. Fears caused by the cold war with the Soviet Union and the demands of the civil rights movement have resulted in direct federal involvement in defining educational priorities and in regulating American schools. The government's major interest in schooling during this period has been in terms of meeting national objectives in the areas of foreign policy and social and economic development; consequently, federal intervention in education has been directed toward achieving specific purposes in terms of national policy.

The basic argument of this book is that federal involvement in education since the end of World War II has reinforced one specific tradition in American education. American public schooling expanded in the nineteenth century for a variety of social and political reasons: as a means of maintaining a political community through the education of a democratic citizen, as a way to increase morality and reduce crime, as a method of Americanizing immigrant populations and preparing the population as a whole for an industrial society.[1] A single volume would be hard pressed to explore all the different shades of meaning and purposes for supporting public schooling in the last century. What is important to this volume is one argument for public schooling that developed in the early part of the twentieth century: public education can increase the efficiency of industrial society by the proper selection and channeling of national manpower resources. This argument supported the rise of vocational guidance, the grouping of students according to ability, the separation of students in high school into different academic programs according to future occupations, and the importance of intelligence testing.[2] This argument gave schools the responsibility for determining student abilities and interests and channeling students through an educational program that would lead them to a specific social slot in the national labor force.

It was this argument that federal involvement in education after 1945 emphasized and made the central feature of American schooling. This was a direct result of national concern about meeting manpower needs in the cold war and the demands of the civil rights movement. It included a concern about the discovery of talented youth in the 1950s and special programs for disadvantaged children in the 1960s. This tradition was swept up in the rhetoric of equality of opportunity in the 1960s, and emerged in the form of career education in the 1970s.

Federal educational policy is the result of complex interactions between a variety of individuals and social forces in and out of government and education. The story of this development begins with the national debate about schooling that occurred in the tense atmosphere of the cold war. From there it moves through the manpower channeling policies of the federal government in the 1950s, the federal influence on the development of national school curriculums, the civil rights movement and the War on Poverty of the 1960s, and the arguments for equality of educational opportunity in the 1960s and '70s.

Public Criticism of the Schools

In 1951 the executive secretary of the National Education Association's National Commission for the Defense of Democracy through Education reported in a slightly hysterical tone that the number of "attacks" upon public schooling had increased rapidly since the closing days of World War II. According to their survey, the pace of "attack" was so swift that more than twice as many attacks occurred in the three-year period since 1948 as in the period before 1948. The phraseology and reaction of educators often made them appear as warriors doing battle with an enemy that was storming the walls of the public schools. Words like *attack, counterattack,* and *siege* were hurled around to describe the plight of the professional educator. The executive secretary of the National Commission for the Defense of Democracy through Education, reporting the increasing criticism of the schools, exemplified the battle mentality. He stressed that the "attacking groups are not as dangerous as they seem .... but we all need to be alarmed as were the Minute Men by Paul Revere in 1775." He went on to call the educational troops together with this plea: "If, like the Minute Men, we are ready to carry out individual responsibilities of intelligent group planning, professional unity, organized action, and friendly contact with our allies, we will be as successful in defending our cause as were the gallant men at Concord." [3]

Criticism of the public schools came from many sectors of American life. One group was a natural product of a society that saw itself in a life-and-death struggle with the Soviet Union and communism. With national leaders wandering throughout the country warning of communist subversion and conspiracy, the dangers of an imminent nuclear war, and the need for planned national defense and security, citizens became gripped by a paranoiac reaction that saw left-wing subversives hiding behind every door. The public schools seemed like a perfect target for communist subversion to win "the hearts and minds" of the American people and erode the foundations of democracy. During the late 1940s and into the 1960s citizen's groups sprang up around the country to get communism and communists out of the schools. These groups found anti-American material lurking on school library shelves and in textbooks. Citizen vigilante groups stormed school board meetings to demand that the schools purge themselves of material that smacked of un-Americanism and socialist and communist subversion. Added to the complaints of these groups was a belief that the school curriculum was too soft and needed to emphasize basic skills and academic training. At times, criticism of the public school curriculum as it had evolved in the twentieth century almost reached the point of claiming that it was the product of a communist plot.

Another group of critics emerged from the university world. They saw antiintellectualism in American life as their enemy. To a large extent their fears originated from the right-wing's hysteria about subversion. The 1950s saw a steadily increasing concern among the academic community about the growing antiintellectual temper of American society. During the 1930s and early 1940s the academic community had experienced a long honeymoon of respect and access to centers of power. Academics were frequently called to Washington in the 1930s to be consulted as part of President Roosevelt's brain trust; during World War II, their services were often engaged in the war effort. But after the war the intellectuals felt they were losing power and respect. This feeling was chronicled by one American historian, Richard Hofstadter, in a book that was very much a product of the period and bore the descriptive title *Anti-Intellectualism in American Life.*

Hofstadter argued that during the 1950s the term antiintellectualism, a term heard only rarely before, became a familiar part of the national vocabulary. In part, he argued, this was the result of right-wing attacks that saw the critical mind of the intellectual as subverting American ideals and traditions. This thinking was exemplified by Senator Joseph McCarthy in the early 1950s with his attacks on subversion in government and in the universities. Antiintellectualism rose to a national issue during the presidential elections of 1952, which pitted the intellectual Adlai Stevenson against the western-novel-reading Dwight D. Eisenhower. In Hofstadter's words, Adlai Stevenson was "a politician of uncommon mind and style, whose appeal to intellectuals overshadowed anything in recent history." The election contest was pictured as one between the "eggheads" and the people of common sense. When Stevenson lost in 1952, *Time* magazine claimed that it disclosed "an alarming fact long suspected: there is a wide and unhealthy gap between the American intellectuals and the people." Hofstadter went on to document antiintellectualism in the 1950s with such facts as these: the growth of the use of "egghead" as an invidious term; President Eisenhower defining an intellectual in a public speech as "a man who takes more words than are necessary to tell more than he knows"; the Eisenhower-appointed ambassador to Ceylon not knowing the name of the prime minister of Ceylon and being unable to pronounce the name of the prime minister of India; and the heated right-wing rhetoric of the 1950s that referred to Harvard professors as "twisted thinking intellectuals" who, while "burdened with Phi Beta Kappa keys," were not "equally loaded with honesty and common sense." [4]

One of the root causes of antiintellectualism, so university people including Hofstadter believed, was the American public school. The schools, it was argued, bred a disrespect for the life of the mind by spoon-feeding a curriculum that consisted of intellectual pablum. Both right-wing communist hunters and status-seeking academicians agreed that a major problem with the schools was the "softness" of the curriculum and lack of academic training. But both groups had different goals and different enemies. Right-wingers wanted more disciplined and academically oriented schools to train loyal and patriotic Americans who would fight communism. Academics wanted a disciplined and academically oriented school to produce a respect for the role of the intellectual. Right-wing groups defined communists, left-wing subversives, and intellectuals as their enemies. Academics defined as their enemy the professional educator.

The picture of the professional educator as enemy of American life was born amid the school controversies of the 1950s. A whole group of critics emerged; along with the academics, they linked the major problems of schooling to the professional educator, who controlled the teacher-training institutions, the curriculum, and the school bureaucracy. As school controversies raged into the 1960s and '70s, this argument would continue —with racism now added to the charges. What occurred during the 1950s was an apparent awakening to the fact that accompanying the expansion of public schooling in the United States was an increasing growth of professional means of governing and controlling public education. The vast number of schools, and the requirements of teacher training and curriculum development, had led to the development of a large corps of educational experts who exercised considerable influence over public schooling. When academics wanted to know why education was in such a sorry condition, it was easy to point to the professional educator as the enemy. After all, this was the group responsible for the introduction of new curriculums and materials. When critics of the school tried to change schooling, they found themselves running head-on into professional control and school bureaucracy. The critics began to argue that meaningful local control of the schools no longer existed and that it had been replaced by a mindless group of professionals.

In addition to the groups fighting communists, antiintellectualism, and professional educators were those who wanted the schools to win the manpower race with the Soviet Union. This group combined all the elements of the other critics with a hysterical fear that the Soviet Union would destroy the United States by educating more engineers and scientists than we did. Although not accepting the right-wing concern of subversion, they maintained a sense of fear about communism by arguing that the American way of life could be preserved only by increasing the academic training in our public schools and emphasizing science and mathematics.

The Anticommunist Crusade

The incident that gave right-wing attacks on the school a national press, and must have left other school administrators in a state of apprehension, was the forced resignation in 1950 of Superintendent Willard

Goslin of Pasadena, California. Goslin was a national figure in professional educational circles. In 1948, the same year he accepted the superintendent's position in Pasadena, he was installed as president of the American Association of School Administrators. School administrators around the country watched with unhappy feelings while the president of their organization was dragged through the wringer of an anticommunist crusade to save the school from subversion. The school controversy in Pasadena was also interesting because it followed a pattern that began to occur in other communities: groups formed around some important local issue and eventually expanded their concerns to the general educational philosophy of the school.[5]

In Pasadena the issue that sparked the school crusade was a request by Superintendent Goslin for an increase in local taxes to support the schools. The year the tax proposal was made, 1949, a local School Development Council had been formed. It set as its first goal the defeat of two socialists running for the school board. When the tax issue was raised, the council wanted to know exactly how much the schools were spending and for what purposes. This launched a crusade against increased taxes and provided a community forum for discussion of educational policies. The council's leadership began to base their attacks on the schools on information and ideas supplied in pamphlets issued by the National Council for American Education headed by Allen Zoll.

The National Council for American Education was one of many national organizations that focused attention after World War II on subversion in the public schools. Other organizations of this type included the American Coalition of Patriotic Societies, the American Council of Christian Laymen, the Anti-Communist League of America, the California Anti-Communist League, the Christian Nationalist Crusade, Defenders of

American Education, the Daughters of the American Revolution, and the Sons of the American Revolution.[6] Allen Zoll organized the National Council for American Education in 1948, the same year Goslin arrived in Pasadena, after a varied career that had brought him into contact with other early right-wing crusaders including Gerald L. K. Smith and Father Coughlin. Zoll reportedly began his crusade with a "Michigan statement" that "we form hell-raising groups to find out what is being taught in the schools, and then we raise hell about it"[7] Pasadena, of course, was not the only community that was influenced by Zoll's pamphlets. In 1951 the *Saturday Review of Literature* devoted a large section of its education issue to school controversies around the country. In Denver, Colorado, Zoll's pamphlets, including one titled *The Commies Are After Your Kids,* were said to have provided a good deal of ammunition for local citizen groups. In Englewood, New Jersey, and Port Washington, New York, there were reports of significant influences from Zoll's writings.[8] In Pasadena the Zoll pamphlet that attracted interest was *Progressive Education Increases Juvenile Delinquency,* which stated that "so-called progressive education, shot through as it is with the blight of Pragmatism, has had a very deleterious effect upon the original character of American education."[9]

Unfortunately for Superintendent Goslin, when local groups began to direct their attention to the issue of progressive education, they found that Goslin had invited one of the more famous progressive educators, William Heard Kilpatrick, to a teacher-training workshop. The fact that Pasadena teachers had come into contact with Kilpatrick led the School Development Council to ask the Board of Education bluntly if the program was "part of a campaign to 'sell' our children on the collapse of our way of life and substitution of collectivism."[10] Concern about progressive education was not isolated to Pasadena but ran through school battles and writings about education during this period. Academics concerned about antiintellectualism attacked progressive education because it seemed to weaken the intellectual content of the curriculum. Rightwing groups attacked progressive education because it appeared antithetical to the American way of life.

What is important to realize about right-wing concern about progressive education is that it represented a widening gap between what some people thought was the ideology of America and the ideology that had transformed the public schools in the twentieth century. Most of the attacking right-wing groups seemed to share a faith that the American way of life depended on free marketplace capitalism where "rugged" individualists competed for economic gain. In the case of Pasadena, many members of the School Development Council were small businessmen and professionals who operated in an economic world that seemed to be defined in those terms. On the other hand, the American public school since the beginning of the twentieth century had organized around the principle that traditional free marketplace individualism was a thing of the past and that a modern urban industrial world depended not on economic individualism but on economic cooperation. This ideology did not imply socialism or communism but a form of cooperative democratic social organization. This ideology led to an emphasis on group activity and social development in the schools. The twentieth century had seen an expansion of these activities and goals in the form of group projects in the classroom, school clubs, sports, assemblies, student government, and other extracurricular activities. By World War II, American public schools had geared themselves to produce through school socialization a cooperative democratic character.[11]

In the late 1940s the term progressive education had often been associated with these developments. Whether in fact those educators who called themselves progressive were responsible for these developments is debatable.[12] What is important in terms of postwar developments is that a group of educators who called themselves progressives launched during the depression years a campaign to bring about radical transformation of the economic system through the public schools. These educators were centered around Teachers College at Columbia University and had among their leaders George Counts and William Heard Kilpatrick. George Counts launched the campaign in 1932 with a speech titled "Dare Progressive Education Be Progressive?" Counts argued in terms of the ideology that had shaped the schools in the early part of the twentieth century, that competition and rugged individualism had been outmoded by science and technology. What Counts did was to take this argument to its next logical step. He declared that what the United States needed was a planned socialized economy. This was to be achieved through indoctrination, and educators should accept that fact and use it for the reconstruction of society. This group of progressive educators eventually issued a magazine, the *Social Frontier*, which became a focus of educational radicalism during the 1930s.[13]

Several effects of the radical progressive education campaign of the 1930s served to link progressive education, in the minds of many people, with an economic radicalism that smacked of socialism and communism and to create a distrust of the educational activities at Columbia's Teachers College. The campaign also tended to link anything new in the schools with the term progressive education, and, consequently, with some form of economic radicalism. For example, in Denver in the late 1940s, progressive education became a blanket term to cover anything in the schools that was not re-

lated to the teaching of basic academic subjects. Under
the term progressive education were cited instances of
teaching hypnotism and contract bridge.[14] In Pasadena
the chairman of the School Development Council
charged that public school teaching was "leading to
Socialism, and there isn't much difference between Socialism and Communism." He went on to complain of
the teaching of sex education to mixed classes because
that led to free love and free love led to communism.[15]

The attack on progressive education therefore carried
with it several related and important elements. First, it
was argued that all teaching in the curriculum not related to the teaching of the basic disciplines should be
eliminated, as a means of combating communism and
socialism. This argument created the feeling that
teaching these basic skills was linked to the promotion
of American ideals and Americanism. An emphasis on
basic skills would return the schools to their original
state, before the invasion of un-American ideas. Second,
it was argued that eliminating "extras" from the curriculum would mean a sizable reduction in school bud-
gets and a lowering of local taxes. The battle against
progressive education and the concentration on basic
skills now supported Americanism and saved money at
the same time.

While un-Americanism was being discovered in the
curriculum, it was also being found in the written materials of the school. The local citizen's group in Pasadena organized an ideological investigation into written
materials. To Goslin's amazement, the school system
was charged with promoting un-American ideas in their
handbook "Audio-Visual Education" because of a passing reference to Rome as a democracy and the supposed
use of "The Star-Spangled Banner" as a warmongering
song.[16] The battle over written material in Pasadena
was mild compared to the battle of the books that began
in Scarsdale, New York, in 1948.

The problems in Scarsdale began about the same time that Goslin became superintendent in Pasadena. Scarsdale was essentially a dormitory suburb for New York executives. Its per capita income was one of the highest in the country, and it claimed the highest proportion of *Who's Who* listings of any town in the United States. The campaign against communism in Scarsdale's schools was begun by a Manhattan broker who had spent four years studying communist-front organizations in America. In 1948, after a study of the school library, he found ten books by a supposed communist named Howard Fast and demanded before the school board that they be removed. He was later joined in his fight by a local minister and a civil engineer who, after buying a 25-cent paperback edition of Howard Fast's biography of Tom Paine, discovered a number of what they thought were obscene passages in the book. The battle was now against both sex and communism in the schools. As the battle progressed, Scarsdale experienced, as would other school systems in the country, a growing attendance and turmoil at school board meetings. During the early stages of the campaign, attendance rose to 250; it later jumped to 1400 during school board elections. After the issue was joined by the battle of the books, voting in school board elections jumped from 58 to 1090. Added to the turmoil were constant petitions and counter petitions circulating throughout the community supporting either retention of the books or their banning. Eventually the fires of controversy in Scarsdale were given added fuel when an executive for Metropolitan Life Insurance demanded that the school board examine its textbooks and teachers for possible communist infiltration.[17]

The issue of possible communist infiltration of the textbook industry was at this time becoming a national concern. In 1949 Lucille Cardin Crain began issuing a quarterly newsletter, the *Educational Reviewer,* which had as its goal the weeding out of subversive material from public school textbooks. Her first target was a popular high school text, *American Government* by Frank Abbott Magruder. She claimed that Magruder's view of democracy led "straight from Rousseau, through Marx, to totalitarianism" and that the book gave a very favorable view of the workings of the government in the Soviet Union. Convinced that the text was designed to undermine the free enterprise system, she gave wide circulation to her critique of the book. Her arguments eventually reached the ears of the national radio commentator Fulton Lewis, Jr., who used portions of Crain's analysis on a coast-to-coast broadcast and added a scare statement, "That's the book that has been in use in high schools all over the nation, possibly by your youngster." Crain's critique of the book coupled with the support of Fulton Lewis, Jr., led to outraged parents attacking the text in Englewood, New Jersey; Port Washington, Long Island; and Washington, D. C.; and to its eventual banning in Richland, Washington; Houston, Texas; Little Rock, Arkansas; Lafayette, Indiana; and the entire state of Georgia. The *Educational Reviewer* received additional national support when the Chicago *Sunday Tribune* in 1950 urged every school trustee and administrator to subscribe to the newsletter.[18]

The work of the *Educational Reviewer* was joined by other groups including Allen Zoll's National Council for American Education, the Daughters of the American Revolution, the Sons of the American Revolution, and the Guardians of American Education in the publication of lists of subversive books and texts. Throughout the country during the 1950s and '60s, community members armed with one of these lists, would demand that certain subversive books be removed from library shelves and from the curriculum of the school. There were even suggestions that textbook writers be required to take a loyalty oath. All these actions alarmed the textbook industry. In 1953 an official statement of the American Textbook Publishers Institute warned against a loyalty oath for authors because it would lower the quality of textbook authorship and material. The institute claimed that the highly individualistic and competitive system in the textbook industry provided adequate safeguards against "the deliberate introduction of harmful or subversive material." To curb local attacks, they recommended that states establish public agencies to monitor complaints about textbooks.[19]

The school battles over subversion in books and the curriculum took different routes in different communities. In Pasadena Superintendent Goslin was forced to resign and eventually take a position at a university. Since he was president of the American Association of School Administrators, this left other school administrators in a state of panic. In Scarsdale the course of events moved in the other direction, with the school board able to stop any form of censorship. But as right-wing concerns mounted around the country, another element of criticism was introduced into the national school debate. Academics, feeling the pressure of loss of status and rising antiintellectualism in the country, began to make important and influential statements about the nature of schooling. Leading the group was Arthur Bestor, a professor of history at the University of Illinois and later founder of the Council for Basic Education.

Antiintellectualism in the Schools

In 1952 Arthur Bestor delivered a paper at the annual meeting of the American Historical Association, "Anti-Intellectualism in the Schools: A Challenge to

Scholars." As part of his presentation Bestor decided to submit a series of concrete proposals for action. He drafted a detailed resolution and began circulating it among scholarly friends for their approval and signature of support. By the time of the meeting he had collected 695 signatures, of whom 199 were historians, 93 were in English, 86 in biological sciences, 77 in mathematics, with the others being drawn from a variety of academic fields. The preamble of the resolution expressed alarm at the "serious danger to American intellectual life arising from anti-intellectual tendencies" and the "anti-intellectualist conceptions of education among important groups of school administrators and educational theorists." The actual resolutions were directed toward establishing a close working relationship between the scholarly community and the professional educator.[20]

Item 1 of the resolution reflected the gap between what people thought schools were supposed to accomplish and the actual historical development of the ideology of schooling. This item argued that the prime function of schooling should be "to provide sound training in the fundamental ways of thinking represented by history, science, mathematics, literature, language, art, and the other disciplines." While the item admitted that education should be concerned with moral conduct, citizenship, and social adjustment, these should be accomplished within the framework of the particular goals of schooling. In other words, stated the resolution, "the particular contribution which the school can make is determined by, and related to, the primary fact that it is an agency of intellectual training."[21]

Now it is hard to find anywhere in the historical record groups of people supporting the development and expansion of public schooling as "an agency of intellectual training." Arthur Bestor consistently argued throughout his writings that the traditional goal of public schooling had been intellectual training and that it was only because of the workings of the modern professional educator that it had deviated from this goal. In Bestor's most famous critical study of schooling, *Educational Wastelands,* he argued, "The founders of our public school system ... believed, quite simply, that ignorance is a handicap and disciplined intelligence a source of power." [22] This statement does contain a grain of historical accuracy in that public school founders were concerned about ignorance, but it was wide of the mark in suggesting an emphasis on disciplined intelligence. If one reads the school reports of the often called father of American public education, Horace Mann, there is little reference to disciplined intellectual training and a great deal of emphasis on using the school as an agency to solve a wide variety of social problems. Primary among these was reducing economic tensions in society by mixing rich and poor in the schoolhouse, and reducing political problems and social decay by teaching a social and political consensus.[23] From the time of Horace Mann in the first half of the nineteenth century through the early twentieth century, the public schools had been promoted as an agency of socialization that would end crime and poverty, Americanize foreigners, provide for adjustment to industrial and urban life, solve labor problems, and a host of other social concerns.[24] The lack of emphasis in the public schools on intellectual discipline was not the result of a sinister group of modern professional educators but an expression of traditional social goals and support of public schooling. Bestor, in arguing for a reinstatement of a traditional goal of intellectual training, was as confused about the historical purposes of schooling as were the right-wing groups who thought the schools should support free marketplace capitalism and rugged economic individualism.

One item of the resolution that reflected Bestor's concern about the socialization goals of education asserted that "an educational philosophy is both anti-intellectual and anti-democratic if it asserts that sound training in the fundamental intellectual disciplines is appropriate only for the minority of students who are preparing for college and the professions." In many ways this resolution resurrected a debate that had existed in the latter part of the nineteenth century over the development of the American high school. In the 1890s the Committee of Ten of the National Education Association, chaired by Charles Eliot, then president of Harvard, was asked to consider if secondary education for college should be different from that given to students who were not continuing their education. The answer of the Committee of Ten was that the preparation of both groups should be the same and that it would be undemocratic to provide different educational programs based on the future social destination of the groups. The argument of the Committee of Ten failed to accomplish anything except to stir up the winds of debate which eventually led to the high school supporting differentiated courses of study based on the future goals of the student.[25]

What Bestor had in mind when he drafted this resolution was his major enemy in recent educational developments and the subject of a great deal of his writings. This was the "life adjustment education movement," which had been launched in 1945 at a final conference on "Vocational Education in the Years Ahead," sponsored by the Vocational Education Division of the U.S. Office of Education. At this meeting a well-known leader of vocational education, Dr. Charles A. Prosser, introduced a resolution that was quickly supported:

"The vocational school of a community will be able better to prepare 20 percent of the youth of secondary school age for entrance upon desirable skilled occupations; and that the high school will continue to prepare another 20 percent for entrance to college." The question was what to do with the other 60 percent of the students. The answer of the Prosser resolution was: "We do not believe that the remaining 60 percent of our youth of secondary school age will receive the life adjustment education they need . . . unless . . . the administrators of public education with the assistance of the vocational education leaders formulate a similar program for this group." In a later draft of the resolution the mysterious figures of 20–60–20 were dropped and life adjustment was called for those who would not benefit from vocational and college training.[26] In part the life-adjustment movement reflected a concern among vocational educators that vocational education in the schools had become a dumping ground for students not preparing for college. What they wanted was more selectivity in determining who would enter vocational education and at the same time to provide some alternative program for those not selected for the vocational or college preparatory track.

One interesting fact about the life-adjustment education movement was that it was an attempt to establish a national curriculum. For those concerned about local control of the schools, it should be pointed out that this issue is made meaningless if decisions about the content of school curriculum are made on a national level. Increasingly after World War II, as the federal government extended its role in education decisions about course content, school materials and curriculum were made at the national level by groups sponsored by the federal government or national professional organizations. This is not to suggest that this trend did not exist before World War II, but to argue that the trend greatly expanded after that period. In the case of life-adjustment education, the original conference sponsored by the Office of Education was followed by a series of regional conferences where the agenda was composed by members of the Office of Education. These regional conferences were held in New York City, Chicago, Cheyenne, Sacramento, and Birmingham, and were attended by leading public school people in each area. One of the agreements reached at these meetings was that "public opinion can be created to support the movement to provide appropriate life adjustment education for these youth." [27] In other words, it was felt that a proper program of public relations and advertising could create a feeling of public need for a curriculum that had not existed in the past. The five regional conferences were followed by the meeting of two national commissions on life-adjustment education which recommended in 1950 the organization of life-adjustment education programs on the state level under the control of state departments of education. This, of course, was part of the plan to spread life-adjustment education to the local level.[28]

What sparked Arthur Bestor's rage about life-adjustment education was this. As a professor at the University of Illinois, he obtained copies of the work of the Illinois Secondary School Curriculum Program which was heavily influenced by life-adjustment ideology. One of the things that Bestor quickly recognized and criticized were the methods used by educators to sell life-adjustment curriculum to the public. He quoted from one of the Illinois studies where it was explained that "given the American tradition of the local lay-control of public education, it is both necessary and desirable that a community (patrons, pupils, teachers) consensus be engineered in understanding support of the necessary changes before they are made." Bestor responded to this

with the statement, "We approach here the real meaning of what educationists euphemistically describe as
'democracy in education.' It is the democracy of the
'engineered' consensus." [29] Statements of this nature by
educators and the whole life-adjustment movement
firmly convinced Bestor that the control of education
was not in the hands of laymen or scholars but in the
hands of the professional educator.

The life-adjustment movement also convinced Bestor
that the professional educator was not only in control of
education but also was responsible for the antiintellectual quality of the American schools. He noted that in
one of the Illinois documents, "Problems of High School
Youth," there was an overwhelming disproportion of
problems dealing with what he called trivia and no
mention of mathematics, science, history, or foreign
languages. He cited as trivia from the list of fifty-five
"Problems of High School Youth" items such as "the
problem of improving one's personal appearance"; "the
problem of selecting a family dentist"; "the problem of
developing one or more 'making things,' 'making it go,'
or tinkering hobbies"; and "the problem of developing
and maintaining wholesome boy-girl relationships." [30]

What Bestor wanted the public schools to reject was
both the traditional emphasis on socialization and the
social-sorting function of schooling. From his perspective the organization of the curriculum should be
around traditional subject-matter disciplines. Bestor
argued that in the schools, "The important books must
be read. . . . Fundamental problems must be studied,
not merely talked about." And this was to occur in a
climate where the basic scientific and scholarly disciplines were presented as systematic ways of thinking
with each discipline organized around a structure and
methodology of its own. These basic disciplines included
mathematics, science, history, English, and foreign lan-

guages. Bestor rejected the notion that there should be a differentiated course of study based on the future social destination of the individual. He accepted the idea that there might be differences in intellectual ability among students but argued, in reference to students of lower mental ability, "Most of them, I believe, can be brought at a slower pace along the same route." By ending the emphasis on socialization and social sorting, Bestor felt, the tide of antiintellectualism could be curbed in society by creating a new respect in the student and in the home for knowledge and cultural achievement.[31]

An important step in achieving these goals was to change the form and substance of teacher education. Two items of the resolution presented to the American Historical Association were directed toward reducing the quantity of education courses for teacher certification and a new emphasis on the subject-matter area the individual was to teach. The great growth in numbers of education courses and certification requirements, Bestor argued, were a product of the interlocking directorate of professional educationists. "Certification standards," he argued, "and the various other requirements imposed upon teachers have far more to do with the power politics of the educational bureaucracy than with the welfare of the schools. The academic empires which can be built by such methods are observable in almost every large state university." In the case of the University of Illinois, where he was employed, he noted that the College of Education offered 61 distinct courses to undergraduates and had a faculty of 124. In contrast, the Department of Chemistry and Chemical Engineering, which he claimed was one of the most distinguished in the country, offered only 42 courses and had a faculty of 42. Professional educators could build academic empires because of the interlocking directorate between professors of education, school administrators, and state education officials, who worked together to increase the number of education courses required for meeting state teacher-certification requirements.[32]

Everything at a university is education, Bestor claimed. His department was a department of history education while others were departments of education in their particular disciplines. It was a mistake to define one separate faculty as a department or college of education. The only legitimate separate field was that of pedagogy or methods of instruction. The proliferation of education courses without a strong subject-matter standing behind them had reduced teacher-certification courses to a low level of intellectual content. Consequently, the students attracted to education courses were usually of very low intellectual caliber. "Good students, it is true," Bestor argued, "are dragooned into pedagogical courses by the operation of teacher certification laws. But among those who actually enroll as majors in education the level of ability is appallingly low." As evidence, Bestor cited the results of the Selective Service qualification tests which showed that in all subject-matter fields except education more than 50 percent received a passing grade. For students majoring in education the figure was only 27 percent.[33]

Bestor was not alone during this period in his concern about the quality and operation of departments and colleges of education. During the year following the presentation of the resolution to the American Historical Association, there appeared on the national scene a book written by a businessman and school committee member in Sharon, Massachusetts, with the eye-catching title *Quackery in the Public Schools*. It leveled a barrage of complaints about the functioning of professional education courses. Albert Lynd, the author of the book, was concerned not only about the quantity of education courses required for certification but also that pay scales for teachers required more education courses for salary advancements. This led to both an overwhelming number of courses and also research as teachers scrambled for master's and doctorates. Admitting that some educational research might be useful, Lynd argued that the majority of studies produced under the title of educational research were useless and displayed a low intellectual tone. Among the many examples he cited was one quoted from the *Encyclopedia of Educational Research* and conducted by the Commission of School Plant Research of the American Council of Education which "revealed that the number of toilet fixtures generally required could be reduced. This study . . . involved observations of the actual use of toilet fixtures in selected schools throughout the regular school day."[34]

As proof of the proliferation of education courses, Lynd noted that Teachers College of Columbia University offered a total of 475 listings in their Summer Session program. Lynd referred to Teachers College as "the paradise of Educationdom; it has been said that American teachers who do not succeed in getting there for a summer in this life look forward to a sojurn there in the next." [35] Lynd's solutions were similar to those of Bestor's. The power of the professional educator had to be broken by changes in certification requirements and reorganization of salary schedules. In Lynd's words, "The most certain insurance against educational quackery is the presence in our schools of a large body of intelligent teachers who are personally educated in something more than the mumbo jumbo of Educationism." [36] Lynd was also concerned about the anti-intellectual condition of American life and wanted to break this cultural syndrome by increasing the intellectual tone of the schools. He felt that an important ingredient in the process was an informed lay vigilance to act as a countervailing power to the stranglehold of the professional educator.

The idea of a countervailing force to the educational bureaucracy was also strongly supported by Bestor. But what he wanted was a national scholarly commission to assume watchdog vigilance over the public school enterprise. In his resolution to the American Historical Association he called upon the group to form with other learned societies a Permanent Scientific and Scholarly Commission on Secondary Education that would be made up exclusively of scientists and scholars from the various disciplines of learning. This group would analyze every major proposal affecting the public secondary school curriculum and programs of teacher training. It would also study the membership and structure of all federal, state, and municipal departments of education and public commissions to assure that the professional educator did not have dominant control. Through public exposure of the workings of professional education and the development of secondary programs, the proposed commission of scholars would gain control of the direction of American education.[37]

In 1952 the American Historical Association could not reach a consensus on Bestor's proposal. In its place was substituted a weakly worded resolution supporting Bestor's basic concerns and calling for further study of the possibility of working with other learned societies. Undeterred by the setback, Bestor searched around for other means of implementing his ideas, and in 1956 helped organize the Council for Basic Education and became its first president. The other early members of the organization were botanist Harry Fuller of the University of Illinois, who served as first chairman of the board, and Professor Harold Clapp of Grinnell College, who was the first executive secretary. Shortly after its founding, Mortimer Smith became the major dynamic force behind the operation.

The Council for Basic Education never fulfilled Bestor's dream of having learned societies watch over American education, but it did maintain a consistent emphasis on establishing the basic disciplines as a focal point of the school curriculum and the need to limit the power of the professional educator. The statement of purpose of the organization reflected many of the ideas Bestor had outlined in his set of resolutions to the American Historical Association. In particular it stressed that the schools should not differentiate the curriculum and that "all students, excepting only those few whose intellectual equipment is clearly too limited, receive adequate instruction in the basic intellectual disciplines." The statement of purpose also looked toward cooperating with school administrators "in resisting pressures to divert school time to activities of minor educational significance, to curricula overemphasizing social adjustment at the expense of intellectual discipline." One item in the original bylaws of the group allowed for any learned society to elect representatives to the council. It was undoubtedly Bestor's hope that the Council for Basic Education would take the form of his dreamed of Permanent Scientific and Scholarly Commission on Secondary Education.[38]

The group that surrounded Bestor when the organization was founded shared similar concerns about schooling. Harold Clapp, the first executive secretary of the council, had proposed in a 1949 article in the *Bulletin of the American Association of University Professors* the establishment of a national commission of "thoughtful" men and women who would investigate the methods of teacher training and selection which to his mind had reduced the schools to a form of intellectual poverty. He also defined the major controlling element as the professional educator, who established the requirements for teacher training. Clapp wrote, "Since these requirements are largely in terms of the courses taught by the Educationists themselves, this approaches the definition of a racket." [39] Harry Fuller, the first chairman of the board of the council, had given national notice about his views on education in a speech titled "The Emperor's New Clothes: or Primus Dementat," which was first delivered as a Phi Delta Kappa address at the University of Illinois in 1950 and was repeated by invitation at the annual meeting of the American Association for the Advancement of Science and reprinted in a 1951 issue of the *Scientific Monthly*. Fuller's speech lambasted the professional educator, and particularly the professor of education, for the supposed intellectual deterioration of the public schools. He referred to professors of education as "dreary intellectual sinks." While admitting that some professors of education were of top quality, he argued they were obscured by a "swirling dust, raised by the hot winds that emanate from the numerous educational opportunists and carpetbaggers who too often dominate our colleges of education and our public schools." Fuller's solution was for parents to protest and act as a countervailing force to the professional educator.[40]

Mortimer Smith, the executive director of the Council, had made his views known nationally in *And Madly Teach: A Layman Looks at Public School Education* (1949) and *The Diminished Mind: A Study of Planned Mediocrity in Our Public Schools* (1954). Smith, like his colleagues, charged the schools with antiintellectualism and domination by the professional educator, but he gave greater emphasis to the idea that the schools were undemocratic. Bestor, it will be recalled, had complained that the differentiation of studies was undemocratic because the schools did not prepare students equally for participation in the world.

The word *democratic* takes on a variety of meanings,

depending on the user. Smith defined the healthy democratic society as "but a step removed from anarchy, a society bound together by the minimum of rules necessary to preserve order and maintain justice." [41] From Smith's perspective, social institutions should exist to serve the individual rather than the individual exist to serve the institution. The problem with education was that it had become increasingly "totalitarian" in the sense that "its aim is to have the school assume responsibility for the total education of youth up to the age of eighteen and to extend its domain into the field of mature education." [42]

Institutions became totalitarian when society lost a clear perspective of their proper functions. Smith likened proposals for universal military training to the development of compulsory public education. He argued that the proper function of the military was defense and warfare but that this function was distorted in proposals to use universal military training as a form of civic training and education. A similar function was true of schooling, whose proper function was to teach basic disciplines, not to assume control and education of the "whole child." Smith complained that the tendency of modern education was to bring under control all the social forces impinging on the individual—the home, school, church, and community—and to aggregate these functions in the school. The creation of the school as a total institution, Smith argued, seemed to be a product of an "uneasy fear which haunts both the advocates of total education and of military training—the feeling that the free agencies of society, and especially the home, have broken down and left youth aimlessly drifting, rudderless." Smith noted that this reasoning had produced the total institutions of Nazi Germany. [43]

Smith was concerned not only that schools had become total institutions but also that they had begun to place social groups and the state above the individual. As an example, Smith quoted the 1947 *Yearbook of the American Association of School Administrators* as to there being an unavoidable choice in education between "the primacy of the individual and the society of which he is a part." The *Yearbook* gave "unreserved priority ... to the unity and well-being of our society as a whole." The statement that angered Smith and convinced him that liberty was becoming a lost word in American society was the call for a fundamental shift in the whole educational program "to the preparation of the individual for the realization of his best self in the higher loyalty of serving the basic ideals and aims of our society." Smith admitted that the schools had not become a political arm of the state in the United States. But he worried that professional educators were rapidly turning the school into a total institution which produced individuals who were educated to serve other total institutions.[44]

Smith, like Bestor, believed that the differentiation of subject matter was undemocratic. Smith believed that as schools had become mass institutions serving a wide spectrum of society, educators were confronted with the difficult task of transmitting culture to the entire population. The choice was between attempting to teach the basic disciplines to those whose home life and social background had not provided adequate preparation for this type of instruction or developing a different curriculum for these groups. Smith argued that educators had chosen the easier path and leaped on the idea of Dewey that it was "the child ... and not the subject matter, which determines both quality and quantity of learning."[45] Wrenching this idea from Dewey's total philosophy allowed the educator to shed the responsibility for handing on the traditional knowledge of the race and teach according to individual interest and needs.

This doctrine enables the teacher, Smith claimed, "who finds Johnny or Mary a little dull-witted in the academic subjects to ease up on them on the basis of supposed lack of interest and ability and to shove them into more courses in manual training or industrial arts or home economics, where mechanical skill takes precedence over thinking."

While educators talked about the democratic right of all to education, what they really meant, according to Smith, was the democratic right of all to *some* education. Modern educators showed a profound distrust of the ability of all to receive an education. Smith wondered if this attitude had not been reinforced by what he considered to be the undemocratic instrument of the IQ test. He argued that it was possible that vocational training in the schools might have expanded "in part from the conviction, fortified by the results obtained by 'scientifically' determining intelligence, that education is beyond the ability of many, and that something must be found to occupy their time. If so, what could be more 'undemocratic.' " [46]

The Council for Basic Education was therefore organized as both a countervailing force to the power of the professional educator and as a group dedicated to overcoming the undemocratic nature of a differentiated curriculum by providing an education in the basic disciplines for all American youth. In pursuit of these two objectives the council sponsored and had published *The Case for Basic Education* (1959). The volume was edited by the new executive secretary of the organization, James D. Koerner, and opened with the statement of purpose of the council: "It insists that only by the maintenance of high academic standards can the ideal of democratic education be realized—the ideal of offering to all the children . . . not merely an opportunity to attend school, but the privilege of receiving there the soundest education."

The book reflected the goal of engaging scholars in each discipline to plan and develop a public school curriculum. It contained sixteen separate essays dealing with individual subject-matter fields that ranged through history, geography, languages, mathematics, and science to what were called "electives," such as art, music, and speech. In addition to the sixteen essays dealing with specific subjects were an opening essay by author and literary critic Clifton Fadiman and a concluding essay by a lawyer and member of the Portland, Oregon, board of education. A distinguished list of scholars authored essays: Ray Allen Billington, William Smith Mason Professor of History at Northwestern University; Douglas Bush, Gurney Professor of English at Harvard University; Stewart Cairns, professor of mathematics at the University of Illinois and former member of the Institute for Advanced Study at Princeton; Carlton J. H. Hayes, Seth Low Professor of History at Columbia University; and M. H. Trytten, director of the Office of Scientific Personnel of the National Academy of Sciences and the man who lent his name to the Selective Service "Trytten plan," which became the draft proposal supported in the 1951 amendments to the Selective Service Act. With such a distinguished list of scholars, this volume was to be the beginning of a counterattack against the professional educator, who had usurped the role of the scholar in the schools.[47]

During the 1960s the work of the Council for Basic Education was highlighted by two books by the executive secretary and later president of the council, James Koerner: *The Miseducation of American Teachers* and *Who Controls American Education? : A Guide for Laymen.*[48] Both volumes followed the Council's original concern over the domination of education by the professional educator and the lack of emphasis on subject-matter fields in teacher training. In *Who Controls American Education?* Koerner analyzed the power structure of education from the federal level through the national professional educational organizations and state educational structure to the local level. Addressing the title of the book, Koerner concluded that the complexity of the situation did not lend itself to an easy answer. But in the tradition of Bestor, Smith, Fuller, and Clapp, he stated that "we have seen that the important decisions in education emerge from a labyrinthine structure of forces and countervailing forces, but that the interests of professional educators tend to be dominant."[49]

In 1956, the year the Council for Basic Education was organized, another influential critic of the American school began to have his voice heard on the national scene. Vice-Admiral Hyman G. Rickover, often called the father of America's nuclear navy, carried his message of the dismal failure of the American school to meetings such as that of the Society of Business Magazine Editors in 1956, the Westinghouse Science Talent Search Award Ceremony in 1957, the Engineering Society of Detroit in 1957, the Harvard Club of New York in 1958, and finally into print in a best-selling book, *Education and Freedom*. Admiral Rickover's basic message was that the United States was losing the technological and military race with the Soviet Union because America's public schools were failing to identify and adequately educate talented youth as future scientists and engineers. In an interview conducted by news commentator Edward R. Murrow, Rickover stated that education "is even more important than atomic power in the navy, for if our people are not properly educated in accordance with the terrific requirements of this rapidly spiraling scientific and industrial civilization, we are bound to go down. The Russians apparently have recognized this."[50] In the past the schools had often been hailed as the first line of defense for a democracy. Rickover identified the schools as a possible cause of destruction of the United States.

Rickover claimed that in the course of twelve years' work on the development of nuclear power plants he had interviewed more than two thousand men for a naval-reactor engineering group which by 1959 numbered about one hundred fifty. The problems encountered in these interviews, and the technical and nontechnical roadblocks to the rapid development of a nuclear navy for national security, convinced him that one of the major problems was the inadequacy of the American educational system. It had failed to produce large groups of individuals who could adapt rapidly to complex and new situations requiring maximum talent and creative ability. The problem with America's educational system was that it failed both to provide adequate training for a modern technological world and to identify and give special training to creative and talented youth.

Rickover described his concerns about education against the background of the cold war strategy of deterrent warfare. The key to maintaining a winning place in the military race with the Soviet Union was to have an adequate lead time in the development of military hardware. Lead time was the time required between the conception of an idea and the production of a finished product incorporating that idea. America's lead time in the development of military weaponry, Rickover argued, had slowly been lengthening since World War II, while the lead time of the Soviet Union had slowly been diminishing. He claimed that during the war the lead time in the United States had been two and a half years, but by the middle of the 1950s it had increased to ten years. On the other hand, the lead time in the Soviet Union had decreased to five years. As examples of the importance of lead time in modern warfare he cited the development of poison gas, submarines, and tanks in

World War I and the V-2 rocket in World War II. He felt
that a shortened lead time for the Germans in the world
wars would have led to their ultimate triumph.[51]

For Rickover the real military race was the race
between educational systems to supply adequately
trained engineers and scientists who could reduce the
lead time. The Soviet Union, he felt, was winning this
educational battle because it had reformed its schools
and was concentrating on providing the highest-quality
education for large numbers of children. According to
figures supplied to Rickover by Allen Dulles, then director of the Central Intelligence Agency, between 1950
and 1960 the Soviet Union would graduate approximately 1,200,000 scientists and engineers as compared
to 900,000 in the United States. By 1960, it was estimated
that the Soviet Union would have more scientists and
engineers than the United States. Rickover warned,
"Let us never forget that there can be no second place in
a contest with Russia and that there will be no second
chance if we lose. But should we lose, it would be largely
by default." [52]

Rickover shared with other critics of the period a
concern about antiintellectualism and disdain for the
professional educator. Rickover felt that the antiintellectualism of the period was hurting the military race
because the American people did not show a proper respect and understanding for the individual of genius.
Unlike the Soviets, Americans were slow to recognize
talent and provide proper rewards and public recognition for it. In part, he felt this was caused by an educational system that emphasized social adjustment and
conformity. Trained in this manner, Americans tended
to display a distrust and dislike for eccentricities, particularly those that might accompany the individual of
genius. As an example, he cited the case of an eminent
scholar who made some important remarks on American

life and was confronted by a commentator who reported only on the color and shape of the scholar's socks. Rickover quoted one toast given in opposition to antiintellectualism which reflected his point of view. The toast urged "Eggheads of the world, unite! We have nothing to lose but our brains. A country neglects its eggheads at its peril." [53] Rickover also believed that the antiintellectual stress on conformity and social adjustment contributed to a lengthening of lead time because it created individuals who were unable to adjust rapidly to changing technological problems.

The professional educator, in the general terms of Rickover's arguments, was the major weak point in America's overall military strategy. Through his control of school curriculums and teacher-certification laws, the professional educator was bringing America to its knees before the superior Russian educational system. On the matter of the professional educator, Rickover's thinking did not differ from that of the Council on Basic Education. He did seem to reach an explosive sense of rage when he saw educators trying to protect themselves against outside criticism. In fact, he warned that professional educators would attempt to punish any person who attempted to take issue with them. As an example, he claimed to have a copy of a statement issued by the National Association of Secondary School Principals after the publication of some critical articles in *Life* and *Time* magazines which told its members : "We know from experience with another magazine a few years ago that your most effective weapon will be to question the continuation of subscriptions to the *Life* and *Time* publications in your school as long as they have an attitude and policy inimical to education." [54] Rickover, like other critics, believed that any attempt in changing educational policies meant a battle with the educational establishment.

What Rickover wanted in education, unlike the Council for Basic Education, was a greater emphasis on the social-sorting function of the public schools. He argued, with a great deal of historical inaccuracy, that the problem was the development of the comprehensive high school, which he saw as a product of the post-Jacksonian upsurge of democracy. The comprehensive high school, to Rickover, was an attempt to maintain a democratic ideal of educating all people together without admitting that there were different levels of intelligence in the population. "At that time," Rickover wrote, "little was known of the differences in intellectual endowments; I.Q. tests had not yet been invented."

Here Rickover erred. The comprehensive high school was a product of the early part of the twentieth century when recognition was given to different levels of intellectual endowment. The debate at the time was over how far differentiation of students should develop on the basis of intellectual capabilities. One side of the debate wanted separate schools for each level of development, while the other side argued that separate schools would destroy America's ideals of common education and would create a democratic community. The compromise was the comprehensive high school with separation according to courses of study and social mixing of all groups in other activities.[55] Rickover objected to the socialization aspect of the comprehensive high school which, in his words, meant "learning to get along with each other, absorbing democratic habits and ideals as by osmosis." Where Rickover stood in this twentieth-century debate was squarely on the side of greater differentiation as opposed to the socialization of the common school tradition.

America's military and technological race with the Soviet Union was to be won by the early identification and accelerated education of the talented and gifted

child. This, for Rickover, was where the battle lines of
the cold war were drawn. Rickover framed this problem
in terms of traditions of democratic thought in the
United States. According to Rickover, and again with
historical inaccuracy, "equality" had become confused
in the head of the professional educator to mean all
people are equal in terms of intellectual abilities. For
Rickover, "equality" meant equality before the law and
in terms of justice but not in terms of physical endowments. In the United States equalitarian philosophy had
led to an assumption that no person could claim to be an
indispensable person. This assumption Rickover agreed
was true, but a resulting conclusion that society does not
have indispensable people was false. Indispensable people in any society were those people "who because of
natural endowment and careful training possess the intellectual, artistic, and moral abilities to build upon existing foundations and to carry forward the momentum
of civilization." Rickover went on to argue that "it has
been estimated that the efforts of less than one per cent
of the total population move the world forward. This
small group is indispensable to the maintenance and
advancement of our civilization." [56]

Rickover essentially was arguing that what a democratic society had to do to survive was to recognize the
need for an intellectual elite, and through schooling and
social recognition to nurture and cherish these movers of
civilization. Reducing lead time and winning the race
with the Soviet Union depended on the cultivation of an
aristocracy of talent.

The Conant Report

Amid the barrage of criticism of the American schools
and professional educators there appeared a national

study which gave support to the traditional concept of the comprehensive high school and argued for changes that would make it a more improved weapon in the technological and manpower race with the Soviet Union. James Bryant Conant's *The American High School Today* was published during the early months of 1959. Part of the book's success was in its timing. As Conant noted in his autobiography, "The timing was perfect. A wave of public criticism of the high schools which had started after Sputnik had reached its crest. School board members all over the country were anxious for specific answers." [57] "Sputnik" referred to the launching of a Soviet space capsule in 1957, which reinforced the criticism appearing after World War II that the American school was failing to provide the manpower necessary for scientific and technological competition with the Soviet Union.

Another reason for the book's success was that it did not attack professional educators or seek to undermine their control over public education. In fact, one of the prerequisites of a good school system, as stated by Conant, was a clear distinction between the policy-making functions of the school board and administration by the superintendent and principals. But what was meant by policy-making function of the school board seemed to deal mainly with arranging extracurricular activities and engineering community support for the schools. Conant clearly stated that school boards should not play a role in determining curriculum or selecting staff. Conant wrote that "if members of a school board become involved in the appointment of teachers and in other matters of patronage, the maintenance of good morale in the teaching staff becomes impossible, however excellent may be the superintendent and the principal." [58] Conant also wrote, "I assume that the school board will leave the development of the curriculum to the administrative officers and the teaching staff but will be kept informed of all developments." [59]

With regard to recommendations for improving education, Conant envisioned the school administrators explaining to the board of education the reasons for needed changes and in turn the school board explaining to the community and winning community support for these proposals. As Bestor had suggested, this was the democracy of the engineered consensus with the professional educator at the top. Considering the large number of attacks on this type of power arrangement in education during the 1950s, Conant's study must be viewed in part as an attempt to stem the tide for greater public involvement in the schools and reduced power for the educator. As Conant admitted, "Those laymen who had been criticizing the public schools most vigorously . . . cried 'Whitewash,' " whereas Conant found the book warmly received among professional educators. "My friends on the Educational Policies Commission, as well as most public school superintendents and high school principals, greeted the findings and recommendations with considerable enthusiasm. . . . For several weeks it was high on the bestseller list, an unusual distinction in these days for a book about schools." [60]

Conant's involvement in the study of the American high school came near the end of a career that had moved steadily through the circles of what sociologist C. Wright Mills has called the power elite.[61] His life was one of a continuing expansion of involvement in national policy decisions. After gaining an international reputation as a chemist at Harvard, he joined the world of national educational politics in 1933 when he was asked to become president of that institution. As a scientist and president of a most prestigious university. it was only natural that his services would be called upon with the outbreak of World War II.

In 1940 Vannevar Bush, at that time president of the Carnegie Institute in Washington, called Conant and asked him if he would be interested in becoming a member of a National Defense Research Committee to be appointed by President Roosevelt. Conant later reflected that if he had not been asked to join this group, he probably would have been offered the position of director of Selective Service. Conant's immediate responsibilities as a member of the National Defense Research Committee were to organize chemists and direct their attention to the problems of modern technological warfare. In 1941 Conant was sent to England to help establish a permanent office of research to aid in the flow of scientific information to the allies. On returning to the United States in 1941, Conant became chairman of the National Defense Research Committee and a deputy of Vannevar Bush, who was now head of the newly formed Office of Scientific Research and Development. In December 1941 the decision was made to proceed full steam ahead on the development and manufacture of the atomic bomb. Conant was selected as liaison between Bush and the project which became known as the Manhattan District. In charge of the Manhattan District was General L. R. Groves; in charge of the S-I Section of the Office of Scientific Research, which was involved in planning the Manhattan project, was James Conant.[62]

There is irony in the fact that an individual who played an important role in the development of the atomic bomb should spend a great deal of his time following World War II exhorting the American people to develop an adequate defense strategy against possible atomic attack from the Soviet Union. As the next chapter explores more fully, one of Conant's primary concerns after the war was to develop and channel scientific manpower. This was reflected in his support of the founding of the National Science Foundation and of universal military training in 1951. Following the war, Conant continued as president of Harvard and remained actively involved in national and international policy decisions. In 1950 he became chairman of a citizens group, the Committee on the Present Danger, which was organized in response to the outbreak of the Korean war. The basic position of the committee was that the United States had to make a strong contribution of troops to the defense of Europe and maintain a strategic reserve. In 1951, after Eisenhower had been appointed supreme commander of the North Atlantic Treaty forces and just before his successful bid for the Presidency, James Conant gave a public radio address in support of Eisenhower's attempts to expand U.S. military forces in Europe. Conant told his radio audience that "the United States is in danger. Few would be inclined to question this simple statement. The danger is clearly of a military nature." He went on to urge support of Eisenhower's plea for increased armed forces in Europe and the need to "build a secure wall for peace." [63]

On December 22, 1952, Conant lunched with the then President-elect Eisenhower and presented him with a memorandum from the Committee on the Present Danger. Considering Conant's support of Eisenhower's military policies, it was not suprising that in the course of the luncheon Eisenhower offered him the post of U.S. High Commissioner for Germany, which Conant accepted. Two years later, the Allied High Commission which had governed Germany following the war was abolished, and Conant became ambassador to West Germany. It was after he left this post, and in the context of his concern about increasing and expanding U.S. military strength around the world, that Conant launched himself into a study of the American high school.[64]

Conant tells the story of his involvement in the study

of the American high school in terms of searching for something to do as the headaches of diplomatic life began to mount. In 1955 he wrote John W. Gardner, the newly elected president of the Carnegie Corporation, that he was interested in leaving diplomatic service after the elections in 1956 and was anxious to explore possible projects. Gardner replied that Carnegie was ready to finance any educational project he might have in mind. In 1956, while vacationing in New Hampshire, Conant received a telephone call from Secretary of State John Foster Dulles offering him the ambassadorship to India. Conant declined and decided to leave diplomatic service. He wrote in his autobiography, "Whether I invented the project of studying the American comprehensive high school right after Secretary Dulles' first telephone call or whether it was already definite, I cannot say." [65]

On March 1, 1957, Conant met with a group of professional educators and members of the Carnegie Corporation and the Educational Testing Service. Conant selected as his staff to work on the study of the comprehensive high school a retiring superintendent from Oak Park, Illinois, and an individual who had just been offered the principalship of a small high school in Connecticut. By the summer of 1957, all the major plans regarding the study had been formulated, and it was decided to conduct the investigation during the 1957–58 academic year. All matters dealing with the employment of staff, travel accommodations, and the negotiations with publishers were to be handled by the Educational Testing Service under a grant from the Carnegie Corporation.

The involvement of the Educational Testing Service was undoubtedly aided by the fact that Conant was one of the people responsible for its organization and for many years had been a member of its board of trustees.

The Educational Testing Service was a mammoth educational enterprise which extended its influence into practically every school in the United States. It was a result of a merger in 1947 of separate and competing testing enterprises, a merger that gave the Educational Testing Service under a grant from the Carnegie Corporation.

Two of the major testing enterprises that were brought together by this merger were the Scholastic Aptitude Test (SAT) and the College Entrance Examination Board (CEEB). The test for the CEEB as it had been organized near the end of the nineteenth century was primarily a written subject-matter-oriented examination. During the 1930s Conant became an advocate of the SAT, which were developed by Carl Brigham as a measure of general scholastic ability. Brigham had worked with the group of psychologists who had developed the first mass IQ test during World War I for the U.S. Army. Following the war, Brigham had conducted a study of the army testing program and published a book with the descriptive title *A Study of American Intelligence* which ranked racial groups in the United States according to levels of intelligence. The study placed Nordic groups above Alpine, Mediterranean, and Negro races on the basis of supposed inherited native intelligence.[66] IQ and aptitude testing was viewed as a means of scientifically sorting students according to native ability. In 1937 Conant first urged that both the CEEB and the SAT be used as a method of determining college ability of entering students. He argued before a meeting of the Educational Records Bureau that this combination would be a better predictor of future college success.[67] In part, Conant's interest in this merger reflected his commitment to the ideal of the school functioning as a social-sorting institution.

In the fall of 1957 Conant and his team began their survey of 103 high schools and 4 school systems located in 26 different states. Conant personally visited 55 of these high schools and 3 of the school systems. The schools he visited were primarily located in cities with populations between 10,000 and 100,000. He decided not to concentrate on schools in metropolitan areas because of the existence in these areas of specialized vocational and academic high schools. Conant's goal was primarily one of evaluating the comprehensive high school that attempted to educate all American youth within one institution. He talked to principals, school board members, teachers, and students in each of the schools he visited and attempted to determine how well they were providing programs for all their students. But even though he was interested in the total school program, it is clear on reading his final report that his major concern was with the education of what he called the "academically talented." He wrote in his book on the survey that "as I discussed with teachers and guidance officers the work of the more able students, I became more and more interested in the program of the academically talented."[68]

When Conant began his trip through the world of the American high school in 1957, he had already developed some fairly clear and definite ideas about what should be the goals of American education. Besides his educational work at the National Science Foundation, Harvard, and the Educational Testing Service, he had also chaired the Educational Policies Commission of the National Education Association and acted as president of the American Council of Education. During the period preceding his acceptance of the role of High Commissioner of Germany he had stated his views in a variety of contexts. His essential argument had been that the educational system was the key element in maintaining the social structure of the United States. One of its most

important results should be maintaining equality of opportunity, which would assure a steady flow of talented
and trained manpower. Central to his goal and the entire
educational system was an adequate guidance program
for identification of ability and planning for its proper
utilization. Social tensions in society were to be reduced
through the socialization program of the school and by
reducing social differentiation based on academic
credentials by providing post-high school education in
general, technical, and vocational institutions. This
concern about adequate manpower utilization and
socialization wove its way through his report on
the American high school.[69]

During the 1958–59 academic year, after Conant had
finished his high school survey and during the period
surrounding its publication, Conant was invited to lecture at Harvard University, Wayne State University,
and Smith College. These lectures elucidated the
ideological underpinnings of the recommendations made
in *The American High School Today.*

Conant's lectures made it clear that in his evaluation
of the American high school his emphasis was on the cold
war and its relationship to American education. He
argued that "many people are quite unconscious of the
relation between high school education and the welfare
of the United States. They are still living in imagination
in a world which knew neither nuclear weapons nor Soviet imperialism." [70] He continually related the recommendations he was making on the improvement of the
high school to U.S. foreign policy and possible Soviet
conquest of the world. For the academically talented he
recommended a program of four years of one foreign
language. In response to the argument that professionals
such as engineers did not need this training, he stated
"that there is a practical reason why our future engineers should learn a foreign language when they are
young. This reason is closely related to our struggle with

the Soviet Union." He went on to argue, "In the competition with the Communists in the uncommitted nations
of the world, we need to send many engineers as well as
other specialists to areas where English is spoken only by
a thin layer of the elite and to other places where English
is spoken not at all." He maintained that four years of
rigorous training in one foreign language made it easier
to learn other languages. This was vitally important
because the school could not provide all the training in
such languages as Arabic, Iranian, and Indonesian required in technical assistance programs in underdeveloped countries. His recommendation could provide
what he called passage through a "sound barrier" which
made for easier acquisition of other languages.[71]

What Conant considered his most important recommendation, and the top priority in educational change,
was the elimination of the small high school. He felt that
a comprehensive high school could not fulfill its true
mission if it had a graduating class of less than one
hundred. He reasoned that a small high school could not
provide the specialized programs required to meet the
needs of all. He claimed, for instance, that it would be
rare if more than 25 percent of the students would benefit from a program for the academically talented. If a
graduating class had forty members, this meant that
advanced instruction in mathematics, science, and foreign languages would have to be provided for a maximum of ten students. This increased the per pupil costs
of these programs to exorbitant levels and in many cases
meant that they would not be provided. A small high
school also made it difficult to provide other programs
Conant recommended: advanced placement programs
for the gifted child, specialized vocational programs,
special programs for slow readers, and, of course, a
quality program for the academically talented.

His plea for the elimination of the small high school

reflected a commitment to the traditional concept of the comprehensive high school. In his lectures following the survey he reminded his audiences of the 1918 Cardinal Principles Report of the National Education Association, which had been the major document to define the goals and structure of the comprehensive high school. Conant accepted the ideas that the school must practice social sorting in terms of manpower needs and at the same time have all students mix within one building and in certain programs as a means of maintaining a political community. Originally, the comprehensive high school had developed a means of increasing industrial efficiency and cooperation. Conant accepted these two goals. In addition, he stressed the urgency of the technological and military race against what he called Soviet imperialism. At the heart of the social-sorting function of the school was the guidance system for sorting students according to ability and interests. Conant recommended that counseling begin in the elementary school and be well organized through the junior and senior high school. He felt there should be one full-time counselor for every 250 to 300 students. When Conant talked about counseling, he clearly did not mean counseling for personal adjustment or character development. The counselor he had in mind would use aptitude and achievement tests, school records, and teachers' estimates to guide the student through an educational program designed to produce what he called "marketable skills."

The sorting function of the school was also to be carried over into the courses that were to be taken by all students in school. Conant advocated a general education requirement of all students that would include four years of English, three or four years of social studies, one year of mathematics, and one year of science. He argued that throughout the school, students should be grouped according to ability, subject by subject. For example, "In

English, American history, ninth-grade algebra, biology, and physical science, there should be at least three types of classes—one for the more able in the subject, another for the large groups whose ability is about average, and another for the very slow readers who should be handled by special teachers." [72] He went on to suggest that the middle group be further divided into two or three sections according to ability.

Conant wanted all Americans to become card-carrying graduates of the high school, to give meaning to its social-sorting function. He recommended that the high school diploma be supplemented with a durable record of courses studied and grades received. He argued that the traditional diploma indicated only that a student had satisfactorily completed work in general education and finished a sequence of elective courses. The record of courses and grades, he stated, "might be a card that could be carried in a wallet." He urged that wide publicity be given to the existence of such a card "so that employers ask for it rather than merely relying on a diploma when questioning an applicant for a job about his education." [73]

A record card was particularly important for students sequenced into vocational education programs. Conant restated the traditional goal of many vocational educators of directly tying the vocational education programs into the needs of the labor market. Specific skills would be taught in the school in terms of the manpower needs of the labor market. Conant wrote, "The school administration should constantly assess the employment situation in those trades included in the vocational programs. When opportunities for employment in a given trade no longer exist within the community, the training program in that field should be dropped." [74] This would make the high school a true channeler of manpower into the economic system. The card-carrying high school graduate would be stamped for life in terms of his or her place in the social structure.

The comprehensive high school's role in developing a democratic political community, Conant recommended, should take place in the homeroom, student government, and a twelfth-grade course on American problems or government. Within these courses and activities, students with differing abilities and vocational destination should be mixed. Conant recommended with regard to homerooms that "students should be taken to have each homeroom a cross section of the school in terms of ability and vocational interest." [75] The homeroom was to overcome the potential undemocratic aspects of ability grouping and vocational tracking. Teachers and administrators were to recognize the importance of the homeroom and allow sufficient time for the development of a sense of community interest and the practice of representative government. From each homeroom were to be elected representatives of a student government to which school administrators would provide important questions each year that could be presented to the homerooms by their representatives. Conant's recommendation reflected the traditional argument for student government as the means of training future voters and learning about representative government. And like these traditional arguments, he did not intend to give students any important rights. Democracy taught in this context was learning to respond to predetermined issues without the exercise of any meaningful power.

The senior social studies course was to be the capstone of building a democratic community. Students of different abilities and vocational destinations were to be mixed and discussions encouraged to "develop not only an understanding of the American form of government and of the economic basis of our free society, but also mutual respect and understanding between different types of students." Conant argued that these courses were essential if the comprehensive high school was to achieve the ideals of a democratic education. Totalitarian governments, like the Soviet Union, provided specialized training in separate schools but not the democratic mixing of the comprehensive high school. Conant wrote in his recommendation for twelfth-grade social studies, "This approach is one significant way in which our schools distinguish themselves from those in totalitarian nations. This course, as well as well-organized homerooms and certain student activities, can contribute a great deal to the development of future citizens of our democracy." [76]

Conant's survey came at the end of a decade of heavy public criticism of the schools. The focus of this criticism was the cold war and a concern that the schools had become undemocratic. One major area of agreement for most critics was greater public control and involvement in the educational process. Extreme anticommunists, nurtured by the flames of the cold war, wanted greater public involvement as a means of ridding the school of what they perceived to be the antidemocratic socialization programs designed to produce cooperative individualism as opposed to the economic individualism associated with traditional American capitalism. These groups agreed with other critics, like the Council for Basic Education, that the schools should reduce their social role and concentrate on teaching the basic disciplines. For the council this meant ending the schools' role as a social sorter, which they labeled undemocratic. In essence, both these groups were demanding some fundamental and radical changes in education. The demand for greater public involvement meant undercutting the power of the school bureaucracy and the idea that education should be controlled by a group of experts identified as professional educators. Stripping away the social goals of schooling would have ended the idea of the school as an institution for social engineering and control. It would have meant getting schools out of the business of trying to end poverty, solve the problem of an urban and industrial society, channel manpower, and build a democratic community. The critics were not opposed to trying to solve these problems, but they were concerned that the school was attempting to solve problems through a system of social engineering guided by the hands of professional educators. In this context Conant's study and recommendations must be viewed as a conservative counterattack against radical attempts to transform American education.

THE CHANNELING
OF MANPOWER
IN A DEMOCRATIC
SOCIETY

2 During the years of national debate about schooling, the federal government was developing policies for the channeling of manpower through the military and educational institutions. Two of the most important results of these policies were the National Science Foundation and an expanded Selective Service System. These policies developed in the context of a growing belief the United States was losing the technological and military race with the Soviet Union because of a manpower shortage of teachers, engineers, and scientists.

Concern about the manpower race with the Soviet Union affected many areas of education. It enlisted the public schools and colleges into a strategy of channeling students into occupations considered vital to the national defense. It also sparked an increased struggle in the schools to provide for equality of opportunity so that manpower resources would not be wasted. This meant increasing educational and occupational opportunities for women and racial minority groups so that their potential could be properly utilized by industry and the military.

Most of the important discussions about education in the 1950s were against the background of an almost paranoiac fear that if the United States lost the manpower race with the Soviet Union, it would mean the end of all democratic institutions. As later chapters will show, this fear in the late 1950s contributed to the passage of the landmark National Defense Education Act and a growing cry for excellence in education. The drive for more scientists and engineers resulted in major changes in school curriculums and an increased value being placed upon ability grouping and tracking. During the 1960s the concern about equality of opportunity through education as a means of increasing manpower resources became a central feature of President Johnson's war on poverty. There was a certain logic in the history of events. Lyndon Johnson, who was chairman of the 1951 Senate subcommittee that weighed the arguments concerning selective service and manpower channeling, later became the President who led one of the most massive federal programs to eliminate inequality of opportunity in the United States through education.

While the fears about a manpower shortage were primarily a result of the cold-war race with the Soviet Union, certain facts also contributed to an apparent manpower shortage. A depressed birthrate during the depression years of the 1930s resulted in a decreased supply of young workers in the late 1940s and early 1950s. This situation was aggravated by a military demand to maintain a large defense establishment. In fact, without the military demand for increased manpower there would not have been a general manpower shortage.

In 1952 the National Security Resources Board, an advisory group to the President, reported the manpower shortage citing a decreasing percentage of the population being of employable age and an increasing demand for manpower by the military and for occupations considered vital to the national defense. Even though the population had increased by 16 million since World War II, the number of males between the ages of eighteen and sixty-four had decreased from 27 percent of the total population to 25 percent. In terms of labor-force potential, it could be considered this way. An estimated 48 percent of the population was utilized during World War II; by the late 1940s, only 45 percent of the population would be available in a national emergency.

One of the chief causes of the supposed manpower shortage was the demand by the armed services to maintain a strength of 3.7 million men. The military made it extremely difficult to provide manpower for other occupations considered vital to national security. The areas the National Security Resources Board viewed as facing manpower problems were public school teachers, engineers, scientists, and experts in foreign affairs. They estimated that the United States needed an additional 160,000 qualified elementary school teachers whereas only 33,000 were being graduated. In terms of engineers, the United States had an annual demand for 30,000 whereas the rate of graduation was predicted to decrease; by 1954 there would only be 17,000 new engineering graduates. The board also noted the inadequacies in providing well-trained manpower to conduct our foreign policy. This was reflected in the fact that between 1948 and 1952 only thirteen Americans had been awarded Ph.D. degrees in the Russian language. The National Security Resources Board concluded, "We are short of people. If we are to do everything we need to do for ourselves and for others, every person must count. We can afford no slippage." [1]

The question of slippage in the allocation of manpower resources raised a host of problems about the relationship of manpower planning to the ideology of democracy. How could a supposedly democratic society based on a doctrine of freedom channel youth into occupations considered vital to national security? This became a particularly difficult problem with the development of plans for universal military training following World War II. The Supreme Court had ruled during World War II that compulsory military training was constitutional under the powers granted by the Constitution to Congress to establish and maintain armies. This ruling was extended to include peacetime compulsory service after the passage of the Selective Training and Service Act of 1940.[2] But even with these Supreme Court rulings to back up compulsory military training, there was still an uneasiness that compulsory service to the government represented a form of totalitarianism.

This problem was amplified during and after World War II because many nonmilitary advocates of universal military training viewed it as a means of creating a compulsory training of all American youth for service to society. In other words, the emphasis was not on *military* training but on training to serve the government and society. The framework of military training was used because it was the only constitutional means by which the government could establish a compulsory educational system. For instance, in 1944, when President Roosevelt proposed a nationwide study of one year's training for youth, he stated that this training need not be exclusively military but could be used to train good stenographers or craftsmen.[3] In 1946, when President Truman appointed an Advisory Commission on Universal Training, he remarked, "I don't like to think of it as a universal military training program. I want it to be a universal training program, giving our young people a background in the disciplinary approach of getting along with one another . . . and what it means to take care of this temple which God gave us." Truman went on to claim that universal compulsory training would instill in youth values which would result in selling "our Republic to the coming generations as Madison and Hamilton and Jefferson sold it in the first place." [4]

For those who advocated universal military training of American youth, the conflict between compulsion and democratic ideology was most often resolved in terms of equality before the law. Universal military training would be considered democratic if it were applied equally to all. This argument lost meaning when a system of deferments was introduced and the draft became selective. With the Selective Service Sytem, the argument shifted to one of choice with persuasion; one could choose future education or a job considered in the interests of national security or the armed forces. The persuasion in this case was a draft law which influenced manpower supply by establishing a limited number of choices for individuals to make when they reached draft age. This system was often justified by comparing it to a totalitarian system where manpower needs were achieved through coercion and direct orders. In the United States the means of achieving manpower needs eventually centered on individual choice influenced by a system of social persuaders. In the public schools these persuaders included vocational guidance, tracking, and ability grouping. Outside of public schooling, the persuaders included the draft law and the availability of financial support for further education.

Manpower Channeling in the Public Schools

The persuaders affecting manpower distribution had already become a part of public schooling by World War II. Vocational guidance counseling had begun in the early part of the twentieth century with the goal of solving labor problems by having the guidance counselor determine the labor needs of industry and plan educational programs for individual students to meet those needs. The school guidance counselor was to help the high school student choose a career needed by society and provide him with the information and educational program required to achieve that career goal. Supporting the counselor was a system of testing, tracking, and ability grouping designed to turn the schools into a social-sorting machine.

The American psychologists who developed the first American group IQ tests during World War I argued that the ideal social organization should be based on the proper classification and use of manpower. In their minds the primary instrument for achieving this would be the intelligence test, which would help social institutions determine the future potential of their individual members. After World War I these group IQ tests became widely used in the public schools and became the models for other tests. In the public schools the tests were used to legitimize an already existing system of social sorting. One of the primary goals of the junior high schools, established just before World War I, was the early differentiation of students according to ability and future occupational destination. This was to be achieved by separating students into different ability groups in the seventh grade and spending the seventh and eighth grade helping the student make a vocational choice. In the ninth grade the student made a vocational choice and was separated into an educational track on the basis of that choice.[5]

Even these early endeavors at using the schools for manpower allocations raised questions about the meaning of democracy. Separation of students in terms of vocational destination appeared to run counter to the traditional goal of public schooling to create a political community. Separating students into different tracks in

the school raised the possibility of this community col-
lapsing and the creation of increased antagonism between different social classes and political groups.

In 1918 a committee of the National Education Association issued the *Cardinal Principles of Secondary
Education,* which provided the model for the development of the comprehensive high school and attempted to
resolve the apparent conflict between the social-sorting
function of schooling and the creation of a political
community. The report accepted the idea of ability
grouping in the junior high school but rejected early
differentiation into vocational groups and recommended
that the decision be postponed until high school. The
junior high school would therefore be a period of career
exploration. The report recommended that when vocational differentiation did occur, it should not result in
the creation of separate schools, e.g., trade and college
preparatory. Vocational differentiation, the report argued, should occur within a single school with the
students separated into different vocational tracks. A
social and political community could be achieved by
bringing all the students together in extracurricular activities such as clubs, sports, student government, and
assemblies. Within the framework of the comprehensive
high school, democracy was defined as a social system
that allowed every individual to develop his or her potential for the good of society. In the words of the *Cardinal Principles,* "The purpose of democracy is so to
organize society that each member may develop his
personality through activites designed for the well-being
of his fellow members and of society as a whole." The
social-sorting function was therefore democratic because it met "individual needs" and grouped the students according to their potential use to society. This
grouping was related to the greater good of the community through the social training of extracurricular
activities.[6]

The social-sorting function of the public school encountered difficulty during the depression years of the 1930s when youth were the last hired and the first fired.[7] The unemployment problems of youth led to a national concern and a struggle between the national government and the schools over who would assume custodial responsibility for youth.[8] The government responded to the youth problem with a number of programs including the Civilian Conservation Corps and National Youth Administration. To a certain extent these programs were early models for what the government could do in establishing national service for American youth. There were even suggestions by the American Legion that voluntary military training under the direction of the War Department be included in the programs of the Civilian Conservation Corps.

Educators within the public schools were faced with the problem of a limited job market for career planning. This situation had an important result that would affect manpower planning attempts in the years following World War II. During the depression, the public school guidance counselors began to shift their emphasis from career planning to counseling directed toward individual social and personality problems. The counselor became less of a labor-market research specialist and more of a therapist.[9] After World II, manpower advocates lamented the fact that the counselors were functioning as therapists and not fufilling their roles as career planners. The counseling profession offered strong resistance to ending the therapist role and constantly frustrated those attempting to maintain the social-sorting function of the school.

Universal Military Training

After World War II, the manpower allocation functions that the public school had assumed became part of a larger attempt to find an effective system of persuaders to channel American youth. The military establishment's early commitment in this debate was for the creation of a universal training program which in the name of democracy would prepare youth for service to society and would apply equally to all youth. The military formulated its manpower plans during the war, and in 1944 they were officially stated in War Department Circular 347, "Military Establishment—General Principles of National Military Policy to Govern Preparation of Post War Plans."

Circular 347 stated as an assumption that Congress would pass a law requiring universal training. With this assumption in mind, the War Department went on to list four advantages this plan would have over that of a large standing army. Three of these advantages were: related to the tradition of citizen armies, ability to select military leaders from a large pool of civilians, and reduced costs. The other advantage was a belief that universal military training would increase the influence of military policies over public opinion. Circular 347 stated this advantage in the framework of what the War Department believed would occur after the conclusion of World War II. The circular read, "As a great majority of the leaders of the war army are included in the civil population in time of peace, an intelligent and widespread public opinion is provided as the basis for the determination of all public questions relating to military affairs." Within this context, one important reason the military supported universal military training was because it gave them the power to mold the opinion of an entire generation.[10]

Immediately following the war, a flood of speeches and congressional bills proposed a variety of universal military training plans. In President Roosevelt's message to Congress in 1945 he proclaimed the need for universal military training as a means of maintaining world peace. In June of the same year the Select Committee on Postwar Military Policy of the Congress proposed a training plan that would "be universal and democratic, applicable to rich and poor alike, and with a minimum of exemptions or exceptions." After President Roosevelt's death in 1945, President Truman quickly seized the banner of universal military training; in a joint address to the Senate and House of Representatives in October 1945, he called for one year of training for all American youth. Truman elaborated the idea of universal military training into a general panacea for the problems of American society. He told the joint session that a plan of this type would not only provide for national security but would also "raise the physical standard of the Nation's manpower . . . lower its illiteracy rate, and . . . develop in our young men the ideals of responsible American citizenship." [11]

During 1945 and 1946 the idea of universal military training encountered a certain amount of resistance in Congress and a certain confusion about the form and length of training. In 1945 three different bills were introduced to establish a system of training, and during the same period a number of bills were introduced in opposition. One of the latter provided that no citizen be liable for compulsory training and service.[12] In 1946 President Truman tried to coordinate the work being done on universal military training by establishing an Advisory Commission on Universal Training. On May 29, 1947, the President's Advisory Commission issued their report, *A Program for National Security.*

One of the striking things about the advisory commission's report was how much the ideology of universal training reflected the ideology of schooling. In one sense universal training was to be a continuation of schooling with the term of training beginning right after high school. The period immediately following high school graduation was viewed as ideal because it was a transition between public schooling and future employment and vocational training. It had the added advantage of getting youth at a period of life in which, in the words of the commission, "he begins to question things seriously and wants to argue about them—at a time when his interests about the world begin to enlarge." [13] The commission even defended universal military training in terms of schooling having established a precedent for compulsion in American life. On the one hand, the commission argued that the program would be democratic because it would be universal and everyone would be equal before the law. On the other hand, the commission responded to charges that compulsory service was un-American and undemocratic with the statement that these same charges had been "hurled against the proposal for universal compulsory education in America. Now we take national pride in this system of education, which we speak of as distinctively 'American.' " [14]

That universal training was to be an extension of public schooling on a federal level was reflected in the recommendations of the commission. Universal training was to include both military training and citizenship building. Basic training under the program recommended by the report would be for a six-month period. During that time there would be a concentration upon development of basic military discipline and skills, and the inculcation of the values of good citizenship. The report paralleled the ideology of the common school when it argued universal training would contribute to reducing social friction and building a democratic community by mixing all social groups within one institutional framework. The commission recommended, in reference to basic training, that one "important phase of such environment must be the opportunity for every boy to mingle on a basis of full equality with others boys of all races and religions, and from every walk of life and many different parts of the country." [15] The commission also argued that the very existence of compulsory training contributed to citizenship because the individual learned that he had an obligation to serve the nation. In the words of the commission, compulsion "should bring home to our youth that they all share in a common responsibility for their country's destiny. Participation in an effort for the common good should give them a very concrete idea of their duties as citizens." [16]

One important ingredient in the citizenship program proposed during basic training was that time was to be spent on relating the general meaning of citizenship to why the recruits were being required to train and why the government was interrupting their civilian lives. It was recommended that this citizenship phase of training be modeled on the program used by the regular army during the war which had been developed by the Information and Education Division of the War Department. These recommendations meant that the citizenship programs would tend to be dominated by the military and would be designed to influence the recruits toward a favorable attitude regarding military policies and actions. In American history the question had always existed, if the common school were to teach basic moral and political values, which group in society would decide what those values were to be? In the case of universal training the source of citizenship values was clearly defined as the military establishment.

Universal military training also reflected other values often associated with public schooling. It was hailed, like the public schools, as one of the panaceas for many social problems. It was argued that a great waste of manpower in the United States was a result of improper health care. A staff report for the commission brought together the facts that the United States in comparison to other nations in the statistical data of the League of Nations was seventh in infant mortality, eighth to eleventh in death rates during childhood and adolescence, and nineteenth to twenty-fifth in death rates for those between ages 35 and 64. Added to this was the fact that for certain minority groups in the United States the mortality rates were even higher.[17] Universal military training was considered as a partial corrective to America's inadequate health care services because it would provide for a system of compulsory national health examinations. These examinations were to be followed by corrective and preventive health services available through the armed forces. It is interesting that whereas the United States has maintained a traditional stance against national government-controlled health services, these have always been allowed in the military. In effect, universal military training was to bring all participants under the care and treatment of government-controlled health services.

The advisory commission also recommended that the social-sorting function of the public schools be continued under universal military training. During basic training an extensive system of vocational guidance would be used to help all men select the right occupation for future education. In fact, the commission wanted vocational aptitude testing and guidance to be a mandatory part of the program.[18] Combined with aptitude testing and guidance would be a remedial program designed to eliminate illiteracy in the United States. The sorting function was also involved in the range of options available after completion of basic training. The individual had the choice of having six months further training or choosing a service option which included enlistment in one of the branches of the armed forces, joining a national guard or reserve unit, attending a military academy or joining a college ROTC unit. There was also the option of inactive duty in an Enlisted Reserve Corps while pursuing an education considered vital to national security. The nature of this education was defined as "enrollment in courses of study in civilian trade schools, vocational schools, or colleges which would provide training in professions, skills, or arts of value to the military in time of emergency and which have been approved by the Secretary of War." [19] This option was therefore to be one of the means used for channeling manpower in terms of national policy. The persuader in influencing individual selection of this option was the exchange of inactive military duty for pursuing a career route determined by the government.

While the issue of universal military training was urged by the President and the military, there was little enthusiasm in Congress to pass legislation of this nature during the early postwar years. Compulsory military training continued under a system of Selective Service established during World War II and was continued by Congress into peacetime. The Selective Service System allowed for deferments for those in occupations or pursuing an education considered vital to the conduct of warfare. This was essentially a wartime measure designed to mobilize and classify all manpower resources in terms of military needs. Its continuation into peacetime created the possibility of channeling manpower resources by giving the individual the option of entering military service or an occupation or educational program defined as vital to national interests. In reality the Selective Service had little impact in the years immediately following World War II because of the small number of men who were drafted. In fact, in 1949 the army suspended all calls to military duty, a policy that was not ended until the outbreak of hostilities in Korea in mid-1950.

The Selective Service Debate

The Korean war provided the final impetus for serious consideration of universal training proposals and issues of channeling manpower. The drama that resulted in the Universal Military Training and Service Act of 1951 and directly affected the career plans of all young men for the next two decades began on the morning of January 10, 1951, when then Senator Lyndon Johnson, chairman of the Preparedness Subcommittee of the Committee on Armed Forces, opened hearings for consideration of universal military training. During the more than three weeks the committee was in session, the major problem was defined as how to balance national security needs for engineers and scientists with military manpower needs. The major witnesses testifying before the committee were the Defense Department and representatives of the academic and scientific establishments in the United States who in general agreed upon compulsory military duty but differed on how deferments should be used for channeling manpower. The university community, of course, was concerned that a sudden introduction of universal training would greatly reduce college enrollments during its first years of operation causing serious disruption and economic strain on universities.

The hearings began with Chairman Johnson outlining the basic bill that was under consideration by the Senate. This bill called for the establishment of a National Training Security Corps which would involve four months of basic training followed by eight months of training in one of the branches of the armed forces. The only deferments allowed under this bill were for completion of high school, mental and physical disabilities, and unspecified reasons vital to national security. Lyndon Johnson then introduced a letter from President

Truman which made it clear that the President did not want deferments for mental and physical disabilities. The armed forces were to assume the role of providing for national rehabilitation. President Truman wrote to Johnson, "We [referring to the President's Advisory Commission on Universal Training] sought to pass a bill requiring universal training of all the young people of the country and be sure that all of them have a go at it—whether they are physically fit or not, because most of the physical defects can be remedied under proper supervision." [21]

The Defense Department took a strong stand against the armed forces functioning as a rehabilitation unit for those classified as physically and mentally disabled. Their concern was with having the first control over all able young men in the United States and not as an instrument for the solution for other social problems. Testifying for the Defense Department was Anna Rosenberg, assistant secretary of the Department of Defense, who stated that the Defense Department was not in agreement with the President and that in their opinion a rehabilitation program could not be made compulsory. Ms. Rosenberg urged that if such a program were to be started, it be undertaken outside the military establishment prior to induction and with the consent of the individual. "We could not legally," she claimed, "require those men to undergo physical rehabilitation unless it would actually be a question of whether their life was endangered." She went on to argue that the armed forces could perform an operation against a man's consent if the lack of it might mean his death, but a man could not be forced to undergo an operation to correct a physical defect unless he agreed. The Defense Department recommended that a program of this type might be established in the Veterans Administration or in the U.S. Public Health Service and that it should be "a rehabilitation program of those who would do it with consent, by consent." [22]

One wonders what would have happened if the Defense Department had not been wary of a national rehabilitation program and had agreed with the President. It might have resulted in a compulsory rehabilitation program which logically would have extended the definition of mental rehabilitation to include emotional disorders. This would have given the armed forces the central responsibility for the psychological and physical welfare of the entire nation and would have greatly extended the role of the military establishment in American life. It is a frightening idea that the military would have defined the emotional and mental standards for the entire nation. What is also interesting is that when the Defense Department did not want to assume a particular function, they were the first to begin talking about individual consent and freedom. This resulted in the rather unusual situation of the Defense Department appearing more interested in the issues of liberty than President Truman.

The Defense Department agreed with the provisions in the bill requiring four months' universal training for all able young men. What they disagreed with was how the period following basic training should be utilized. On the one hand they were concerned about manpower planning and the effect of universal training on the colleges. On the other hand they wanted the military to have charge of the entire manpower pool of able young men. The Defense Department wanted all able young men drafted at the age of eighteen or upon graduation from high school into four months of basic training with an obligation of twenty-three months' further service. After the four months of training, the individual would be given a series of options for fulfilling the rest of his service.

One option was continued service in the armed forces followed by three to six years in a reserve component. Another option would be that after four months of training, the individual could enlist in a college ROTC unit, and after completing his college education serve two or three years in the military. The last option, which dealt specifically with manpower planning, would have given the President the power to suspend temporarily the active-service requirement of up to 75,000 students after completion of four months' training. These students would be allowed to complete their college or vocational training. The method of determining who would receive this deferment would be in civilian hands using procedures determined by the President and Congress. The primary criterion for selection would be the relationship between an individual's ability, interests, and career choice and the manpower needs of national security. It was recommended that these selected students might receive financial aid in the form of national scholarships. After graduation this group would have an obligation to perform some type of military duty, but this could be deferred. The Defense Department argued that if individuals under this option entered careers considered in the national interest by the President or Congress, they could receive continued deferment for a ten-year period, at which time they would be released of all obligations.[23]

The Defense Department plan, as presented to the committee, in effect undercut the whole argument that universal military training, even during peacetime, would be democratic if it were truly universal and applied equally to all men. By first rejecting the idea of accepting the physically and mentally disabled and then proposing a system of deferments after basic training, they introduced a system of inequality. The Defense Department justified a deferment system as necessary for maintaining a college system in the United States and the defense needs for scientists and engineers. In fact, when the assistant secretary of defense talked about deferments for 75,000 to attend college, she meant for further scientific and technical training. When Senator Johnson asked Ms. Rosenberg whether the deferment proposal was made primarily to have people study science in school or assure college enrollments, she replied, "We feel, senator, that with our shortage of manpower it is essential that we make it up in skills; that the skilled manpower, the scientific manpower, the highly trained manpower is essential for the national interest."

She also argued that such a plan would improve and increase manpower resources because it would provide for equality of opportunity. This was an argument that was beginning to reverberate through all discussions about manpower shortages. Manpower problems, it was felt, could be corrected if equality of educational opportunity were provided for minority groups and the poor. In this case the Defense Department was proposing to provide equality of educational opportunity through selection of 75,000 from a controlled manpower pool of all American young men and provisions for financial aid. The assistant secretary of defense argued, "No man should be deprived of the opportunity to make his fullest contribution to the national welfare because he lacks the financial means to acquire an education." Combined with deferments for ROTC, this would have meant that the majority of male students in college would have received their education in the framework of obligations to the military and national security.[24]

One group that was very nervous about proposals for universal military training was the Association of American Colleges, which represented many of the smaller universities and colleges in the United States.

Their great fear was that universal training would dry up the flow of students to the smaller schools without any relief through an expanded ROTC program or through the plan to select 75,000 for further college training. From the perspective of these schools, ROTC and the Defense Department's deferment plan would benefit only the larger schools. In a rather anxious tone James Baxter, president of Williams College and chairman of the Committee on Manpower of the Association of American Colleges, explained to the Senate committee that the colleges he represented "have no Army, Navy or Air Force ROTC; but, as you gentlemen know, they would dearly like to have one or, if they can't have one, to have some other share in the work of military training." The resolution submitted by Baxter from the Association of American Colleges supported the idea of universal training which would be shared equally by all male youth with exemptions allowed only for extreme mental and physical disabilities. In order to protect their own interests, they strongly urged that after four months of basic training those recruits who wished to go to college should be allowed to complete their education and return to active duty after graduation. In essence, this extended the Defense Department plan to include all potential college students rather than a select 75,000. This plan, it was felt, would do the least damage to the existing educational system.[25]

In opposition to simply letting any recruit return to school but supporting some system for the channeling of men into science and engineering were the leaders of the scientific establishment. By the scientific establishment is meant those growing groups of scientists who during and after World War II began to move freely between centers of power in government, industry, and the military. These scientists began to exert a growing influence on national policy and were listened to with a great deal of sympathy during discussions of manpower policy and education. Appearing before Lyndon Johnson's Preparedness Subcommittee in January 1951 were some extremely important leaders of this growing power base of the scientific community. One such person was Dr. Charles A. Thomas, chairman of the Scientific Manpower Advisory Committee of the National Security Resources Board and executive vice president of Monsanto Chemical Corporation. The Scientific Manpower Advisory Committee had been established to advise the President of the United States, and its membership consisted of those who had the greatest stake in the training of more scientists and engineers, namely, the military, industry, and universities. The universities were represented on the committee by the dean of the faculty at Princeton and the presidents of the California Institute of Technology, the Carnegie Institute of Technology, and the University of South Carolina. Industry representation included the chairman of the board of Jones & Laughlin Steel Corporation, the vice president of General Electric Company, the vice president of Rohm & Haas Co., and Dr. Thomas of the Monsanto Chemical Company.[26]

The President's Scientific Manpower Advisory Committee supported the Defense Department's plan for four months of universal training followed by a series of options including the deferment of 75,000 for future education. The real interest and concern of this advisory committee was in the selection and use of the 75,000 receiving deferments. They wanted this group to be designated as a Reserve Specialist Training Corps and even suggested that uniforms or distinctive badges might be worn by this group while attending school. They wanted the selection of these men for deferments to be conducted by a National Scientific Personnel Board appointed by the President. This board would determine scientific and engineering manpower in industry and the military, and through a selective device applied to the pool of all young men undergoing four months of training, would channel them into scientific and technical education. Added to this were to be further deferments for those selected for graduate studies. The Scientific Manpower Advisory Committee made it quite clear that "the fields of study open to members of the Reserve Specialist Corps should be primarily the fields of science, engineering, medicine, and others determined by the Government to be essential to national security." [27]

What is important about the argument of the President's Scientific Manpower Advisory Committee was that it assumed that an adequate supply of engineers and scientists could not be achieved unless some form of universal military training resulted in a system of channeling. In other words, if universal military training were not instituted, it was felt the United States would face a manpower shortage in those areas. From graphs depicting manpower supply in the United States, it was argued that at the present rate of enrollment engineering graduates would drop from a peak of over 50,000 in 1950 to 17,000 in 1954. Added to this was the argument that the number graduating in scientific fields was not sufficient to meet present and future demands. This meant that without universal military training and channeling there would be a severe shortage in these areas. Rather than universal military training having a negative effect on the supply of scientists and engineers, it would actually improve it through a system of channeling. The opening line of the statement of purpose of the document submitted by this group to the Senate subcommitte in support of universal training clearly stated, "The objective of the Committee is to propose a method by which an adequate supply of scientific manpower can be maintained and channeled most effectively into the Armed Forces, industry, education, and Government." [28] Universal training in this framework was viewed as primarily a means by which the government, acting on the advice of industry and the military, could control and manipulate the occupational decisions of all American young men.

Another important and influential representative of the scientific establishment to support universal military training was Vannevar Bush, the architect of government scientific policy during and after World War II and the major person responsible for the establishment of the National Science Foundation. Bush supported the idea of universal military training and the selection after basic training of talented young men to pursue a scientific education. This selection, he argued, should be by competitive examination and the judgment of a competent selection board and while the individual attended college he should be required to wear a uniform and be subject to immediate return to active duty. [29]

Vannevar Bush's support of universal military training as a means of channeling scientific manpower must be understood in the context of his activities as director of the Office of Scientific Research and Development during World War II and his reasons for promoting the establishment of a National Science Foundation. In 1944 President Roosevelt asked Bush to prepare a plan for continued government involvement in research following the war. Bush responded with an enthusiasm which reflected his own belief that science was the panacea for the world's problems.

Bush was one of those people who had an unlimited faith in the power of science and technology to accomplish good. Even in his autobiography, written during the turmoil and rebellion of the 1960s, he expressed a faith that science and technology would end poverty, save the environment, and be the foundation stones of a better world.[30] In 1945 Bush issued his reply to the President in the form of a report with the glowing and hopeful title *Science—The Endless Frontier.* Bush argued that continuation of basic scientific research was essential for maintaining full employment, world leadership, national security, and national health. The key to increasing scientific capital was, first, to have plenty of men and women trained in science, and second, to support basic research in colleges, universities, and research institutes. This could be accomplished, Bush felt, through the establishment of a National Science Foundation which would not take over other governmental agencies' involvement in the support of science but would become a focal point for planning and supporting expanding scientific capital.[31]

Two of the important functions of the National Science Foundation, as envisioned by Bush, besides the support of basic research, were the improvement of science education in the public schools and a system of undergraduate and graduate fellowships for training and fundamental scientific research. Bush felt that the improvement of science teaching in high schools was imperative if latent scientific talent was to be properly developed. There was a great danger, he felt, if high school science teaching failed to awaken interest or provided inadequate instruction. This goal of the National Science Foundation would have an important effect on public education in later years when the foundation began to support studies of science curriculum and helped to introduce many new programs into the public schools.

It was also proposed that the National Science Foundation would provide 6000 undergraduate scholarships and 300 graduate scholarships each year as a means of maintaining a steady supply of scientists. Under the plan as given in the 1945 report, those who received scholarships would be enrolled in a National Science Reserve and would be liable for call into government service during a time of war or other national emergency. The idea of a National Science Reserve was similar to the proposal made by the Scientific Manpower Advisory Committee to the Senate subcommittee in 1951 for a Reserve Specialist Corps composed of those selected for scientific training. Bush was a member of this advisory committee, and it might have been his influence that resulted in the proposal for the establishment of this paramilitary scientific corps.[32]

Bush appeared before the Senate Preparedness Subcommittee in 1951, shortly after he had accomplished his goal in the form of the National Science Foundation Act of 1950. The battle to establish the foundation had been primarily over the issue of executive vs. independent control. The first act to establish a National Science Foundation had been passed by Congress in 1947 but was vetoed by President Truman because he felt the board of the foundation was given too much independent power and he wanted the director to be appointed by the President. When the bill passed, Bush claimed that he was able to convince President Truman not to veto it because an independent board that selected its own director would have an easier time working with the university community. The establishment of the National Science Foundation did not dissuade Bush from seeking other measures to increase scientific manpower.[33]

Bush's testimony before the Senate subcommittee was given on behalf of a group called the Committee on the Present Danger which stated that it believed the first key step in the free world's defense was military manpower legislation which would act "both as a deterrent to a major aggression and as a defense if war should come." The membership of this group included thirty-three powerful leaders from the military, industry, and universities. Some of the important members were the chairmen of the boards of Johns Manville and General Mills; the president of the Carnegie Corporation; the presidents of Princeton University, the University of Chicago, and the University of California; and several former assistant and undersecretaries of war. This powerful industrial and university group emphasized the much repeated idea that "we need not only trained men but also the most modern weapons. . . . This means we need both a reservoir of trained men and a continuing advance on every scientific and technical front." [34]

Another member of the Committee on the Present Danger who testified in support of universal military training and the channeling of manpower into science and engineering was James B. Conant, the president of Harvard University and first chairman of the board of the National Science Foundation. Conant, like Vannevar Bush, represented the new breed of scientists who were gaining influential positions and exerting power over national policy. Conant is important in the discussion of the issues surrounding the channeling of manpower not only because he was a leader of the scientific establishment but also because later in the decade he was to gain national prominence through his study of the American high school. His support of universal military training and the channeling of manpower provided the basic framework for his later discussions about the American high school.

Conant's ideas on manpower channeling were first explicitly stated before a congressional hearing in 1947 when he was asked to testify on behalf of bills supporting the establishment of the National Science Foundation. Conant told the committee that he was primarily concerned with the provisions in the bills for a National Science Foundation that were related to the granting of scholarships and fellowships. He stated, "It is men that

count. And today we do not have the scientific manpower requisite for the job that lies ahead." [35] The important thing for Conant was to tap the latent talent of
many high school students who either did not enter a
scientific career or were unable to pursue a college education because of financial reasons. A system of scholarships would assure that superior high school students
who needed financial aid could continue their education,
and they could be channeled into science because their
financial support would depend upon following that
type of career. During the discussion, one congressman
asked Conant if he thought the public schools could
accomplish more toward channeling scientific manpower by setting apart superior students and giving
them special training. Conant replied that this, of
course, was to a certain extent being done in the public
schools, but it required a greater emphasis. To broaden
the meaning of this idea Conant submitted an abstract
of a speech he had given two days before to the American
Association of School Administrators on "The Dilemma
of American Education."

The dilemma, as described by James Conant, was
similar to the dilemma facing the consideration of universal military training. How do you make it equal but
at the same time make provisions for channeling superior manpower into needed occupations? Conant never
resolved the dilemma but suggested that, "We pay a
price for the fundamental democracy of our undifferen-
tiated system of public schools . . . if we are wise the price
need not be as high as it is at the present moment."
Reducing the price of democratic schools meant for
Conant increasing their roles as social-sorting institutions by placing greater emphasis on the guidance and
counseling of superior students and by setting a greater
intellectual pace for these students by requiring them to
take four years of mathematics, three years of a foreign
language, and to gain a mastery of the English language.

These superior students would be the pool from which scholars would be selected for federal subsidy of higher education. Conant made it clear before the congressional committee that he did not advocate a federal subsidy so that all students could go to college—only those who would be considered superior and would enter professions considered necessary to the national interests. He also stated his own interest in tying federal support to the idea of obligation and establishing a National Science Reserve.[36]

Pressure from the scientific and industrial community for the channeling and control of scientific and technical manpower and the fear of small colleges that universal military training would mean economic disaster almost assured that the argument for compulsory service—it would be democratic because it would apply equally to all—would not be sustained. The pressures almost made certain that some type of special provision would be made in terms of future manpower supply. Added to this was a fear among certain congressmen that if selection for deferment for further education were made after universal military training it would concentrate power in the executive branch of government and greatly increase the social control of the President. During the subcommittee hearings in 1951, Senator Wayne Morse told the chairman of the Scientific Manpower Advisory Committee that he could not accept their plan to establish a National Scientific Personnel Board to select deferments because of "the power it gives the President." Senator Morse argued, "I do not see any reason why we have to do what you propose to do by vesting more power in the President. He already has entirely too much power from the standpoint of exercising discretion." [37]

The need for channeling manpower combined with a fear of increased presidential power and concern about the future of small colleges led to the shelving of the idea that the draft should be made democratic by requiring universal service. The resolution of the problem led in future years to complaints that indeed the draft was unfair because the middle class and rich went to college while the poor went into the armed forces. The solution arrived at was to continue the Selective Service System but use a combination of aptitude tests and class standing as a means of assuring a steady flow of manpower through the colleges. This plan had been presented to the subcommittee in 1951 by M. H. Trytten, director of the Office of Scientific Personnel of the National Academy of Sciences and chairman of the Scientific Committees of the Selective Service System. Trytten presented the plan with the remarks that highly trained personnel are "now fundamental to the proper functioning of our civilization, to its economy and to its military strength." He went on to paint a gloomy picture of how the Soviet Union was outdistancing the United States in the production of highly trained technicians and scientists. But he also expressed a fear that the 75,000 figure to be used for deferments would not be adequate because of a possible attrition of 20,000 of those students.[38]

The Trytten plan originally called for deferment on the basis of a national objective test and college performance. This was modified after complaints that the use of a specific test score plus class standing would work to the disadvantage of students from localities having poor educational facilities. In their final form the new deferment standards were passed as amendments to the original selective service act rather than passing a new act establishing a universal military training corps. The amendments of 1951 provided for the control and channeling of manpower by authorizing the President to defer individuals whose academic training was necessary to the national health, safety, or interest. Students could be deferred in college by receiving a certain score on the national Selective Service College Qualification Test or by maintaining a certain class rank. Ultimate power over the system was placed in the hands of local draft boards, and restriction of presidential power was assured by the draft boards being specifically exempted from the obligation to defer students solely on the basis of any federally established criteria.[39]

The National Manpower Council

The first major complaint about the inequalities inherent in this system of deferments was contained in a special report on *Student Deferment and National Manpower Policy* issued by the National Manpower Council and presented to the newly elected President Dwight D. Eisenhower in 1952. This report was the first work undertaken by the National Manpower Council after its establishment in 1951 at Columbia University under a grant from the Ford Foundation. During the 1950s and until its final report, *Manpower Policies for a Democratic Society*, in 1965, the National Manpower Council was the major public organization for studying and issuing recommendations on national manpower objectives. Very often during its life it was assumed to be a government group because of its wide publicity and the attention given its recommendations. The National Manpower Council complained in its final report, "The Council is still sometimes mistakenly identified as a governmental body. It is not. It is a body of private citizens . . . who share a common deep concern with the state of the nation's manpower resources." [40]

This group of private interested citizens was primarily drawn from the leadership of major industrial, educational, and labor organizations. The primary impetus for establishing a National Manpower Council came from Eisenhower's leadership when he served as president of Columbia University before running for the presidency of the United States. During World War II,

General Eisenhower encountered shortages of manpower in the North African Campaign and in the European Theater. At the time he was experiencing these shortages he knew that many young men were being rejected for military service because of mental and emotional problems. After the war, Eisenhower became very much interested in using the personnel records of World War II to investigate the nation's human resources. In 1949, as president of Columbia University, Eisenhower helped to establish the Conservation of Human Resources Project under the direction of Eli Ginzberg. The sponsorship of this project reflected the interest that major industrial groups had in the issues of manpower utilization. The Conservation of Human Resources Project received funding from the Ford Foundation and fifteen leading American corporations. Included in the list of sponsoring organizations were the American Can and Continental Can Companies, E. I. Du Pont de Nemours and Company, General Dynamics Corporation, General Electric Company, General Foods Corporation, Standard Oil Company (New Jersey), and the Coca-Cola Company.[41]

During the 1950s the Conservation of Human Resources Project issued a series of reports, the most important being the three volumes which came under the general title *The Ineffective Soldier*. The first volume, *The Lost Divisions*, looked closely at why many young men were unable to serve during World War II and the implications of this for future manpower planning. Their major conclusion was that the failure to provide adequate educational facilities during the 1920s and 30s and the failure of many young persons to take full advantage of existing educational resources resulted in the loss to the armed forces during World War II of at least 372,000 men, which was equivalent to twenty-five 15,000-man divisions and in excess of all battle deaths suffered by the United States. The report strongly recommended, based on their findings, increased educational opportunities in the United States and proper manpower utilization and planning.[42]

In 1951 the staff of the Conservation of Human Resources Project began to work closely with the newly founded National Manpower Council with Eli Ginzberg assuming the role of director of research for the council. When the National Manpower Council issued its first report on student deferments in 1952, its membership was sixteen and included the presidents and deans of six universities, the presidents of two unions, four industrial leaders, a newspaper manager, a professor of political philosophy, a management consultant, and a lawyer. In its first report the council strongly supported student deferments as necessary "to insure a continuous supply of college-trained people whose general education and specialized knowledge are essential to the nation's civilian and military strength." [43] The council was concerned about certain inequities that had apparently been built into the Selective Service System. One of these was the possibility that a student deferred for college might continue his deferment after college by being granted a dependency deferment because of marriage and children. The council argued that this in effect turned the student deferment system into an exemption system which could be corrected only by the elimination of dependency deferments. Unless this were done, the council felt, there could be no justification for selective service in terms of democratic ideology. All must be required at some point to serve the nation.[44]

The other concern of the Manpower Council was that student deferments tended to discriminate against certain geographical areas and against the poor and minority groups. The system as it was established after 1951 and continued through the 1960s provided deferments on the basis of class rank or score achieved on the Selective Service College Qualification Test as administered by the Educational Testing Service. In figures presented by the Educational Testing Service to the National Manpower Council it was shown that in terms of the estimated number of deferable freshman in each region of the country, as compared to the number of all males of college age in that region, there were some major regional differences. In the Northeast section of the United States 9 percent of all males of freshman age were deferable, while in the North Central and West the figure was 7 percent. The startling fact was that in the South the figure fell to 3 percent.[45] The Manpower Council warned, "To the extent that the educationally handicapped states need college graduates in order to improve their educational systems, it may be said that the present deferment method does them some disservice." [46]

The council was also concerned that the system was basically unfair to promising young men who did not go to college. They noted that "among Negroes and in other minority groups, discriminatory bars to college entrance and the difficulties that college-trained persons of these groups encounter in finding appropriate employment may discourage even those who strongly desire a college education." [47] Added to this was the fact that many young men had the ability and desire to attend college but lacked the financial resources. Based on the 1952 report of the Manpower Council, one could have predicted that the system of deferments established under selective service as a means of channeling manpower would result in the manpower of the armed forces being disproportionately drawn from the South, minority groups, and the poor.

After the issuance of their first report on student deferment, the National Manpower Council began to hold a series of large-scale conferences at Columbia University to which were invited leaders in education, government, labor, and industry. The conferences were designed to focus on some topic relating to manpower problems and had as their objective the publication of a major report on that subject. The first such series of conferences concentrated on scientific and professional manpower and were held from April through December, 1952 with over one hundred public leaders attending. Some of the participating organizations included the American Management Association, Bell Telephone Laboratories, National Association of Manufacturers, Educational Testing Service, National Education Association, Atomic Energy Commission, Department of Defense, National Science Foundation, National Security Resources Board, Office of Defense Mobilization, and Selective Service.[48] The organizations and individuals participating in these conferences represented those who had the greatest interest in the channeling of manpower. The report issued by this conference was *A Policy for Scientific and Professional Manpower* (1953). It was followed by a series of other reports produced by similar types of conferences. These reports included *Proceedings of a Conference on the Utilization of Scientific and Professional Manpower* (1954), *A Policy for Skilled Manpower* (1954), *Improving the Work Skills of the Nation* (1955), *Womanpower* (1957), *Work in the Lives of Married Women* (1958), *Education and Manpower* (1960), *Government and Manpower* (1964), *Public Policies and Manpower Resources* (1964), and *Manpower Policies for a Democratic Society* (1965).

One of the underlying problems that threaded its way through all these reports was the reconciliation of a desire to channel manpower with the ideology of a democratic society. The report on scientific and professional manpower argued that totalitarian societies could use direct coercive methods of assuring the achievement of manpower objectives. The rival of the United States in the race for manpower was, of course, designated as the Soviet Union, who through its current Five Year

Plan could call for specified increases in the numbers of its scientists and engineers. The disadvantage of the United States was that it could not call upon the power of a monolithic state to achieve its manpower targets.

"A democratic society," the report argued, "promises each individual the opportunity to develop his potentialities as fully as he can in accordance with his own desires." [49] This meant that manpower channeling in the context of democratic ideology had to concentrate on influencing individual choice through indirect methods. Defined in a different manner, this meant that freedom was considered the sense of freedom an individual had when he was able to do those things he desired. Freedom and social needs could be maintained by controlling individual desire through training and organization of the social structure. Individuals would choose and act in a manner consistent with social needs if their desires had been properly conditioned by education and social persuaders. The key, then, to channeling manpower in a democratic society was to develop the social means of controlling individual choice. This, of course, was the reasoning used in the discussions of universal military training as a means of channeling manpower. The National Manpower Council accepted this role of selective service and tried to find additional means of persuading individual choice through provisions for equality of educational opportunity, financial support for certain types of education, making certain types of occupations more attractive, and through strengthening the role of the public schools as channelers of manpower.

In its report on skilled manpower in 1954 the National Manpower Council directed its attention toward the role of the secondary school. The council argued that the primary objective of secondary education in the United States should be preparation for work. The primary ingredients in meeting this objective were to be the teaching of basic skills, the development of good work habits, and effective vocational guidance. Under the heading of basic skills were included ability to read, communicate, and perform basic arithmetical processes. These were considered part of the foundation upon which future training and employability could be built.[50]

The other part of the foundation was to include work habits the individual gained through attendance at school. This argument emphasized the idea that the very process of attending school provided a form of socialization which prepared the individual to enter the world of work. The council report stated that "the school environment exposes youngsters to conditions and experiences comparable, in a number of important ways, to those which they will encounter when they go to work." These school conditions which reflected the world of work were given as, "The school enforces a regular schedule by setting hours of arrival and attendance; assigns tasks that must be completed; rewards diligence, responsibility, and ability; corrects carelessness and ineptness; encourages ambition." It was argued that of all cultural institutions youth encounters, including the church, family, and peer group, demands of schooling came closest to those demands made by employers. The school was therefore central to manpower planning because "the school's manner of operation resembles the employment situation, it can be viewed as a training and preliminary testing ground in the work habits and methods, motivations, and attitudes that will be considered desirable when the student seeks employment."[51]

The argument that schools should and would be the central socialization agency for an industrial culture was not a new argument but one that had existed from the nineteenth century and had been reiterated at various stages of industrial development. Historian Michael Katz has shown that the argument for developing good work habits for an industrial society through school attendance was one of the prime motives behind the support of developing secondary schools in the nineteenth century.[52] In the early part of the twentieth century one of the most widely used textbooks in elementary teacher training stressed that the habits gained through marching to and from the playground and class, through drill and classroom routine, were all preparation for the world of industrial work.[53] What should be recognized about these socialization arguments is that they were primarily directed toward increasing industrial efficiency by increasing managerial control. The habits learned in school were mainly related to obedience and compliance with institutional policies. What the National Manpower Council did was to emphasize again these ideas against the background of a global race with the Soviet Union for technological superiority.

The Council also argued that motivation in school work would increase if education demonstrated its value in terms of future work. This meant that all the important processes of education including teaching, socialization, and motivation were to be directed toward career goals. For the Manpower Council this would give the high school diploma increased meaning to future employers. High school graduation would demonstrate not only the learning of basic skills and good work habits but also indicate "a youngster's commitment to his own development and, therefore, of his willingness to undertake further training." In different language this meant that the high school diploma symbolized a motivation to learn those things that increased industrial efficiency and allowed for the proper utilization of individual talents to achieve manpower goals.[54]

Key to the use of secondary education for manpower planning was vocational guidance. The importance of guidance, so the Manpower Council argued, was in helping the individual to make effective use of freedom. This meant that individual career choice must be influenced and guided in such a manner that it did not result in society's loss of individual talent. It was felt that if a person made an educational or occupational decision without consideration of his strengths and weaknesses, it would lead to a wastage of manpower resources. The role of guidance was to analyze individual abilities effectively in terms of national manpower needs and help the individual freely choose a career route. This could be achieved, the Council argued, only if guidance counseling ended its concern with personality adjustment and concentrated on vocational issues. The Council lamented that one of the major obstacles to using the schools effectively as part of manpower planning was the ever-growing emphasis on counseling for overall adjustment. The council strongly stated that the proper function of guidance should be vocational.[55]

The other concern of the council in eliminating manpower wastage in the social system was providing equality of opportunity for areas of the labor pool that were discriminated against in terms of employment and education. From the perspective of the council, motivation to achieve in education could not be obtained unless one could realize a market value for the education. For minority groups, such as blacks, equality of educational opportunity depended on equality of occupational opportunity. This meant legislation to curb job discrimination and the opening of all avenues of advancement for all racial and minority groups. Discrimination had to be ended to avoid manpower wastage in the race with the Soviet Union. Of particular importance were women, representing the largest of the manpower resources discriminated against in the American economy. The 1957 report of the National Manpower Council on *Womanpower* stressed that along with effective schooling and vocational guidance, policies must be developed by which employers "hire, assign, train, and promote all individuals regardless of sex on the basis of their personal qualifications . . . and both employers and unions take additional steps to apply the principle of equal pay for equal work." [56]

The final report of the Manpower Council directed attention to one of the fundamental criticisms of the manpower concept. At the 1953 conferences of the council, Kenneth E. Boulding had argued, "The manpower concept is basically, I suspect, an engineering concept. . . . Society is conceived as a great machine, feeding Manpower in at one end and grinding maximum quantities of the Single Well-defined End . . . at the other." Boulding went on to charge that the concept of manpower fits well into a slave society where human beings are treated as domestic animals but not for a free society where the individual was the creator of both demand and supply.[57]

Boulding's criticisms centered on the possible incompatibility of manpower concepts with a democratic ideology. Spokesmen for manpower concepts had achieved a partial solution in arguing that manpower policies should not be coercive but should influence the choice of the individual. On the other hand, manpower spokesmen consistently throughout the 1950s and even later in the 1960s and '70s, referred to the "waste of manpower" and the development of "individual potential" to meet manpower needs. The concept of "waste of manpower" was primarily directed toward the needs of society and not of the individual. A waste of manpower implied that wastage occurred when an individual did not perform a task needed by society. For instance, if a brilliant engineer or scientist decided that contentment meant living a reclusive life in the woods or driving a taxi, this would be a waste of manpower in terms of social needs but not in terms of the individual. The same thing was true of the concept of helping individuals "fulfill their potential." This concept implied that every individual had some maximum level of brainpower which had to be obtained in terms of an hierarchical structure of occupations. A "brilliant" person achieved his maximum by becoming a scientist or engineer; another individual, with a little less brainpower, would achieve his potential by becoming a high grade technician. Potential was therefore defined primarily in social and not individual terms. There was no room within the concept for the "brilliant" individual who freely chose not to develop her or his brainpower in terms of a hierarchical occupational structure.

In its final report the National Manpower Council attempted to answer the problems inherent in the rhetoric of manpower utilization by arguing that manpower was not at variance with the ideals and values of a free and democratic society because it "places man and the realization of his potentialities at the center of the stage of the drama of democratic life." What manpower concepts underscored, it was argued, was "that the ideals and values of a free and democratic society impose obligations upon government and private individuals and organizations alike to discover and help create conditions of life under which the potentialities of all men may be realized." [58]

In concrete terms this obligation meant a system of social persuaders for channeling manpower which included the compulsion of selective service, the social sorting and occupational orientation of the public schools, and public policies that brought everyone into the social race by providing for equality of education and opportunity. Involved in this was a belief that individual needs and social needs were inseparable and that individual fulfillment was the same as increasing social efficiency. This meant that freedom and democratic life had very specific meanings in terms of manpower discussions. Freedom meant the ability to develop individual potential for the good of the entire society. Democratic life meant a form of social organization that maximized its own efficiency and development by allowing proper utilization of manpower resources. This concept of democracy was not very much different from the one that justified the development of the social-sorting function of the comprehensive high school in the early part of the twentieth century. As quoted earlier in the chapter, it had been argued with regard to the high school that "the purpose of democracy is so to organize society that each member may develop his personality through activities designed for the well-being of his fellow members and of society as a whole."

THE DEVELOPMENT
OF A NATIONAL
CURRICULUM

3 The basic issues of cold-war strategy, manpower channeling, and criticisms of the public schools all contributed to the development and national distribution of new curriculums in science, mathematics, and foreign languages. These three areas of education were considered most vital in the international race for global power with the Soviet Union. Improved science and mathematics were important in the technological race, while foreign languages were essential to effective foreign policy actions in the areas of cultural relations and technical assistance to underdeveloped countries.

What made possible the development of national curriculums was a combination of federal government and foundation support for the development of new curriculum materials and the distribution of monies by the federal government so that local schools would be able to purchase some of the products of these new curriculums. Federal support of curriculum innovations was channeled through the National Science Foundation established in 1950 under the leadership of Vannevar Bush and James Conant. The goals of the National Science Foundation were to increase American scientific capital by supporting basic research and the scientific education of talented students, and by improving science education in the public schools. Two important curriculum groups supported by the foundation were the Physical Science Study Committee organized in 1956 and the School Mathematics Study Group organized in 1958. Federal support of curriculum developments in foreign languages came through Title VI of the National Defense Education Act of 1958.

Rapid national distribution of new curriculum materials was possible because of the nature of the textbook industry in the United States and the money made available through Title III of the National Defense Education Act. Title III provided money to each state for the purchase of equipment and materials for programs in science, mathematics, and foreign languages. This occurred just at the time innovations were taking place in the areas of mathematics and science.

National distribution was also aided by the existence of a national textbook market. Certainly one of the most important influences on the content of teaching in the public schools is the textbook. By the late 1950s less than a hundred textbook companies dominated the public school textbook market. Approximately one-half of these concentrated on elementary school textbooks while the rest published high school texts. None of these companies offered a complete line of textbooks for every course at every grade. This meant that for any particular course, there were relatively few alternative textbooks. In 1959 ten publishing houses published all the high school physics textbooks. In 1960 about a dozen texts were available in chemistry and fourteen in biology. Almost all textbooks were distributed on a national basis and had to conform to state statutes which covered things like the physical appearance of the book and marketing procedures.

Textbook prices were essentially nationalized in 1934 with the passage of an Ohio law which stated that the price for any textbook sold in Ohio could not exceed the lowest price for a particular textbook sold anywhere else in the country. A majority of states followed the example of Ohio with the result that textbook prices became a matter of nationwide competition. Added to these factors was the similarity of state and local study guides which influenced the content of textbooks. This meant that the major distinguishing characteristics between textbooks in different study areas were authorship, editing, and method of marketing.[1]

One result of the concentration of textbook publishing and the national market was the virtual creation of a national curriculum. A person could travel from Maine to California and find a similarity between what was taught in the schoolhouses across the nation. Another result of these features of the textbook industry was the ability to influence curriculum nationally by changing the nature and content of the textbooks. This became a very important strategy of curriculum developers like the School Mathematics Study Group. Their task was aided by the fact that major publishers could not afford to spend money on curriculum research.[2] This meant that the federal government could sponsor curriculum research which then would be welcomed by private publishing companies. This situation explained why groups like the School Mathematics Study Group could so swiftly, and to the amazement of parents, convert the public schools to something called the "new mathematics." It also meant that in a roundabout fashion the federal government was determining the nature of curriculum in certain areas in schoolhouses throughout the nation.

The National Defense Education Act

The major influence over federal policy regarding education in the 1950s was the scientific establishment, which was supported by and had intimate connections with cold-war military research. As previous chapters have shown, this was true of the National Science Foundation and exemplified by scientists like Vannevar Bush and James Conant. It was also true of the National Defense Education Act of 1958 (NDEA), which represented the major federal support of public education during the 1950s. In fact, the NDEA symbolized the triumph of the arguments of the scientific establishment over those of professional education groups like the National Education Association in determining federal policy with regard to education.

The story of the passage of the NDEA of 1958 was related to cold-war concerns about education, the development of new national curriculums, and the problems of federal aid to education. As noted, President Dwight D. Eisenhower had a major interest in the channeling and utilization of manpower beginning in World War II and in his support of the National Manpower Council and the Conservation of Human Resources Project while he was head of Columbia University. He was also a military expansionist. As head of NATO in the early 1950s, he called for an increased number of U.S. troops in Europe as a means of building "a secure wall of peace" against the Soviet Union. Involved in both these concerns was the technological and military race with the Soviet Union. The situation which dramatized all the cold-war arguments and brought immediate calls for action was the launching by the Soviet Union of *Sputnik I* on October 4, 1957. This event seemed to confirm the dire predictions that the United States was losing the cold war because of the failure of its educational system. It also resulted in Eisenhower stating what he felt should be national educational policy in the cold war and a special message to Congress which provided the basis for passage of the NDEA.

In Oklahoma City on November 13, 1957, President Eisenhower outlined the relationship between education and cold-war strategy in the context of national fears about the launching of *Sputnik I*. Eisenhower began his speech by pointing out that the Soviet Union in only forty years had converted itself from a nation of peasants to an industrial nation which had accomplished major technological achievements and established a rigorous educational system. He went on to warn, "When such competence in things material is at the service of leaders who have so little regard for things human, and who command the power of an empire, there is danger ahead for freemen everywhere." Eisenhower argued that the Soviet threat must be met on its own terms by outmatching them in military power, technological advance, and specialized education and research. In terms of military power, he outlined his basic defense strategy, which included a strong nuclear retaliatory power as "a primary deterrent to war," military cooperation with other countries, a strong home defense, and reserve strength. Essential to this program of national defense was increased military research, which would be directed toward the production of intercontinental ballistic missiles. Eisenhower tried to assure the nation that it was well on the way to the development of adequate missile power. "Today," he stated, "a principal deterrent to war is the retaliatory nuclear power of our Strategic Air Command and our Navy. We are adding missile power to these arms and to the Army as rapidly as possible." He also urged increased attention and support of economic aid to foreign nations as a means of warding off the threat of Soviet domination.[3]

Eisenhower's stress on defense requirements provided the framework for his discussion of educational policies. In one sense his speech introduced the nation to the new world of missiles and space technology. As the school system had been called upon to prepare the nation for a world of atomic warfare, it was now called upon to prepare the nation for the space age. "Young people now in college," Eisenhower emphasized, "must be equipped to live in the age of intercontinental ballistic missiles." The most important problem in preparing for this new age was the production of more scientists and engineers to match the increased quantity and quality of graduates from the Soviet educational system. In fact, Eisenhower claimed in his speech, "My scientific advisers place this problem above all other immediate tasks of producing missiles, of developing new techniques in the armed services." Within this context and in terms of the overall speech, improvements in the educational system were to be the number-one priority in maintaining national defense. Specifically, Eisenhower called for a system of nationwide testing of high school students and a system of incentives to persuade students with high ability to pursue scientific or professional studies. He also urged a program "to stimulate good-quality teaching of mathematics and science" and an increase in laboratory facilities. And of vital importance was a system of fellowships to increase the number of qualified teachers.[4]

On January 27, 1958, Eisenhower delivered a special message to Congress outlining his program of education for national defense. The first item on his list of recommendations was a fivefold increase in appropriations for the scientific education activities of the National Science Foundation. Eisenhower argued that the scientific education programs of the foundation "have come to be recognized by the education and scientific communities as among the most significant contributions currently being made to the improvement of science education in the United States." In terms of specific programs of the foundation, Eisenhower urged increased spending for summer institutes to train science and mathematics teachers. As will be shown later in the chapter, these summer institutes had a significant role in the spreading of the new national curriculums in science and mathematics. He also urged an increase in funds to stimulate the improvement of the content of science courses at all levels of schooling. Eisenhower stated, "The efforts of even the most dedicated and competent teachers will not be effective if the curricula and materials with which they work are out of date or poorly conceived." Undoubtedly what Eisenhower had in mind was the already important work of the Physical Science Study Committee in the development of a new curriculum for high school physics. It was clear that Eisenhower saw these curriculum changes taking place on a nationwide scale. Eisenhower also urged expansion of the foundation's programs for encouraging students to consider a career in science, and for graduate fellowships to give students better scientific training. This part of the package for education for national defense was to be located under the control of the National Science Foundation.[5]

The other part of the package of education for national defense was to be under the jurisdiction of the Office of Education of the Department of Health, Education, and Welfare. Eisenhower's first recommendation in this part of the message was for a reduction in the waste of national talent by providing grants to states for improved testing programs, guidance and counseling services.[6] This, of course, had been one of the prime concerns of all the manpower studies in the 1950s and considered of vital importance in the proper channeling of manpower. It was the fundamental element in the use of the school as a social-sorting instrument in terms of national needs. This recommendation eventually became Title V of the NDEA of 1958 as it was finally approved in September of that year.

Title V appropriated $15 million for each of four succeeding fiscal years for guidance, counseling, testing, and identification of able students. The money was specifically allocated to states for a program of testing in secondary schools and for guidance and counseling programs that would advise students of the best course of studies for their abilities and urge capable students to take the necessary courses for admission to institutions of higher education. Money was also appropriated under Title V for guidance-training institutes for secondary school guidance personnel.[7] One important factor about Title V was the clear intention of Congress and the President to support guidance for testing and program planning and not for psychological therapy and counseling. One of the central concerns of manpower advocates (see chapter 2) was that secondary school counselors minimize their role in dealing with personality problems.

Eisenhower's second recommendation in his message to Congress called for federal funds for improving the teaching of science and mathematics through the hiring of additional science teachers and purchase of equipment and materials. This recommendation became Title III of the NDEA. It appropriated $70 million for each of the next four fiscal years which was to be used for equipment and materials and for the expansion and improvement of supervisory services in the public schools in the areas of science, mathematics, and modern foreign languages. Eisenhower's third recommendation was for a graduate fellowship program to prepare more students for college teaching careers. This became Title IV of the NDEA and produced the National Defense Fellowship program. Congress appropriated 1000 fellowships for the first fiscal year and 1500 for each succeeding fiscal year.

The issue of foreign languages and their relationship to national security occupied the text of Eisenhower's fourth recommendation. This was of importance because the improvement of science and mathematics curriculums had already found a home in the National Science Foundation. Eisenhower's recommendation would place the responsibility for improving foreign-language curriculums as part of education for national defense in the Department of Health, Education, and Welfare. Eisenhower argued, "Knowledge of foreign languages is particularly important today in the light of America's responsibilities of leadership in the free world. And yet the American people generally are deficient in foreign languages, particularly those of the emerging nations in Asia, Africa, and the Near East." The foreign language aspects of the NDEA were clearly seen as part of our competition with the Soviet Union for influence over the developing nations of the world. Title VI appropriated moneys for language institutes and for language centers and research. Title VI also appropriated money for studies of history, anthropology, political science, economics, sociology, and geography about geographical areas where adequate instruction in those areas was nonexistent in the United States. This part of Title VI reflected a concern that the Soviet Union was outdistancing the United States in world influence because of a lack of knowledge in America about many regions of the world.

One effect of the NDEA was to expand and increase the importance of the Office of Education. As a final recommendation Eisenhower asked Congress to authorize the Office of Education to give grants to states for improving the collection of statistical data which in turn would be reported to the Office of Education. This was provided for by Congress under Title X. Eisenhower ended his congressional message with the argument that the federal role was to assist and not control local, state, and private effort. While there was no statement of control in Eisenhower's message and in the final NDEA, it certainly could not be overlooked that such immense sums of money would have a persuasive effect on the direction of education in the United States. Eisenhower described his recommendations for expansion of the National Science Foundation and education for national defense as an "emergency program" which stemmed "from national need, and its fruits will bear directly on national security."

The final form of the NDEA included several important additions by Congress to the original program as presented by Eisenhower. One was a student loan program under Title II which in terms of appropriation was to leap from $47.5 million in the first fiscal year to $90 million in 1962. The student loan program was to include a series of social persuaders to channel manpower. The social persuaders in this case were special preference for students of superior capacity or preparation in science, mathematics, engineering, and modern foreign languages. In addition, graduates who entered a teaching career in elementary and secondary schools could cancel 10 percent of their loans for each year of teaching for a period of five years, or 50 percent of the loan. One wonders how many individuals in the 1960s went to college on an NDEA loan as a means of avoiding the draft into the military services and then, to maintain their draft exemption and pay off their NDEA loan, became public school teachers. Congress also added sections to the NDEA for the support of experimentation in educational media, a science information service, and vocational education.

The whole emphasis and direction of federal aid to education as provided under the NDEA ran counter to the desires and wishes of many powerful national education organizations. This was made clear in the testimony of William G. Carr, executive secretary of the National Education Association, when he appeared before the Senate Committee on Labor and Public Welfare. The committee opened hearings on the issue of science and education for national defense on January 21, 1958, seven days before President Eisenhower's special message to Congress. It was this Senate committee that was to be charged with consideration of Eisenhower's proposals. The committee was chaired by Senator Lister Hill of Alabama and was composed of twelve other members including Senators John F. Kennedy of Massachusetts, Wayne Morse of Oregon, Strom Thurmond of South Carolina, and Barry Goldwater of Arizona. The two committee members who eventually dissented against the NDEA were Goldwater and Thurmond. Carr of the National Education Association appeared before the committee on February 20 and opened his testimony with the statement, "I do not know how many times I have sat in this chair and faced this committee ... to plead with the Congress ... to accept what we in the National Education Association consider to be a proper share of the national responsibility." [8]

Carr's many trips before congressional committees had been made to support some form of general federal aid to public schools in the United States. The attempt to get general federal aid had begun before World War II, but after the war these attempts had rapidly escalated with the pressure of increased public school enrollments. In 1945 two major federal aid bills were presented to Congress under the sponsorship of the National Education Association and the American Federation of Teachers. These bills, after many amendments, were eventually approved by the Senate in 1948 as the Thomas-Hill-Taft Bill; it eventually was killed when considered by the House committee. Several other bills were attempted but underwent the same fate as the Thomas-Hill-Taft Bill. In 1950 Congress passed two aid bills for construction and operating costs to schools in areas affected by federal activities such as military installations and research centers. These two bills, of course, did not answer the demands for general federal aid to education. In 1949 it was proposed that the federal share of oil revenues from tideland oil fields be given to states for educational purposes, and in 1952 a bill containing these provisions was passed but was vetoed by President Truman. In 1950 the arguments for general federal aid began to concentrate on federal support of school construction. Support of school-construction bills did not mean the abandonment of hope for federal support of school operating expenses and teachers' salaries. A school-construction bill eventually reached the House floor in 1956 but was defeated. School-construction aid had been the central focus of President Eisenhower's program for education but was objected to by the National Education Association and other education groups because it provided too little federal assistance. The House debate in 1956 was the first formal House debate on a federal aid bill in the twentieth century. Many blamed Eisenhower's lukewarm support of the construction bill as one of the reasons for its defeat.[9]

The difficulties encountered by general federal aid bills came from many sources. One issue dividing congressional support was that of flat grants vs. some form of equalization formula. The flat grants would have distributed a fixed sum per pupil to each state, whereas under equalization formulas money would have been distributed on the basis of need. In general, congressional representatives divided on this issue according to how much benefit their own state would receive under either method. Representatives of wealthy northeastern states preferred flat grants because equalization formulas would have meant less federal income even though they would have been paying a higher percentage of federal taxes. Poorer southern states, of course, favored some form of equalization.

Two other major divisive issues were racial segregation and support of private schools. Many southern states viewed any federal intervention as a potential source of forced integration, particularly when many of the congressional bills had amendments attached which denied aid to school districts in which there was racial segregation. Catholic education groups and other private school groups tended to seek aid for nonreligious textbooks, health services, and transportation rather than general aid for school operating expenses and salaries because of the constitutional issue of federal involvement in religion. Added to these controversies was the opposition of some federal representatives to any form of federal involvement in education. There were also controversies over the percentage of federal aid that should be allocated for salaries and operating expenses. The American Federation of Teachers as opposed to the National Education Association wanted a higher percentage of federal aid to be used for teachers' salaries. All these conflicting issues made it extremely unlikely that any form of general federal aid to education would win a majority of congressional support.[10]

Against this background of congressional battles over federal aid, Carr of the National Education Association testified before the Senate committee in 1958. A general tone of defensiveness permeated Carr's testimony because of the strong national criticism of the schools occurring in the 1950s and the use of Sputnik as a symbol that the American schools had indeed lost the educa-

tional race with the Soviet Union. Carr presented a long
statement defending the public schools and arguing
that, contrary to the national criticism of the schools, a
majority of Americans supported the current organization of schooling. Carr argued that in terms of national
defense the schools were doing an important job in
preparing loyal citizens to serve in the armed forces. In
terms of international relations, Carr stated, "I believe
that one thing that will draw the underdeveloped nations of the world into the democratic rather than the
totalitarian camp might well be our free and versatile
system of public education." He argued that, contrary to
recent discussions about schooling, the school system
was a product of the American people and reflected their
strengths and weaknesses. "There are, of course," Carr
noted, "critics [who] say that our public schools are
educator dominated, whatever that means." [11]

Senator Gordon Allott of Colorado reacted sharply to
the general tone of Carr's statement and told him, "All
you have to do is go out and talk with any one of tens of
thousands of fathers and mothers to find that they are
not happy with what is happening and nothing seems to
be done about it." [12] Carr reacted to this by submitting to
the committee seven pages of opinion polls which purported to show general public approval of schooling.
Senator Allott, who had obviously done his homework in
the area of public school criticism, explained to Carr, "I
do not want this thing of 'educating' children for social
adjustment as the beginning and the end and the whole
means of education." A debate then ensued between
Carr and Allott over the amount of homework children
received in the public schools. Carr cited a study which
purported to show that high school students averaged
two hours of homework a day, but in the debate that
followed it turned out that the study was limited to
college preparatory students in Pittsburgh and the in-

formation had been gathered by asking students. Carr found himself similarly trapped when he tried to provide other evidence of the effectiveness of schooling, such as the fact that more students were studying Latin in 1949 than in 1900. Carr then made the mistake of quoting Admiral Rickover that education was the most important ingredient in national defense. The senators on the committee were obviously acquainted with Rickover's views. H. Alexander Smith of New Jersey snapped back with another quote from Rickover, "We are in our present predicament because education in America had deteriorated in quality for lack of standards." [13]

It was within this atmosphere of hostility toward professional educators that Carr was asked two important questions by Chairman Lister Hill. Hill asked if special emphasis in federal support of education should be placed on the training of scientists, engineers, and technicians, and if special funds should be provided for guidance. Carr responded to both of these questions with a flat no. What Carr and the NEA wanted was for the federal government to give each state $25 per child for the first fiscal year and to have this raised to $100 over a four-year period. Under this plan, state and local authorities would have a maximum amount of discretion in the use of the funds with the only limitations being that the money would have to be used for salaries, basic instructional equipment, and classroom construction. Carr argued that the probable division of these funds based on past history would be 65 percent for salaries, 30 percent for classrooms, and 5 percent for equipment. There was to be no special emphasis on foreign languages, mathematics, and science unless this was decided upon by the local school authorities.[14]

In a sense, the proponents of general federal aid as represented in the proposals by Carr were watching their efforts slip away as the committee considered Eisen-

hower's recommendations. The final approval of the
NDEA was a defeat for general federal aid and the formula of local control proposed by the National Education Association. The specific provisions of the NDEA
and the work of the National Science Foundation would
have a greater influence on directing the actions of local
school officials than would have the flat grants in the
general federal aid bill.

In contrast to the hostile treatment given the executive director of the National Education Association was
a very cordial reception by the senators of the many
scientists who made up the majority of witnesses testifying before the committee. Many of these scientists had
direct connections with the new curriculums being developed for the public schools. The first witness called
before the committee on January 21 was Detlev W.
Bronk, then chairman of the National Science Board,
which governed the National Science Foundation, and
president of the National Academy of Sciences and of
the Rockefeller Institute of Medical Research in New
York. At this stage of the Senate hearings there was just
general consideration being given to what should be
done by the federal government with regard to education and national defense. Bronk was accompanied by
two other members of the National Academy of Sciences
who were to testify at a later date, on February 24. These
two important figures who exercised important influence
over national policy were M. H. Trytten and R. M.
Whaley, the executive director of the Advisory Board on
Education of the National Academy of Sciences. Trytten, it will be recalled, was responsible for the adoption
of the "Trytten plan" for selective service in 1951 and
had worked with the Council for Basic Education.
Whaley was later to have a major impact on educational
thinking when he developed the idea of calling a national
conference on new curriculum developments at Woods

Hole, Massachusetts, in September 1959. The report of this conference, planned and arranged by Whaley, was written by Jerome S. Bruner and became the very influential book on curriculum theory in the early 1960s, *The Process of Education.*

The testimony of the scientists reflected concern about antiintellectualism and the need to stress the basic disciplines in the school. In addition, their statements indicated the direction of the new curriculum developments in science and mathematics. This was particularly true in the case of Detlev Bronk, who as head of the National Science Foundation exercised important influence over the support of these new developments.

The Senate committee had presented each witness with a series of topics for the preparation of a formal statement. The most important one was "The deficiencies in American education as related to national defense." In his reply it was obvious that Bronk accepted and shared many of the criticisms of public schooling that had been made during the 1950s. First, Bronk stated his concern about the socialization aspects of schooling and the need to emphasize the basic disciplines. He told the committee that "rather than have the elementary schools concerned with many of the things which should be the responsibility of the home and the parents and the church, I would like to see the schools giving emphasis to those fundamentals upon which all of the future education of man must depend." [15] In stressing this point he made a distinction between the accumulation of facts and the ability to think as a basis of education. This was to be a theme echoed through the new curriculum movement. Bronk told the senators about how his father, when departing to dig gold in California in 1849, selected Chaucer and Newton's *Principia* as traveling companions and would in the evening read under a lantern slung from the axle of his covered wagon. This intellectualism on the part of a traveling gold miner, he argued, was a product of a school system that emphasized rigorous thinking. "So I would say," Bronk argued, "that another of the deficiencies . . . is inadequate leadership of our young people into the habits of rigorous thinking. There is inadequate revelation to students of the joys and pleasures of the intellectual life which was a foundation for our great Nation." [16]

Of great concern to Bronk was the antiintellectualism that seemed to run rampant through the school systems of the United States. He talked of the need to develop a greater respect for learning among all the people of the country. "We need to recreate," he claimed, "a widespread regard for persons who have a curiosity and who wish to develop trained minds, and who will work hard intellectually as well as physically." [17] The development of curiosity and the creation of a satisfying intellectual life were to become another important objective of the new curriculum movements, and these were goals that must be understood against the background of concern about antiintellectualism.

Increased status and recognition for the intellectual was considered necessary in the cold-war race. As mentioned in an earlier chapter, this feeling was a product of perceived threats from the radical right to the status of intellectuals. By changing the nature of schooling and emphasizing intellectual skills, it was believed that these threats to status could be overcome. In part, the new curriculums with their emphasis on thinking and discovery were to contribute to the overcoming of these antiintellectual tendencies in American life. They were to show that the intellectual life could be as exciting as the high school football game. Bronk told the committee that one of the foremost of national needs was "the encouragement of a cultural environment in which there is more regard and respect for the thoughtful man." [18]

Bronk argued that the most important thing in renewing respect for intellectual endeavors was the development of new curriculums such as those being sponsored by the National Science Foundation. He referred to the development of the Physical Science Study Committee as a great experiment in the improvement of the quality of teaching and urged greater federal support of developments in science education. He stated, as Vannevar Bush had in original proposals for the National Science Foundation, that "one of the great needs of our country in the field of scientific education is a better quality of teaching in our high schools because this is where the students' interests are often aroused and molded." [19] In addition, there was a need for greater stress in teacher education upon knowledge of the subject matter.

It seems natural that Bronk's testimony would give support to the work of the National Science Foundation since he was chairman of the governing body of the organization. But his thinking also found support among the other scientists appearing before the committee. Trytten told the senators that "national survival depends upon the success or failure of our educational institutions to provide the intellectual, the scientific, the diplomatic leaders sorely needed to solve complex problems." He located the soft spots of American education in the concern about social problems and questionable educational philosophy which diverted school administrators and teachers from the central objective of "developing the mind." His list of proposals reflected essentially those of the Council for Basic Education in a demand for a broad basic education for all youth and greater stress on science, languages, and mathematics. The role of federal government should be that of catalyst in the development of new programs, which meant activity like the current endeavors of the National

Science Foundation. He also restated his long-standing concern about the need for channeling manpower through an adequate system of guidance.[20]

Even scientists who had never been directly connected with any American educational institutions seemed to have been strongly affected by the national criticism of the schools. Wernher von Braun, who had been educated in Germany and worked for the Nazi government as technical director of the Peenemünde rocket center until the end of World War II when he had been brought to the United States to work on V-2 rockets, told the committee, "I do not . . . believe in all these newfangled type of things that are being taught at some schools and colleges these days, like 'life adjustment' or 'household economy.' "[21] Von Braun admitted that he had little acquaintance with American schools since all of his research had been conducted in government centers and he was currently working as director of guided-missile development at the Redstone Arsenal and the Army Ballistic Missile Agency. But even with lack of contact with American schools, he was able to state all the current criticism of the schools. He was certainly a good example of how criticism along with cold-war policy had come to permeate all discussions about education.

Other scientists emphasized the need for greater intellectual rigor in the schools and the need for a stress on theory over facts in teaching. Edward Teller, the physicist who played a crucial role in the development of both the atomic and hydrogen bombs, argued that the teaching of mathematical theory should begin at an early age, to develop proper habits of thinking. This, of course, was to become one of the goals of the "new math" developed by the School Mathematics Study Group. Teller told the committee, "One of the very important reasons why the Russians are pulling ahead of us in science is . . . the fact that they drive their children on toward a very solid education, particularly in science, and they drive them on in a really merciless manner." [22] Lee A. DuBridge, then president of the California Institute of Technology and former member of the Atomic Energy Commission, the Naval Research Advisory Committee, and the Air Force Scientific Advisory Committee, urged additional funds for the National Science Foundation so that "science and mathematics be restored to a respected place in the curriculum of our elementary schools, our high schools, our colleges and universities." [23] He also argued that the major corrective to the poor intellectual content of teacher training would be the summer institutes for teachers organized by the National Science Foundation.

The New Curriculum

The combination of the National Science Foundation and the NDEA was, therefore, to stem the tide of antiintellectualism and U.S. losses in the race with the Soviet Union by the development of new curriculums, teacher training, manpower channeling through improved guidance, loans and fellowships, and the availability of money to purchase new scientific and mathematics equipment and materials for the schools. The new curriculums were to heighten intellectual excitement and greater respect for the life of the mind by stressing theoretical material, curiosity, and creativity. The first of these new curriculums to be developed under the sponsorship of the National Science Foundation was by the Physical Science Study Committee (PSSC) of a new high school physics course.

One thing about the new curriculums developed under government sponsorship was that they were not cheap. Probably at no other time in the history of

American education had so much money been lavished on curriculum development. Between the original organization of PSSC in 1956 and 1961, $6 million were spent by this group. This total did not include costs of teacher retraining conducted by the summer institutes of the National Science Foundation.[24] Jerrold Zacharias, who directed the original PSSC group, wrote that traditionally those engaged in curriculum development had been poorly paid in comparison to what they could have earned in industry. He stated with regard to PSSC, "There has been, however, an attempt to elevate the rate of payment, and there has been a stubborn refusal to enlist assistance free or at bargain rates on the plea that it is 'good for the country.' "[25]

The PSSC was the brainchild of physicist Zacharias of the Massachusetts Institute of Technology. He decided in the mid-1950s that one way of getting around the shortage and mediocrity of high school physics courses was the production of teaching films and classroom equipment to accompany the films. He proposed that there be ninety twenty-minute films with commentary and questions and answers for students and teachers. He also proposed that these films introduce a new content into high school physics by stressing the study of particles as opposed to the traditional emphasis of Newtonian mechanics on the laws of motion and force.

In 1956 the proposal was approved by the administration at MIT and submitted to the National Science Foundation (NSF) where its success was assured by the fact that the chancellor of MIT, who submitted the proposal, was on the governing body of the foundation. While the proposal was being considered, the PSSC was formed with membership including scientists of international reputation and one Nobel laureate in physics. A statement of purpose was issued at the initial meeting which called for changes in the content of courses in physical science as a means of finding "a way to make more understandable to all students the world in which we live and to prepare better those who will do advanced work. It is probable that such a presentation would also attract more students to careers in science." [26] The scientists at this meeting agreed that the attractiveness of science was in its ideas and not in its applications. Discussions of applications in course content were to be secondary to scientific ideas and methods of inquiry. In this statement of purpose was a complete reversal of the ideas of life-adjustment and curriculum theory which sought to tie learning directly to the needs of social life. It also paved the way for a curriculum where student motivation was to be a product of enjoyment of the life of the mind and the intellectual pleasure of dealing with abstract ideas. In one sense, it was to be a war against antiintellectualism conducted with a certain degree of vengeance.

The original group constituted itself as a steering committee and appointed a Curriculum Committee to develop the new physical science course. The evaluation of the new course materials was to be under the direction of that rapidly expanding educational conglomerate, the Educational Testing Service (ETS). The ETS, which had already expanded its influence into the world of selective service, was now moving into the arena of national curriculum development. The steering committee expanded its original membership to include a high school chemistry teacher, an expert on secondary education, and a number of other scientists and public leaders, including the president of the ETS and the important cold-warrior of the scientific establishment, Vannevar Bush. With this type of membership and institutional connections, the continued financial support of the group was guaranteed.[27]

At the second meeting of the PSSC in 1956, a report was submitted on high school physics textbooks which argued that they spent too much time on the applications of physics and too little on the nature and structure of physics. The group agreed that either the film project would have to replace all current textbooks or a new textbook would have to be written. When the initial grant from the NSF came through, it was for $303,000 to prepare recommendations for the new program. Two-thirds of the money was to go to support those preparing the recommendations. As Zacharias had stated, they were not going to be underpaid workers. The work of that first year was in the development of an outline of basic concepts in physical science and one set of examples of these concepts. During an eight-week summer workshop in 1957, a draft of one-fourth of a new text and one experimental film were produced with teachers' guides and examinations. During the fall of 1957 these materials were tested in eight secondary schools. At the end of 1957 the National Science Foundation rewarded the work of the PSSC with another grant for $245,000.

After the launch of *Sputnik I* and Eisenhower's recommendations to Congress for increased support of the work of the NSF, the appropriations of NFS increased by $9 million. During 1957 the PSSC received additional money from the NSF and $750,000 from the Ford Foundation and the Alfred P. Sloan Foundation. With the new congressional appropriations for NSF in 1958, the PSSC received a grant for $1.8 million; this was renewed by the NSF in the next year for another $1.4 million. The PSSC began to spend more than a million dollars a year to give American schools a new curriculum in physics.

During the spring of 1958, a motion-picture studio was put into operation; and during the summer five institutes trained three hundred teachers in the use of the new materials. Another eight-week summer work-shop continued the development and revision of new materials. During the 1958–59 academic year, 250 schools experimented with the material, and this was followed with more summer workshops and teacher-training institutes. After testing in 500 schools in 1959–60 and final editing during the summer of 1960, the course "entered ordinary commercial channels."[28]

National publicity and marketing of PSSC materials proved relatively simple because of the national feeling of concern about the progress of science and the technique of using NSF institutes. The project was bound to attract attention because of the international reputation of the scientists involved and the publicity given by the NSF. Articles on PSSC appeared in *Time* and *Life* magazines and the top people in PSSC were invited around the country as speakers to scientific meetings and schools. But the most important method of spreading the products of PSSC to classroom teachers was the summer institutes.

The method of organizing these institutes was for a college or university science department to propose a summer institute and for the NSF to pay for it. The local institution would take care of all the details of administration and instruction while the NSF would pay the entire bill including a percentage for overhead. Teachers attending the summer institutes would pay no tuition and would receive some form of monetary compensation. In addition, many institutions gave academic credit for attendance. In the case of most teachers, this meant a movement upward on the pay scale of their local school district.[29] The complete NSF summer-institute package was one that was difficult for science teachers in the public schools to resist. The NSF supplemented their teacher-training activities in 1956 with in-service institutes which brought teachers together once or twice a week during the regular school year. The PSSC began its work in training and testing its material at NSF in-service institutes in 1957–58. This was followed over the years with NSF summer institutes where teachers were trained and introduced to PSSC material.

Federal government support of, first, the development of PSSC material, and second, the summer and in-service institutes as a means of spreading PSSC materials, raised the question of government control over education. This problem has to be approached at two different levels. On the surface there was no government control because the NSF did not specify what the content of PSSC materials was to be or the content of in-service and summer institutes. Also it was clearly stated that PSSC materials were not to compete with those produced by private companies. But beneath these surface features was a network of interests and understandings. In the first place, it is difficult to talk about government control in the United States because of the conflicting personalities and agencies that form the government. Even within the three major branches of government, conflicting interests make it difficult to specify control as the work of a single monolithic institution. For instance, to speak of congressional control is meaningless unless one specifies what part of Congress and the nature of institutional organization. The conflicts between congressional representatives are often bitter, and the nature of the committee structure of Congress defines the real organization of power.

The work of the NSF did not represent government control but control by the scientists who controlled the NSF. Certainly the NSF depended upon the support of the President and Congress for continued funding, but in the context of the cold war and firing of *Sputnik I* this was not a difficult problem. The nature of NSF control over the curriculum developed by the PSSC was both formal and informal. Formally, the NSF by providing major monetary support to PSSC essentially approved the nature of the curriculum that was being developed and assured the spread of the content of their materials. It would have been difficult for any curriculum group wishing to develop a new physics curriculum to have competed with the amount of money the NSF poured into the PSSC and the in-service and summer institutes. Informally, there was a close understanding between the members of the governing board of the NSF and the members of the PSSC. As mentioned previously, the initial grant for the PSSC was assured because it was supported and introduced to the NSF by a member of the governing board. In addition to these connections was the international reputation of the scientists involved in the project. In the academic world of the United States, this meant friendships with important colleagues throughout the country. This was why it was possible in 1958 to arrange that five NSF summer institutes strategically located around the country would offer PSSC material even though the content of the institutes was at the discretion of the host institution. In 1958–59, through this network of formal and informal relationships, the PSSC arranged to have its material used in 15 in-service institutes in Boston, New York City, Cleveland, Portland, Dallas, and Detroit. During the summers of 1959 and 1960, 67 summer institutes using PSSC material were conducted at 42 different host institutions.[30]

While PSSC material was not to compete with materials issued by private companies, there was a direct intention to influence the publishing of textbooks in physics and the manufacturing of laboratory equipment. Certainly, companies took notice of the fact that by the fall of 1958, within two years of the founding of the PSSC, there were 250 classrooms teaching PSSC materials even though the work was incomplete, its use restricted and still experimental. By 1959, the PSSC was marketing its own material and gaining increased publicity through NSF institutes. No private company could have afforded the cost of this type of publicity. When the total number of PSSC institute participants, who as a result taught the course between 1958 and 1961, was divided into the total cost of these institutes paid for by the NSF between 1958 and 1960, the resulting figure was $3300 per teacher. In addition, the PSSC distributed free materials between 1957 and 1959 which averaged out in cost to $680 per class.[31]

Beginning in 1958, the distribution of PSSC materials was aided by the passage of the NDEA. At this time, even though the PSSC was not to compete with private industry, the PSSC began to sell their materials. There was almost perfect timing between the work of the PSSC to produce a new curriculum and the actions of Congress to allow local schools to purchase new science equipment. All the new PSSC laboratory equipment and teaching aids could be bought by local school districts by matching grants under the NDEA. The textbook and laboratory manual were not reimbursable under Title III but they were both sold for a competitive $7 for both volumes. Small wonder, considering the amount of money spent on development and distribution, that within four years of the founding of the PSSC, commercial companies moved in to take over their accomplishments. In 1959–60, after discussion with the larger publishing houses, the PSSC turned over to one of them the right to publish all their written material. In the same manner the production and sale of films and laboratory equipment were turned over to private companies.[32]

In many ways the School Mathematics Study Group (SMSG) was more sophisticated than the PSSC in their marketing techniques and dealings with publishing companies in the development of a national mathematics curriculum. The "new math" spread through the country like a rapidly burning brush fire. The SMSG was officially organized in 1958 under the direction of Edward G. Begle of the Department of Mathematics at Yale University and financed by an initial grant from the NSF of $100,000. The grant was given for devising "a practical program which will improve the general level of instruction in mathematics in elementary and secondary schools." [33]

The initial writing session began during the summer months of 1958 with twenty-one participants drawn from college departments of mathematics and twenty-one from high schools. In addition, there were representatives from the RAND Corporation, the Bell Telephone Laboratories, and the American Association for the Advancement of Science. During the first summer writing session at Yale, it was agreed that the most important single factor in determining subject matter content was the textbook. In terms of mathematics, it was argued that the textbook determined almost exclusively what was taught and when things were taught. It was decided that if SMSG was to influence mathematics curriculum, it would have to be through influence exerted by sample textbooks. The goal of SMSG was therefore to issue new mathematics textbooks which contained a new curriculum that was recognizably superior to any in existence and would stimulate commercial publishing firms to produce new and improved books of a similar nature.[34]

The work of several other school mathematics groups was to have a direct influence on the type of curriculum developed and textbooks written by SMSG. One of these was the University of Illinois Committee on School Mathematics (UICSM) begun in 1952 by Max Beberman of the laboratory school of the College of Education at the University of Illinois and Herbert E. Vaughan of the Department of Mathematics. Vaughan was later a member of the first writing session of SMSG during the summer of 1958.

The emphasis of the UICSM program was upon understanding rather than manipulation of numbers and equations. A student would come to understand mathematics when the teacher and textbook used precise mathematical language and when the student was allowed to discover generalizations. On the basis of this belief, two important principles developed for the teaching of school mathematics. One was the need for precision of language which led to stress on the meaning of number and function. Related to the need for precision of language and discovery was the introduction of set theory. This was the beginning of later confusion among parents in the 1960s when traditional methods of teaching arithmetic were replaced by the theory of sets, and many found themselves unable to do their children's homework. The idea of using sets as a method of teaching was to allow the student to discover relationships and invent new arrangements to meet new problems. A set was any collection of things which could be points, lines, vectors, or any philosophical notion, such as brotherhood. By thinking in terms of sets, children were to learn to understand relationships and discover hidden patterns. Supposedly, after developing this habit of thinking, the student would retain a mental discipline that would be useful in advanced mathematical techniques. The work of the UICSM reflected the general pattern of making school work a "life of the mind" by stressing abstraction, structure, and discovery.[35]

Two other groups to influence the work of SMSG were the University of Maryland Mathematics Project and the Commission on Mathematics of the College Entrance Examination Board. The Maryland project, which began in the fall of 1957, was directed toward the problems of junior high school mathematics and a concern that much of grades 7 and 8 were devoted to the social application of mathematics with only a few new mathematical ideas being introduced. The objective of this group was to introduce material with less review and drill and more emphasis on abstraction and understanding.[36] The Commission on Mathematics issued recommendations in 1959 which were similar to those of the Maryland project and UICSM. This commission had been appointed in 1955 and after three years of work reported that the traditional method of teaching mathematics did little in developing an understanding of mathematics and in developing a positive attitude toward mathematics.[37]

The influence of these groups on SMSG was clearly in the direction of creating greater understanding of mathematics and a higher degree of abstraction. The first summer writing project of SMSG in 1958 was devoted to outlining a series of textbooks in mathematics for grades 9 through 12 and the writing of a series of units on specific topics for students in grades 7 and 8. The decision of the group working on grades 7 and 8, which worked under the direction of the head of the University of Maryland project, was to refrain from a treatment of algebra and emphasize logical patterns, mathematical vocabulary, and informal deduction and induction. It was decided that the ninth grade should concentrate on algebra with a stress on number theory and precision of language. The tenth grade was to be devoted to geometry with the replacement of traditional methods of teaching geometry with modern geometric concepts and a stress on accuracy of language and thought. The eleventh grade would stress the structure of algebra and trigonometry, which provide an introduction into the nature of mathematical thought. After debate about the introduction of calculus in the twelfth grade, it was decided to write two textbooks for each semester of the course, the first directed toward the study of elementary functions and the second devoted to an introduction to modern algebra.[38]

In the fall of 1958, after the outlines had been written during the summer months, the NSF gave SMSG an additional $1.2 million. During its first year of work SMSG received a total of $1.3 million from the NSF. With the additional funds, SMSG established centers around the country for experimenting with the new curriculum material. This meant that within six months after the founding of SMSG, its materials were already beginning to find their way around the country. In addition, panels were established to supervise the actual writing of the textbooks. In February of 1959 a conference was held on elementary school mathematics where it was agreed that a comprehensive study of mathematics from kindergarten through high school should be undertaken. It was suggested that a special panel on elementary school mathematics be appointed, but the work of this group was not begun until the spring of 1960.

The second summer writing session in 1959 established the rather staggering goal of writing six textbooks and six teachers' manuals in a nine-week period. The work was subdivided into grade-level groups. The junior high school groups met in Ann Arbor, Michigan, and by the end of the session in August they had produced volume 1 of *Junior High School Mathematics* for students at the seventh-grade level. A series of sample units of the eighth-grade book was developed and bound together as volume 2. The writing session for the ninth through twelfth grades met in Boulder, Colorado. At the close of its summer's work, the SMSG had a complete set of textbooks covering grade levels 7 through 12. During the fall of 1959 the testing of the sample textbooks was begun with 26,000 students at 49 experimental centers around the country. The final revision of this textbook series was to take place during the summer of 1960.[39]

One of the bold decisions made by SMSG was not to differentiate the content of the curriculum on the basis of student ability. In this decision they were in agreement with Bestor and the Council for Basic Education that if something was worth teaching, it was worth teaching to all students. The SMSG series was originally written for the top 25 percent of the ability range of high school and junior high school grades. When SMSG met in the spring of 1960 to discuss the type of material to be offered to the other 75 percent, it was decided that the basic ideas in the developed series were so important from both a cultural and a utilitarian standpoint that they were appropriate for the needs of all students. A series for this ability group was needed to introduce the mathematical ideas of the original series at a slower pace. Consequently, with another grant from the NSF of $1.7 million in 1960, the third summer writing session included the final revision of the first series of textbooks and the beginning of writing a slower-paced volume for the noncollege bound. In addition, the summer of 1960 would witness the beginning of writing on the elementary school series. In the fall of 1960 the NSF provided another $1,184,200 for the work of SMSG.[40]

As mentioned earlier, one goal of SMSG was to influence the textbooks marketed by the larger commercial publishing companies. With the completion of the junior and senior high school series it was decided to establish a committee which each year would review all mathematics textbooks on the market to determine if texts comparable to the SMSG were available, and if so, to remove the SMSG text that was in competition with the commercial publication. This procedure was designed to put competitive pressure on the textbook industry. With the final revision of the series in the summer of 1960, the Yale University Press was given exclusive rights to print, advertise, and sell all SMSG textbooks. During the 1960–61 academic years the Yale University Press sold 130,000 books. Sales increased in the next academic year to almost 500,000 volumes. Since an estimated 10 million students were in grades 7 through 12, 5 percent were using SMSG.[41] But because the original material was intended for only the top 25 percent of this group in ability, it meant that within four years of the organization of SMSG its material was being used by 20 percent of its intended market.

SMSG always claimed that the one thing it was not doing was establishing a national curriculum. It certainly was not imposing one, but the results of its work were leading in that direction. Its competitive pressure on the textbook industry forced them to begin marketing similar textbooks in 1961 and 1962. The review committee of SMSG agreed that just because a text contained the word *modern* in its title did not mean that it would be viewed as a substitute for SMSG material. Before SMSG material was removed from the market, commercial texts had to conform to the standards of the new SMSG curriculum.[42]

The PSSC and SMSG were landmarks in the new curriculum developments of the late 1950s and early 1960s. Their work became models in many other areas of the school curriculum. In 1959 the American Institute of Biological Sciences Curriculum Study (BSCS) received a grant from the NSF and began working on the BSCS curriculum for the public schools.[43] Between 1960 and 1963 the Chemical Education Material Study (CHEM Study) produced a text, a laboratory manual, a teachers' guide, a set of motion pictures, and supplementary equipment.[44]

Eventually these new curriculums were to spill over into other areas but without the heavy financing of the NSF and the ability to spread the material through NSF in-service and summer institutes. This was seriously to hamper attempts to copy the revolutionary changes that took place in the science, mathematics, and modern-language curriculums. In 1962 the American Council of Learned Societies and Educational Services Incorporated organized a conference to plan the development of a new curriculum in the humanities and social studies. But these efforts encountered difficulties because they lacked the vast funding received by other projects. A member of the American Council wrote about the conference, "Shortage of funds held the conference down to two weeks' duration and deprived it of full representation in the humanities so that nothing so revolutionary as a unifying approach to the entire humanities and social studies curriculum was formulated." [45]

The new curriculum movement was born out of the cold-war race with the Soviet Union and complaints about antiintellectualism in the schools. As the curriculums developed, they tended to counter the complaints about antiintellectualism by creating a cooperative endeavor between university scholars and school people, and by stressing structure, abstraction, discovery, and curiosity. In fact, these curriculum endeavors spoke almost directly to the criticisms voiced by Arthur Bestor and the Council for Basic Education. This did not mean that there was a direct connection between these groups but that the new curriculum movement reflected the general climate of opinion. The one major deviation was that critics such as Bestor wanted these endeavors to range through the entire school curriculum. That concentration occurred in the sciences, mathematics, and foreign languages was a result of the cold war.

The Process of Education

Underlying the new curriculum movement were a host of questions dealing with the philosophy and psychology of learning and knowledge. In September, 1959, a conference was called at Woods Hole, Massachusetts, to explore these issues. The initial idea and planning of the conference were the work of Randall Whaley, director of the Education Office of the National Academy of Sciences; the final report of the conference was Jerome Bruner's *The Process of Education*. The support of the conference came from the NSF along with additional aid from the Office of Education, the air force, and the RAND Corporation. The conference was attended by ten psychologists, six mathematicians, four physicists, five biologists, one medical expert, two educators, two cinematographers, a member of the Educational Testing Service, and to add a flavor of the humanities there were two historians and one classicist. Included in this group were the directors of the PSSC, SMSG, and BSCS.

The conference spent its opening days in evaluating the work of the new curriculum groups. It saw demonstrations and it heard progress reports from the SMSG, the PSSC, the University of Illinois Committee of School Mathematics and two other mathematics groups. Within a few days after the opening of the conference, the participants were divided into five work groups to study the sequence of a curriculum, the apparatus of teaching, the motivation of learning, the role of intuition in learning and thinking, and the cognitive processes in learning. Each of these groups prepared lengthy reports and submitted them for debate to the entire group. Jerome Bruner, the director of the conference, prepared a final report by selecting what were the major themes and conclusions of the conference. Copies of the report were then distributed to conference members for comments and criticism. The major objections to Bruner's final report by conference members was an overemphasis on the ideas of psychologist Jean Piaget and the neglect of the problem of teaching aids. Piaget remained in the report, and an additional chapter was added at the end on the range of teaching aids including films and programmed learning devices.[46]

The final report was a beautiful example of how historical trends can come together to reinforce one another and blend into a total product. While the cold war was sparking demands for changes in education and the development for new curriculums, psychologists were developing psychological theories that would justify those changes. In essence, what happened at Woods Hole was that psychologists were able to tell the new curriculum innovators that their work was correct because of recent psychological studies. In turn, the curriculum innovators could reinforce already existing trends in psychology by providing concrete models. The final cement in this blend of views was the concern about the cold war. The opening statement of the report stated there had been an increased concern about the quality and intellectual aims of education that was "accentuated by what is almost certain to be a long-range crisis in national security, a crisis whose resolution will depend upon a well-educated citizenry." [47]

The first major issue the report concentrated on was the structure of knowledge and the teaching of the fundamentals of a discipline. Critics of education during the 1950s had been arguing for the necessity of returning to structure and fundamentals. The new curriculums that were being developed also reflected a belief that structure and basic ideas needed to be taught in the schools. The major problem, of course, was the meaning of fundamentals and structure and their relationship to the process of learning. There seemed to be general agreement that fundamental ideas were those ideas selected by leading scholars in a particular discipline as fundamental. There also seemed to be agreement among the new curriculum projects that these fundamental ideas would provide the general conceptual framework for understanding the discipline. This was particularly true in the mathematics projects where the stress was to be on understanding as opposed to manipulation. But even with these general agreements, the murky problem of the meaning of these terms and their value in education remained. On these major issues, psychologists were able to provide aid.

Jerome Bruner was a psychologist and had been one of the leaders in the Cognition Project at Harvard University between 1951 and 1956. The research findings of this project were to provide a major contribution to the understanding of concept development and the psychological views expressed at the Woods Hole conference. Bruner's interest in this area stemmed from his work during World War II on propaganda and the manipulation of public opinion which led to an interest in the study of opinion formation. The Harvard Cognition Project looked at this problem from the wide perspective of perception, thought, learning, and language. It was influenced by certain new ideas in the stimulus-response theory of learning, ego psychology, and information theories dealing with the molding of public opinion. In a sense the interest in opinion formation and information theory was as much a product of the cold war as the new curriculums.[48]

The final report of the Harvard Cognition Project, of which Bruner was the principal author, stressed that most human thinking involved dealing with classes of things rather than unique objects and events. This meant that most human learning involved the categorization of objects and events into concepts. The process of concept formation and attainment, it was argued, provided for economy in learning. The report of the

Cognition Project claimed, "the establishment of a category based on a set of defining attributes reduces the necessity of constant learning. For the abstraction of defining properties makes possible future acts of categorizing without benefit of further learning." The key element in this was the learning of defining attributes as opposed to just knowing the membership of a class of objects or events. That is, memorizing the objects in a certain class, such as all trees in a neighborhood, did not guarantee that when a person encountered a different tree outside of the neighborhood, it would be recognized as a tree. But by achieving concept attainment where the defining attributes of trees were learned, future recognition of different trees would be greatly aided. Or in the words of the report, "Learning by rote that a miscellany of objects all go by the nonsense name BLIX has no extrapolative value to new members of the class." [49]

At the Woods Hole conference the terms *structure, fundamental ideas,* and *understanding* were placed in the framework of concept formation and attainment. In the language of Bruner's final report the word *concept* was replaced with the term *general idea.* Structure and fundamental ideas were all related to the teaching of general ideas. The teaching of general ideas or concepts was to provide for a continual transfer of learning or ability by the understanding of the defining attributes of the concept. Bruner wrote, "Learning initially not a skill but a general idea, [it] can then be used as a basis for recognizing subsequent problems as special cases of the idea originally mastered. This type of transfer is at the heart of the educational process—the continual broadening and deepening of knowledge in terms of basic and general ideas." [50] It was also argued that learning concepts or general ideas made the subject matter more understandable because the individual learner could see the interrelationships between the parts that made up the concepts. And it was argued that teaching concepts improved memory because "unless detail is placed into a structured pattern, it is rapidly forgotten."[51]

In this psychological argument was support for the new curriculum developments. But the one underlying assumption was that leading scholars could agree upon the general ideas that were to be taught. This assumption seemed to be correct, Bruner argued, by the work of SMSG and PSSC. But the problem with using these examples is that they were in mathematics and science where agreement about general ideas might be more possible than in other disciplines. It would be hard to imagine a Marxist and a laissez-faire economist agreeing on the fundamental concepts of economics.

When Bruner tried to apply concept learning to disciplines outside of mathematics and science, all sorts of problems were immediately apparent. For example, Bruner's report in arguing that understanding fundamentals made a subject more comprehensible used an example from social studies which stated, "Once one has grasped the fundamental idea that a nation must trade in order to live, then such a presumably special phenomenon as the Triangular Trade of the American colonies becomes altogether simpler to understand.[52] The concept of trade, as Bruner would have been forced to admit, is meaningless unless it has some defining attributes. These attributes probably could not be agreed upon by a radical historian interested in imperialism and a conservative historian interested in free trade. The assumption of Bruner and the rest of the participants at Woods Hole was that a consensus of views existed in other disciplines which made it possible to apply their scientifically oriented curriculum developments to all areas of knowledge.

The second major issue in the report was extremely important to the new mathematics curriculums at the University of Illinois and in the work of SMSG. This was the question of how early general concepts of a subject matter could be introduced. For instance, could set theory be introduced in the first grade and be understood? Bruner's final report stated in terms that were to be echoed through the educational world, "Any subject can be taught effectively in some intellectually honest form to any child at any stage of development." To support this proposition, Bruner introduced the ideas of Swiss psychologist Jean Piaget. Some conference members were a little uneasy at the heavy stress on Piaget, but they were satisfied with the argument that the general ideas of a discipline could be introduced at an early age. Bruner had helped to arrange that a psychologist, Barbel Inhelder of the Institute Rousseau of Geneva, who was familiar with Piaget's work, be in attendance at the conference. One possible result of the stress on Piaget in the final conference report was to spread Piaget's ideas through educational groups in the United States.

Piaget's ideas, as expressed at the Woods Hole conference by Inhelder, defined specific developmental levels through which the child progressed. The first stage of development, which ended in the fifth or sixth year of growth, consisted mainly in the establishment of relationships between experience and action. The major concern of the child during this period was with manipulating the world through action. Also during this stage of growth, the child learned to manipulate symbols with the learning of a language. The second stage of development, after the ages of five or six, was the stage of concrete operations. During this period the child developed an internalized structure by which the child could represent the world in symbolic systems. This meant that problem solving for the child no longer had to be a process of external trial and error but could be performed internally through symbolic structures. The third stage of development, placed somewhere between

the ages of ten and fourteen, was one of formal operations when the child was able to operate on hypothetical
propositions rather than being limited to what had been
experienced.

To the joy of the developers of the new science and
mathematics curriculums, Inhelder stated in a special
memorandum to the conference that it was incorrect to
delay the teaching of subjects like geometry and physics
because "basic notions in these fields are perfectly ac-
cessible to children of seven to ten years of age, provided
that they are divorced from their mathematical expression and studied through materials that the child can
handle himself." [53]

What this meant in terms of the statement in
Bruner's final report that any subject could be taught to
any child at any age was that the basic concepts or
general ideas had to be taught in terms of the child's
cognitive level of development. Or, as Bruner phrased it,
"What is most important for teaching basic concepts is
that the child be helped to pass progressively from concrete thinking to the utilization of more conceptually
adequate modes of thought." [54] Also involved in this
idea was the nondifferentiation of the content of the
curriculum. A major concern of critics of the 1950s had
been that large numbers of students were shortchanged
by not introducing all of them to the basic disciplines.
The psychological arguments regarding conceptual attainment and stages of cognitive development clearly
favored the idea that the structure of a discipline could
be taught in some form to all students. Bruner's final
report emphatically stated, "Good teaching that em-
phasizes the structure of a subject is probably even
more valuable for the less able student than for the
gifted one, for it is the former rather than the latter who
is most easily thrown off the track by poor teaching." [55]

The third major issue was the nature of analytical
and intuitive thinking. One of the things the new cur-

riculum developments wanted to convey to the student was the excitement of the researcher working on the frontiers of knowledge. It was argued that a great deal of what a research scientist or mathematician did was a result of the good intuitive guess. An important ingredient in developing this cognitive style and learning basic concepts, it was argued, was the discovery method. This method had been utilized in the mathematics curriculum developed by Max Beberman at the University of Illinois where the students were presented material by which they could discover the basic concepts of mathematics. The discovery method and conceptual learning were to develop the ability to leap about in the subject matter and make good guesses that could later be checked by more analytical methods. The discovery method was to convey to the student the joy of the life of the mind.

The important social issues raised by the new curriculum developments were the focus of the discussion of motivation in learning. Obviously, one theme of motivation was the need to reduce the importance of extrinsic rewards such as grades and competition in the school for more intrinsic rewards of intellectual achievement and delight in the process of learning. It was argued that "our cultural climate has not been marked traditionally by a deep appreciation of intellectual values." [56] This, it was claimed, was quickly changing with the rapid advances of the Soviet Union in technology and conquests in space. There were calls for technological speed-ups and federal support of education geared to meeting the world crisis. Bruner's final report warned, "Both of these trends—increasing emphasis on technological progress and federal aid in the interest of coping with the competitive crisis ... are likely to lead to one result that has questionable consequences for American education and American life unless change is planned well in advance." [57]

The danger, as expressed in the report, was the creation of a meritocracy where through a system of competition "students are moved ahead and given further opportunities on the basis of their achievement, with position in later life increasingly and irreversibly determined by earlier school records." This danger was highlighted by the then current trend to move the able student ahead faster, particularly if the student showed promise in technical or scientific subjects. Another dangerous trend was the development of national examinations. While not directly mentioned in the report, it could be assumed that part of the concern was with the heavy national reliance on the examinations of the Educational Testing Service. Of specific concern in the report was that future jobs might be tied to the winning of National Merit Scholarships. One of the interesting things about the report's discussion of meritocracy was that a meritocracy was feared because it might result in a wastage of talent and not because of its potential elitism. The report argued, "The late bloomer, the early rebel, the child from an educationally indifferent home—all of them, in a full scale meritocracy, become victims of an often senseless irreversibility of decision." [58]

In addition to the danger of a meritocracy was the creation of a technological society that would lose the ingredients of traditional culture. Federal aid to education was leading to an unbalanced stress upon science and mathematics that might widen an already apparent gap between the community of science and the humanities. Society could not afford, it was argued, to alienate the literary intellectuals from the advances in science. The report urged that as much energy should be expended in the development of curriculums in the humanities and social sciences as had been spent in the sciences and mathematics. But what was not considered in this context was whether schooling, which focused on the "life of the mind" and general concepts, and where knowledge was not taught in relationship to social needs and processes, would produce individuals who had an uncritical awareness of the social consequences of rapid technological and scientific advances.

One of John Dewey's major concerns at the beginning of the twentieth century had been that unless knowledge was directly linked to the life of the community, individuals would lose control of the direction of social change. This meant the life of the community and the school had to merge if education was to produce individuals who understood the social implications of knowledge and technological change. Jerome Bruner, in an essay titled "After John Dewey, What?" dismissed this aspect of Dewey's thinking and argued the school "is primarily the special community where one experiences discovery by the use of intelligence, where one leaps into new and unimagined realms of experience, experience that is discontinuous with what went before." [59] The idea that the school should be linked to the life of the community, Bruner argued, was primarily suitable to primitive societies. For Bruner, the school was to be a special social agency for nurturing intellectual excellence.

Bruner also attacked Dewey's idea of how subject matter should be organized in the school. Dewey had wanted to link knowledge with social activities as a means of teaching the individual the power of knowledge in social criticism and understanding. Bruner claimed that Dewey had misunderstood the nature of knowledge and how it could be mastered. For instance, Bruner wrote, "If set theory . . . had to be justified in terms of its relation to immediate experience and social life, it would not be worth teaching. Yet set theory lays a foundation for the understanding of order and number that could never be achieved with the social arithmetic of interest rates and bales of hay at so much per bale." He went on to argue, "Mathematics, like any other subject, must begin with experience, but progress toward abstraction and understanding requires precisely that there be a weaning away from the obviousness of superficial experience." [60]

But what seemed to have been neglected by Bruner was a clear understanding and answer to Dewey's concern that knowledge taught in abstraction and separate from social processes created an individual who understood the subject matter but not the social consequences. For instance, a clear knowledge of the concepts of mathematics and science did not provide a basis for understanding that the application of these disciplines could result in the destruction of the environment by pollution, the heightening of international hostilities through the development of new weapons, the creation of a technological culture which might be destructive of human values, or a technological organization which served the rich of the world while the poor starved. Training only in intellectual excellence of a discipline could not prepare the future medical researcher for deciding whether research in heart transplants was more important than community health problems in underdeveloped countries. Without a critical awareness of the social implications of knowledge, the scientist and mathematician could be easily manipulated by those who controlled the research money. The danger of Bruner's arguments and the new curriculum developments was the creation of a social elite of technocrats who would push forward the frontiers of knowledge without regard for the social consequences of their actions.

The NSF, NDEA and the new curriculums were all products of the cold-war global race for world power. But they were not inevitable products of the history of that period. There were alternatives. One wonders, for instance, what would have happened if rather than establish the National Science Foundation, we had established a National Peace Foundation which sought to increase America's understanding of world peace by supporting basic research in peace studies and provided money for developing new school curriculums organized around the concept of world peace. But such historical fantasies seem unrealistic when faced with the historical fact that World War II had made the military establishment and the scientists two of the most powerful groups in American society.

THE CIVIL RIGHTS MOVEMENT

4 One of the major results of the civil rights movement of the 1950s and '60s was increased federal control of American education. An inherent problem of American federalism has been to maintain some type of balance between constitutional rights and states' rights. The circumstances surrounding the denial of constitutional rights to black citizens forced the civil rights movement to seek redress from the federal government and, consequently, resulted in the extension of federal power. The situation that brought this about was as follows.

In the southern and border states, laws and local ordinances required segregation in transportation, public facilities, and schooling. In addition, a variety of techniques were used in these areas to deny voting rights to black citizens. Thus, black citizens could not use the power of the ballot to eliminate unfair laws and ordinances. Even in 1963, after a long period of struggle, it was reported that in six counties in the South where blacks represented a majority of the population, not one black citizen was able to register to vote. [1] The only recourse was to seek action through the courts to have the segregation laws declared unconstitutional. The first major step in this direction was accomplished in 1954 in the Supreme Court ruling in *Brown* v. *Board of Education of Topeka* which declared segregated schooling unconstitutional. The second step was gaining some form of compliance with Court decisions. In part, this was achieved through the Civil Rights Act of 1964, which extended the power of the federal government into many areas of American life and defined a method for controlling basic policies in American education.

Civil Rights and the Cold War

The 1954 Supreme Court school desegregation decision occurred in a climate of increasing concern about the effect of American race relations on foreign policy. It was difficult to present to the world an image of the United States as a bastion of freedom against the totalitarianism of the Soviet Union with the existence of segregation laws and the continued problems of lynchings and race riots. The pattern of concern about race relations on international politics began to emerge during World War II, when President Roosevelt in 1941 issued Executive Order No. 8802 which called for an end to racial discrimination in defense-related industries. One of the significant things about Roosevelt's action was the use of the government contract as a means of attempting social change. This would be one of the primary methods utilized in the 1964 Civil Rights Act. Private industry was to be granted a government contract only if it adhered to guidelines established by the government. In terms of Executive Order No. 8802, this meant equal hiring procedures for all racial and religious groups. In later years this would be one of the important techniques for implementing social change in the schools. As federal aid to education expanded in the 1960s, its primary method of social persuasion was the denial of federal funds if certain standards of civil rights were not adhered to by local school systems and institutions of higher learning.

President Roosevelt issued Executive Order No. 8802 under pressure from a national civil rights movement against discriminatory hiring which seriously threatened America's foreign policy. In February of 1941 A. Philip Randolph, president of the Brotherhood of Sleeping Car Porters, called a conference of top black leaders to discuss the discriminatory patterns in the defense industry and the armed forces. Black leaders were concerned that the ending of the depression had not resulted in any significant increase in employment opportunities for black people in the United States. Randolph told the leaders that "if American democracy will not give jobs to its toilers because of race or color; if American democracy will not insure equality of opportunity ... it is a hollow mockery and belies the principles for which it is supposed to stand." [2] He proposed that ten thousand blacks march on Washington for jobs in national defense and equal integration into the fighting forces of the United States. Out of this conference developed the March on Washington Movement which proposed to use mass nonviolent direct action to achieve its goals. It established July 1, 1941 as the target date for the march. President Roosevelt, fearing the effect of the march on national unity and international relations, issued his executive order calling for full participation in the defense program of all people regardless of race, creed, color, or national origin. The order required that all contracting agencies of the government include in all defense contracts a provision obligating the contractor not to discriminate and established a Committee on Fair Employment Practice. [3]

Concern about America's international image in terms of race relations continued after World War II and was pushed to the forefront by the ideological war to win the hearts and minds of the world's people. Increased racial tension following the war created a concern about America's image in the foreign press. In 1946 there were six reported lynchings of blacks in the South; and racial terror was reported in Louisiana, Georgia, South Carolina, and Tennessee. [4] In September 1946 the executive secretary of the National Association for the Advancement of Colored People (NAACP) went to the White House to plead with President Truman for executive action to protect the rights of black people. Truman responded by establishing the President's Committee on Civil Rights which issued its report, *To Secure These Rights,* in 1947. In 1948 Truman incorporated the basic recommendations of this report in a special message to Congress and made them the heart of his civil rights program.

The 1947 report of the President's Committee on Civil Rights reflected major national concerns about race relations. The report stated three major reasons for the need for action to strengthen civil rights in the United States. The first, of course, was the blatant contradiction between democratic ideals and race relations. The report stated, "The pervasive gap between our aims and what we actually do is creating a kind of moral dry rot which eats away at the emotional and rational bases of democratic beliefs." [5] The other two reasons were directly related to cold-war concerns about manpower and international relations.

In terms of manpower it was argued that economic discrimination resulted in the loss of a potential market for goods. This created a vicious circle where depressed wages and incomes of minority groups resulted in a reduction of purchasing power which in turn reduced overall production. The report depicted this argument in a two-page pictorial chart. One page showed black workers and white workers separated into two labor groups with an X drawn through the black laborers. Arrows on the chart led the reader from the segregated labor force labeled "inefficient use of our labor force" to a pile of money marked "less purchasing." From there the chart moved in a circle through an item marked "less consumer demand" to one of "less production" and finally to an item labeled "and a lower living standard for *all*" which led back to the segregated labor force. The other page had a similar circle which depicted an integrated work force labeled "full and efficient use of all our workers." This group of integrated workers marched around a circle through "greater puchasing power," "greater consumer demand," "full production," and "a higher living standard for all." The report warned, "The United States can no longer afford this heavy drain upon its human wealth, its national competence." [6]

The international reason for strengthening civil rights was America's foreign image. The President's committee argued, "We cannot escape the fact that our civil rights record has been an issue in world politics. The world's press and radio are full of it." The committee cited a letter from Acting Secretary of State Dean Acheson which warned that the existence of discrimination against minority groups had an adverse effect upon U.S. relations with other countries. Frequently, Acheson argued, it was impossible to formulate a satisfactory answer to foreign criticism because "the gap between the things we stand for in principle and the facts of a particular situation may be too wide to be bridged." He went on to claim, "An atmosphere of suspicion and resentment in a country over the way a minority is being treated in the United States is a formidable obstacle to the development of mutual understanding and trust between the two countries." In addition, the committee cited an article from a United Press dispatch in which it was claimed that British diplomatic circles felt that recent lynchings provided excellent propaganda ammunition for the communists. The President's committee concluded the section on international reasons for strengthening civil rights with, "The United States is not so strong, the final triumph of the democratic ideal is not so inevitable that we can ignore what the world thinks of us or our record." [7]

When President Truman presented some of the recommendations of his committee to Congress in 1948, it caused a storm of protest from the South.[8] The proposals included a Commission on Civil Rights, antilynching and voting rights legislation, and the establishment of a Fair Employment Practices Commission to prevent unfair discrimination in employment. This legislation had little chance of passage through a Congress where the seniority system gave southern legislators powerful positions on congressional committees. In fact, when these proposals were included in the 1948 Democratic platform, some southern Democrats bolted from the Democratic party and formed a States' Rights party. This split almost cost Truman the 1948 election. [9] In many ways, the Truman program failed because public opinion had not been effectively mobilized to counter southern intransigence. Later civil rights acts of 1957, 1960, and 1964 were debated against a background of public opinion that had been aroused by boycotts, sit-ins, and battles to desegregate the schools.

Brown v. Board of Education

Within the climate of the cold war, the NAACP was setting the stage for a Supreme Court decision on the constitutionality of school segregation. The key legal item was the interpretation of the Fourteenth Amendment. This amendment to the Constitution had been ratified in 1868, shortly after the close of the Civil War. One of its purposes was to extend the basic guarantees of the Bill of Rights into the areas of state and local government. The most important and controversial section of the Fourteenth Amendment stated, "No State shall make or enforce any law which shall abridge the privileges or immunities of citizens ... nor ... deprive any person of life, liberty, or property, without due process of law; nor deny to any person within its jurisdiction the equal protection of the laws." [10] The important question was declaring segregation laws in southern states unconstitutional.

The first major test of this issue had been in 1895 when Homer Plessy, who was one-eighth black and seven-eighths white, was arrested for refusing to ride in the colored coach of a train as required by Louisiana state law. The Supreme Court ruled in this case that segregation did not create a badge of inferiority if segregated facilities were equal and the law was reasonable. The Supreme Court in establishing the "separate but equal doctrine" failed to clearly define what constituted equal facilities and what was reasonable. [11] Truman's civil rights committee in 1947 had expressed hope that the Supreme Court was moving toward a broader interpretation of the Fourteenth Amendment. It noted that, beginning in the 1930s, the Supreme Court had begun to declare certain state and local laws unconstitutional because they infringed upon due process and equal protection of the laws. [12]

The overturning of the "separate but equal doctrine" and the broader application of the Fourteenth Amendment came in 1954 in the historic and controversial Supreme Court decision *Brown* v. *Board of Education of Topeka,* which declared segregated public education

unconstitutional. Supreme Court decisions do not occur in a social vacuum. Supreme Court justices are
influenced by public opinion and national and international issues. [13] Two important influences on the Supreme Court's decision were the cold war and what were
described as the "findings of social science."

The issues of the cold war and the findings of social
science were included in the briefs submitted to the
Court by the NAACP. The NAACP had been struggling
for years to get the Supreme Court to overrule the
"separate but equal doctrine" and declare school segregation unconstitutional. In 1953 *Brown* v. *Board of
Education of Topeka* was only one of five school segregation suits to reach the Supreme Court. It became
the first case simply because all the cases were put in
alphabetical order. The *Brown* case began in 1951 when
Oliver Brown and twelve other parents represented by
NAACP lawyers brought suit to void a Kansas law
which permitted but did not require local segregation of
the schools. In this particular case Oliver Brown's
daughter was denied the right to attend a white
elementary school within five blocks of her home and
forced to cross railroad tracks and travel twenty-one
blocks to attend an all-black school. The Federal District Court in Kansas ruled against Oliver Brown on the
argument that the segregated schools in the case were
substantially equal and fell within the separate but
equal doctrine.[14]

The NAACP in preparing its brief for the Supreme
Court defined two important objectives. One was to
show that the climate of the times required an end to
segregation laws. The other objective was to show that
the separate but equal doctrine contained a contradiction in terms, that is, separate facilities were inherently
unequal. In terms of painting a picture of current international problems the NAACP brief to the Court
argued, "Survival of our country in the present interna-

tional situation is inevitably tied to resolution of this domestic issue." The NAACP brief submitted as friend and adviser of the Court argued that discrimination against minority groups had a negative effect on our relations with other countries. The brief warned, "Racial discrimination furnishes grist for the Communist propaganda mills, and it raises doubts even among friendly nations as to the intensity of our devotion to the democratic faith." While the Supreme Court did not say anything directly about foreign affairs in its decision, it did not dismiss the arguments as immaterial. In fact, the *Brown* decision became widely used in America's propaganda offensive to show that racial justice did exist in the United States.[15]

Of greater importance to the actual wording of the Supreme Court decision was the argument presented by the NAACP that recent findings in the social sciences showed that separate facilities were inherently unequal. This provided the basis for overturning the separate but equal doctrine. It also caused a storm of protest that the Supreme Court was basing it decisions on nonlegal arguments. Throughout the South, the Court was seen as being persuaded by communist-oriented social scientists. Billboards began to appear on highways demanding the impeachment of Chief Justice Earl Warren for his role in subverting the Constitution. Charges were made that the Supreme Court had overstepped its role of interpreter of the Constitution and had entered the field of legislation.[16]

What the Supreme Court argued in the *Brown* decision was that "in the field of public education the doctrine of 'separate but equal' has no place. Separate educational facilities are inherently unequal." To support this argument the Supreme Court wrote one of the most controversial single sentences ever to appear in a Court decision. The sentence read, "Whatever may have been the extent of psychological knowledge at the time of *Plessy* v. *Ferguson*, this finding is amply supported by modern authority." Following this sentence was footnote 11 which cited a number of social science documents, the most important being the works of Kenneth Clark and Gunnar Myrdal's *An American Dilemma*.[17]

The NAACP had put a lot of effort into marshaling evidence to prove to the Court that separate educational facilities were inherently unequal. Kenneth Clark, a social psychologist at the College of the City of New York, acted as general social science consultant to the legal staff of the NAACP. The beginning of the development of evidence for this argument was not in the *Brown* case but in another school segregation case that appeared on the Supreme Court docket at the same time. This was the case of *Harry Briggs, Jr.* v. *R. W. Elliot,* which was initiated in South Carolina six weeks before the first *Brown* case. In this case social scientists appeared in the state court and in federal district courts to testify on the deleterious effects of segregation on motivation, ability to learn, and personality development.

Other segregation cases being pursued by the NAACP also began to be used as a testing ground for the introduction of social science data. When the school segregation cases began their way to the Supreme Court, a special committee was formed to work closely with the legal staff of the NAACP to prepare an Appendix to the briefs being submitted to the Court. The responsibility for formulating the Appendix was given to Kenneth Clark, Isidor Chein, and Gerhart Saenger. Clark and Chein were to have the honor of being cited in footnote 11 of the Supreme Court decision. The final draft of the Appendix was submitted and accepted by the Supreme Court in 1952 under the title "The Effects of Segregation and the Consequences of Desegregation: A Social Science Statement." [18]

One very important thing about the social science material submitted by the NAACP and the studies cited in footnote 11 was that they reflected current opinion about both the effects of segregation and how the problems of poverty caused by racial discrimination could be cured. These arguments provided the framework for later discussions about the use of education as a means of ending poverty by providing equality of opportunity. This was particularly true of Gunnar Myrdal's *An American Dilemma,* which was not only a resource for the Supreme Court but also a major book that outlined the problems of racial discrimination to an entire American generation.

It should be noted that all the references cited by the Supreme Court in footnote 11 were used in the development of the social science Appendix. One of the most important was Kenneth Clark's "Effect of Prejudice and Discrimination on Personality Development" which was prepared for the fact-finding report of the Midcentury White House Conference on Children and Youth.[19] This report provided the major arguments in the first section of the social science Appendix submitted to the Supreme Court.

The basic argument in Clark's original paper and in the NAACP brief was that officially sanctioned segregation by a state or local government organization caused personality damage to the children of both the minority and majority groups. Minority-group children became aware of their inferior status and often reacted with feelings of inferiority and a sense of personal humiliation. This created an internal conflict between a need for a sense of personal worth and the lack of respect provided by the majority group. As a means of coping with this conflict, it was argued, there developed certain patterns of behavior related to the socioeconomic class of the minority child. "Some children," it was written, "usually of the lower socio-economic classes, may react by overt aggressions and hostility directed toward their own group or members of the dominant group. Anti-social and delinquent behavior may often be interpreted as reactions to these racial frustrations." [20]

What Clark and the NAACP were essentially arguing to the Supreme Court was that segregation caused behavioral patterns that led to crime and violence among lower-class blacks in the United States. In terms of middle-class and upper-class minority children, it was argued, racial frustration was likely to result either in withdrawal and submissive behavior or in rigid comformity to middle-class values and standards. For all minority-group children racial segregation was believed to cause a lowering of morale and a depression in the level of educational aspiration. For majority-group children, it was stated, "confusion, conflict, moral cynicism, and disrespect for authority may arise . . . as a consequence of being taught the moral, religious and democratic principles of the brotherhood of man . . . by the same persons and institutions who, in their support of racial segregation . . . seem to be acting in a prejudiced and discriminatory manner." [21]

One of the things that emerged from the social science Appendix was the argument that a culture of poverty existed which was directly related to racial discrimination. The term *culture of poverty* was not used in the written material but was implied in the basic argument. What was argued was that racial segregation caused behavioral patterns that reinforced the beliefs of the dominant group about the necessity for segregation. For instance, crime and violence among lower-class blacks and conformity among middle- and upper-class blacks convinced the white majority that continued segregation was both necessary for self-protection and acceptable to the black population. In addition, segregation, by reducing economic and social aspirations, had created behavioral patterns which resulted in depressed economic and educational achievement. These behavioral patterns in turn reinforced an already depressed economic situation and resulted in continued poverty and support of existing behavioral patterns.

In the 1960s this type of reasoning contributed to the educational war on poverty as a means of breaking this culture pattern. In the 1940s and '50s this argument found its strongest expression in Gunnar Myrdal's *An American Dilemma,* which influenced the Supreme Court decision. In 1937 Myrdal was asked by Frederick P. Keppel, then president of the Carnegie Corporation of New York, to begin his study of American blacks. Myrdal was a Swedish social scientist and the justification for inviting a Swede to conduct a study of the American black was given in the original letter of proposal from Keppel to Myrdal as a desire to invite someone from "a nonimperialistic country with no background of domination of one race over another." [22] Myrdal began his work in 1938 with a two-month tour of southern states and library work and consultation with American scholars. The Carnegie Corporation provided Myrdal with a staff of over fifty people to be used in formulating a plan for the study. Kenneth Clark was one member of the original working staff. During the summer of 1939 Myrdal completed a detailed plan for the study, but with the outbreak of war in Europe he returned to his country in 1940. In his absence the staff supervised the publication of three volumes on the American black and gathered a large number of unpublished manuscripts to be used in the study. In 1941 Myrdal returned to the United States to complete the final writing of the manuscript. The study was completed in 1942 and was finally published in 1944.[23]

The overall thesis of Myrdal's study was that Americans faced a major moral dilemma between the ideals of American democracy and actions with regard to race relations. The "American Dilemma" was defined as the conflict between "the valuations preserved on the general plane . . . of the 'American Creed' " and "the valuations on specific planes of individual and group living." [24] Included in the areas of group and individual living were social, economic, sexual, and community problems related to race relations. This dilemma, Myrdal's study argued, had a direct effect upon behavioral patterns.

On the one hand, it was argued, a cultural unity existed in the United States through a sharing of the "American Creed." On the other hand, this cultural unity existed in a context where people held values that were in conflict with the values that provided for cultural unity. For instance, the study argued, an uneducated white person living in the rural South, who was violently prejudiced against blacks and intent upon depriving them of civil rights and human independence, had also a whole compartment in the sphere of values which included a belief in liberty, equality, justice, and fair opportunity for everybody. People who acted in conflict with their belief in the American Creed had to find a means of defending their behavior to themselves and others. This was accomplished by twisting and mutilating social reality and by the production of emotionally loaded rationalizations for particular behavior. As a result of this distortion of social reality, firmly entrenched popular beliefs developed concerning blacks which the study labeled as "bluntly false and which can only be understood when we remember the opportunistic ad hoc purposes they serve." [25] The purpose of the study was to undercut these false belief systems and help to end the "American Dilemma" by providing a true picture of social reality and a careful depiction of the actual life conditions of American black people.

What was titled as "Our Main Hypothesis" was the theory of the vicious circle. This was a theory of the oppression of black people in the United States which saw an interrelated set of social circumstances which reinforced patterns of racially prejudiced behavior and created a culture of poverty. The basic argument was that when slavery ended, a caste system remained which gave the average black a disadvantageous start in each generation. The continued discrimination was rooted in a system of economic exploitation and justified by a false set of racial beliefs. These economic and social conditions in turn created behavioral patterns among blacks that provided some semblance of proof for white people that black behavior was typified by "low standards of efficiency, reliability, ambition, and morals." [26] White people exaggerated their view of these behaviors and used them to justify continued belief that black people were not capable of handling machines, running a business, or learning a profession. Myrdal's study argued that these behavioral deficiencies were not inborn and that "we must conclude that they are caused, directly or indirectly, by the very poverty we are trying to explain, and by other discriminations in legal protection, public health, housing, education and in every other sphere of life." [27]

The hypothesis of the vicious circle proposed a method for solving the problem of black poverty. Since within this hypothesis was an interrelated set of causal factors, no single solution or final cause could be defined. What was involved were three sets of interrelated causative factors defined as "(1) the economic level; (2) standards of intelligence, ambition, health, education, decency, manners, and morals; and (3) discrimination by whites." [28] Since these three sets of factors were interrelated, it was argued, a change in any one of them would cause a change in the other two. For instance, if white prejudice were decreased, this would likely cause an increase in black standards of living and education, which in turn would further decrease white prejudice. A rise in black employment, for instance, would increase family income, nutrition, health, and housing which would increase the possibilities of providing black youths with more education. In turn this would mean possibilities for better employment and improved standards and begin to undercut the belief system that supported white prejudice. This theory of social change was stated in the language of social science as "any change in any one of these factors, independent of the way in which it is brought about, will, by the aggregate weight of the cumulative effects running back and forth between them all, start the whole system moving in one direction or the other." [29]

In many ways this hypothesis provided a social scientist's dream for controlled and planned social change. The government could work on one of the factors, i.e., education, as a means of creating a chain of reaction in the other factors. Or the government, because of consideration of social lag, equilibrium, or accommodation, might choose to work in the areas of health or housing.[30] However, this social scientist's dream had little relationship to the power and methods of southern congressional leaders and the workings of the government in the 1940s and '50s. To a certain extent the Supreme Court decision in the school segregation cases could be viewed as one method in starting this chain of reaction. Desegregated schools, it could have been argued, would decrease prejudice and improve the education of blacks, which in turn would raise standards of employment, health, and housing; and all these things could lead to a further decrease in prejudice and improved education.

The arguments contained in the social science brief and in the *American Dilemma* were certainly the major factors in causing the Supreme Court to reverse the "separate but equal doctrine" and declare segregated schooling unconstitutional, but they provided no certain method by which the Court decision could be implemented. The social science Appendix presented to the Court had argued that most of the evidence on whether desegregation increased or decreased racial tension established that "desegregation has been carried out successfully in a variety of situations although outbreaks of violence had been commonly predicted." [31] As an example, the peaceful integration of the armed forces that had occurred after President Truman issued Executive Order No. 9981 in 1948 was cited as proof that violence would not occur. But this proof had little relationship to the years of turmoil and violence that would later greet attempts to desegregate southern schools and public facilities.

In 1955 the Supreme Court issued its Enforcement Decree for the desegregation of schools. One problem facing the Court was the lack of machinery for supervising and assuring the desegregation of vast numbers of locally segregated school districts. The Court resolved this problem by relying upon federal district courts as the determiners of equitable principles for desegregation.

The Court argued that each local school district had its own set of problems with regard to how desegregation would effect the use of buildings, school transportation systems, and the determination of boundaries of school districts. These problems, it was felt, could best be handled on a local basis through the district court. A major problem with the Enforcement Decree was that it did not define the nature of equitable standards of enforcement or provide guidelines for desegregation. The only ground rules provided by the Supreme Court was a statement that "the courts will be guided by equitable principles. Traditionally, equity has been characterized by a practical flexibility in shaping its remedies and by a facility for adjusting and reconciling public and private needs." In addition, the Court stated the often quoted guideline that district courts should issue orders and decrees "as are necessary and proper to admit to public schools on a racially nondiscriminatory basis with all deliberate speed the parties to these cases." [32]

The problem of enforcement through local federal courts was not only a matter of inadequate guidelines and the meaning of "all deliberate speed," but also the fact that federal judges lived in local communities and felt the heavy hand of local pressure. It was also a very cumbersome and time-consuming process for local groups who were dissatisfied with local attempts at desegregation or lack of desegregation to take the issue into court.[33] Following the Supreme Court decision, many school districts were desegregated. Within one year of the decision, desegregation occurred in school districts in Arkansas, Delaware, Maryland, Missouri, Texas, and the District of Columbia. But in many areas there was considerable resistance and attempts to evade compliance.

One method was to create groups to study desegregation problems as a method of delaying implementation. This method was used in Atlanta, Georgia, in a number of cities of North Carolina, and in Mobile, Alabama. Houston, Texas, delayed action by claiming the need to build new buildings and prepare black students for the transition. In a number of southern towns White Citizens Councils developed with the major purpose of disrupting attempts at integration. Violence by white groups occurred in towns throughout southern states. In little towns like Mansfield, Texas, attempts at desegregation were greeted by angry white people waving signs that read, "A dead nigger is the best nigger," and "Coons ears $1.00 a dozen." [34]

One obstacle in gaining compliance with the Supreme

Court decision was the failure of President Eisenhower to use the power of the executive branch effectively. In fact, Eisenhower avoided taking a public stand of approval or disapproval on the Court decision. He made the very weak claim "that if I should express, publicly, either approval or disapproval of a Supreme Court decision in one case, I would be obliged to do so in many, if not all, cases." [35]

Eisenhower stated his whole approach to the integration problem would be one of moderation. In a letter he wrote to evangelist Billy Graham, in which he urged the Reverend Dr. Graham to influence southern ministers to calm public opinion, he stated, "I shall always, as a matter of conviction and as a champion of real, as opposed to spurious, progress, remain a moderate in this regard." [36] When civil rights groups in 1955 demanded federal troops be sent to Mississippi to do something about the murder of a fourteen-year-old black named Emmett Till, Eisenhower refused and claimed that the Communist party was behind the demand. Eisenhower freely interjected the image of a communist conspiracy into the civil rights movement. He claimed, "The Communist Party of the United States, doing its best to twist this movement for its own purposes, was urging its members to infiltrate the NAACP . . . and had launched a program to drive a wedge between the administration and its friends in the South in the election year of 1956." [37] One could interpret this statement to mean that Eisenhower believed that a communist conspiracy in the civil rights movement was designed to cost him southern votes.

When Eisenhower was finally forced to act, a major motivating factor was the potential damage of southern resistance to America's cold-war foreign policy. The situation that set the stage for action was in Little Rock, Arkansas, in the fall of 1957. The Little Rock school district planned to begin integrating their schools by admitting nine black students to the Central High School. Governor Orval Faubus took action to block the integration of the schools by ordering the National Guard into Little Rock. Faubus announced that the National Guard was to be used to maintain order and that order would not be possible "if forcible integration is carried out." When black students appeared to enroll in the previously all-white school, they found the doors of the schoolhouse blocked by the National Guard and were informed the school was off-limits to "colored" students. Such an open and flagrant violation of the Supreme Court decision forced Eisenhower to take action. Also, such an open and planned violation had immediate exposure through the mass media and foreign press. It seems clear that one of Eisenhower's concerns was the effect on America's foreign image of a governor of a state openly using troops to maintain the race line.

President Eisenhower tried to negotiate and persuade Governor Faubus to withdraw the troops and abide by the Little Rock plan for integration. Finally, the courts issued an injunction against Governor Faubus to withdraw the Guard. With the troops withdrawn and the Little Rock population already stirred up by the governor, the stage was set for mob violence. Eisenhower later reflected that before September, 1957 a line from the musical *South Pacific* in which a Frenchman mistakenly called the heroine's hometown "Small Rock" was meaningless to foreign audiences. "Thereafter ... the name Little Rock, Arkansas, would become known around the world. But the world's disapproval should not have been for a city, only for a man and a handful of its population." [38] When violence did occur in Little Rock, Eisenhower federalized the Arkansas National Guard and sent regular federal troops into the city. The pressures of the cold war had finally forced executive action in a dramatic fashion. Eisenhower was later to write, "Overseas, the mouthpieces of Soviet propaganda in Russia and Europe were blaring out that 'anti-Negro violence' in Little Rock was being 'committed with the clear connivance of the United States government.' " [39]

Little Rock represented such a dramatic reversal of Eisenhower's previous lack of action and lack of approval of the Supreme Court decision that he felt compelled to go on national television and radio to explain his actions. On September 24, 1957, Eisenhower justified to the American public the sending of federal troops in terms of maintaining the law and demonstrating "to the world that we are a nation in which laws, not men, are supreme." Eisenhower warned the American public that the incidents in Little Rock were threatening the security of the world. He stated that "at a time when we face grave situations abroad because of the hatred that communism bears toward a system of government based on human rights, it would be difficult to exaggerate the harm that is being done to the prestige and influence, and indeed to the safety, of our nation and the world." He went on to claim, "Our enemies are gloating over this incident and using it everywhere to misrepresent our whole nation." The speech, which was presented to the American people to justify Eisenhower's first significant involvement in the school desegregation controversy, ended with a statement that when Arkansas citizens ended interference with the law, federal troops would be removed and "a blot upon the fair name and high honor of our nation in the world will be removed. Thus will be restored the image of America and of all its parts as one nation, indivisible, with liberty and justice for all." [40] Black students eventually entered Central High School not because of Eisenhower's devotion to civil rights but because of his devotion to winning the cold war against the Soviet Union.

The Civil Rights Movement

The circumstances that forced President Eisenhower to act highlighted the techniques civil rights groups felt would be needed to bring about federal action to achieve compliance with the Court decision. A key element was the use of the mass media. Television made it possible to bring pictures of social conflict into every American home. Television broadcasts of troops and mob violence in Little Rock projected more reality of a situation than thousands of words on radio or in newspapers. In some ways this reality was portrayed in an overly dramatic fashion because the cameras focused mainly on the most exciting events and could leave the impression that Little Rock was entirely a battleground for troops and mob violence.

The evolution of mass media in the 1950s made it possible to turn local problems into national problems. Presidents in the twentieth century had treated the institutions of the South with a great deal of deference because of the importance of the white southern political structure. With newspapers and radio to report on events in the South, Presidents could easily call these problems local and delay action. There was a major difference in terms of national impact between reporting lynchings of black people in the newspaper and providing two minutes of television film depicting the actual lynching. The enforcement of the Supreme Court school desegregation ruling depended on civil rights groups making effective use of television. In a way it became a battle of public images. There was concern about America's international image as pictures of racial injustice flashed around the world. There was also the President's public image which was often threatened when examples of racial injustice were shown to millions of television viewers and the question was asked,

What is our president doing about this situation now?

The most important and dramatic technique used by civil rights groups was that of nonviolent confrontation. The massive nonviolent confrontation of black people in the South against an array of cattle prods, clubs, and fire hoses wielded by cursing southern law-enforcement units provided dramatic and shocking television viewing for the nation. CORE, SNCC, and the Southern Christian Leadership Conference under the leadership of Martin Luther King provided the national drama and the final push for national civil rights legislation.

The introduction of nonviolent confrontation into the civil rights movement came from the Christian student movement of the 1930s which under the leadership of the Fellowship for Reconciliation, was committed to the use of the Gandhian technique of *satyagraha,* or non-violent direct action, in solving racial and industrial problems in the United States. The techniques Gandhi had used in India against British imperialism provided an apparent model for how love and nonviolence could defeat evil and violence. The executive director of the Fellowship for Reconciliation was A. J. Muste, a labor leader and radical school reformer of the 1920s, who had attempted to establish an alternative system of schools for organized labor at the Brookwood Labor College and the Manumit School for workers' children.[41] In 1942 two Methodist members of the Fellowship for Reconciliation, James Farmer and George Houser, organized the Congress of Racial Equality (CORE) at the University of Chicago. Early support for CORE came from the Methodist youth movement. Muste stated, "The Youth Movement of the Methodist Church ... is the most progressive of our Protestant youth movements."[42]

The two basic doctrines of the early CORE movement were those of being interracial, blacks and whites together, and the use of Christian nonviolent techniques.

CORE leaders argued that interracial action was necessary because it was false to speak of the Negro problem; rather, it was the problem of the brotherhood of all people. Any organization that was predominantly black or white worked against the ultimate goal of brotherhood. Nonviolence was supported not only because it symbolized a Christian community of love but also because it was viewed as the only practical technique to achieve racial justice. The early CORE program stated "that it is suicidal for a minority group to use violence, since to use it would simply result in complete control and subjugation by the majority group." [43]

CORE did not rise to national prominence until the late 1950s when another Christian leader, Dr. Martin Luther King, made nonviolent confrontation the central drama of the civil rights movement. King was born in Atlanta, Georgia, in 1929 into a family of Baptist ministers. His maternal grandfather had founded the Ebenezer Baptist Church, and his father had made it one of the largest and most prestigious Baptist churches in Atlanta. King entered Morehouse College in Atlanta in 1944 where he claimed to have been influenced by the reading of Thoreau's *Essay on Civil Disobedience*.[44] He later wrote about the essay, "Fascinated by the idea of refusing to cooperate with an evil system, I was so deeply moved that I reread the work several times. This was my first intellectual contact with the theory of non-violent resistance." [45]

In 1948 King entered the Crozier Theological Seminary in Chester, Pennsylvania, where for the first time he became acquainted with the pacifist position in a lecture by A. J. Muste. King wrote that at the time he considered Muste's pacifist doctrine impractical in a world confronted by the armies of totalitarian nations. Of more importance to King's intellectual development was his exposure to the social-gospel philosophy of Walter Rauschenbusch which developed during the late

nineteenth century and saw the church actively involved in social reform as a means of creating a Kingdom of God on earth. King rejected Rauschenbusch's
optimism about establishing a Kingdom of God but accepted the social responsibility of religion. King wrote,
"It has been my conviction ever since reading Rauschenbusch that any religion which professes to be concerned about the souls of men and is not concerned
about the social and economic conditions that scar the
soul, is a spiritually moribund religion only waiting for
the day to be buried." [46]

While at Crozier, King also began to read the works of
Karl Marx and Lenin. As a Christian, he rejected the
materialist interpretations of history in these works because they had no place for God. He also rejected the
moral relativism of Marx and Lenin and the development of political totalitarianism in communist countries. Despite these rejections, King was attracted to
Marx's analysis of capitalism. King claimed that since
his early teen years he had been deeply concerned about
the gulf between wealth and poverty. King wrote,
"Although modern American capitalism had greatly
reduced the gap through social reforms, there was still
need for a better distribution of wealth. Moreover, Marx
had revealed the danger of the profit motive as the sole
basis of an economic system: capitalism is always in
danger of inspiring men to be more concerned about
making a living than making a life." [47]

King's partial acceptance of the social gospel and the
radical critique of capitalism were united into a doctrine
of action by the study of the lectures and works of
Gandhi. The Indian leader's work convinced King that
the Christian doctrine of love could be a force used for
social change. King wrote, "Gandhi was probably the
first person in history to lift the love ethic of Jesus above
mere interaction between individuals to a powerful and

effective social force on a large scale." Like the early members of CORE, King became convinced that the nonviolent resistance philosophy of Gandhi "was the only morally and practically sound method open to oppressed people in their struggle for freedom." [48] With this intellectual development based on the social gospel and Gandhi, King graduated from Crozier in 1951 and the following fall entered Boston University as a doctoral candidate in philosophy.

In 1953, as King was finishing his doctoral dissertation, he made a decision that began a chain of events that would have a profound effect on the history of the United States. After receiving several offers from eastern churches, he finally accepted one in the South at the Dexter Avenue Baptist Church in Montgomery, Alabama. On September 1, 1954, the same year as the Supreme Court's school desegregation decision, King and his family moved into the parsonage of the Montgomery church and King launched his career as minister. King entered the ministry in the South exactly at the time when hopes were increasing that the Court's actions would end segregation. In addition, Montgomery was to provide King with lifelong companionships in the struggle for civil rights. Around the corner from King's parsonage was the home of the Reverend Ralph Abernathy, the man who was to become King's alter ego in the civil rights movement.

The incident that launched Martin Luther King's civil rights activities and provided scope for his Gandhian form of the social gospel occurred on December 1, 1955. On that date, Rosa Parks, who had spent a regular day's work as a seamstress in one of Montgomery's leading department stores, boarded a bus and took the first seat behind the section reserved for whites. Later on the journey home, several white passengers boarded the bus. The driver ordered Rosa Parks and three other black passengers to stand so that the white passengers could have seats. Rosa Parks refused and was arrested. The black ministers in the community quickly organized in response to this incident, and on December 5 the Montgomery bus boycott was begun.

The bus boycott lasted over a year with black citizens either walking to work, forming car pools, or riding in cabs. The media found Montgomery ideal drama for the national news. Around the country the story of the bus boycott spread and with it a realization of the conditions existing in towns like Montgomery. In addition, the nonviolent technique was made part of the boycott and proved extremely effective in causing moral indignation against the white citizens of Montgomery. While no acts of violence were initiated by the black community, there were bombings by white citizens of four black churches and three homes, including those of Martin Luther King and Ralph Abernathy. The bus boycott ended on December 21, 1956, when, after a Supreme Court decision against segregation on buses, the transit system of Montgomery was officially integrated.[49]

King emerged from the Montgomery boycott as a national figure in the civil rights movement. He had demonstrated a method of resistance that could be used in communities throughout the country. In January 1957, black religious leaders meeting in Atlanta organized the Southern Christian Leadership Conference (SCLC) with Martin Luther King as its president. One of its first actions was to request that President Eisenhower venture into the South to make a major policy speech supporting the decisions of the Supreme Court. They also suggested that Vice-President Richard Nixon tour the South and confer with black and white leaders. And finally they asked the attorney general to conduct a fact-finding tour of the South. All three requests were refused as the Eisenhower administration tried to walk the thin line between not denying civil rights and not antagonizing the white southern voter.[50]

On May 17, 1957, Martin Luther King gave his first national address in Washington, D.C., to a Prayer Pilgrimage organized by A. Philip Randolph in the tradition of his early March on Washington Movement. King's speech outlined his basic civil rights strategy. Speaking at the Lincoln Memorial, King attacked the Eisenhower administration for its failure to provide leadership and action in the field of race relations. He argued that the national administration should accept its responsibility to enforce desegregation. Second, he urged that white sympathizers be moved to a position of positive commitment to the civil rights struggle. In addition, southern white moderates must be used to assure at least minimal implementation of Court decisions. But the most important strategy was that of gaining voting rights for black citizens in the South. For years, excluded from voting by literacy tests, poll taxes, and discrimination, the black citizen of the South was unable to exercise meaningful political power. King told his audience, "Give us the ballot and we will quietly, lawfully, and non-violently, without rancor or bitterness, implement the May 17, 1954, decision of the Supreme Court." For King, meaningful school desegregation would depend upon the power of the black voter.[51]

Civil Rights Legislation

The Montgomery bus boycott and King's rise to national leadership accompanied by the unfavorable international publicity in the area of race relations forced Eisenhower to take a stand on civil rights. Feeling the pressure of the Montgomery bus boycott and the Supreme Court decisions, Eisenhower, in his State of the

Union message in 1956, called for civil rights legislation. The most important item in his proposal was the creation of a civil rights division in the Department of Justice which would have the power to institute suits in the courts against violation of civil rights laws. The expenses of these suits were to be borne by the federal government. This provision would have given the government the power to move into the South and assume part of the burden of effectively taking civil rights cases into the courts. It would have provided an end to the federal inaction complained about by black leaders. But when the bill reached the Senate Judiciary presided over by Senator James O. Eastland of Mississippi, it was never reported out. Eisenhower probably knew that the bill would never get through congressional committees dominated by southerners. But Eisenhower noted with pleasure that in the elections of 1956 "I enlarged the sizable vote I had received four years earlier among Negroes of the North and through the South." [52]

Heartened by the results of the 1956 election, Eisenhower again introduced his civil rights program. This time, successful efforts were made to bypass Senator Eastland's committee and report the bill directly to the floor of the Senate. The most important concern for southern senators was the provision providing power for the attorney general's office to institute legal action. Southern senators countered this provision by attaching an amendment which eliminated the authority of the attorney general to bring civil action against violators of civil rights other than voting rights. Another amendment was passed requiring trial by jury which, in the South, meant a jury composed of whites who were sure to rule against any black litigant. Black leaders protested the bill as it was reported out of the Senate and urged Eisenhower to veto it. A. Philip Randolph wrote Eisenhower, "In the name of the officials and members of the Brotherhood of Sleeping Car Porters, urge veto of Civil Rights Bill. It is worse than no bill at all." [53] In the Senate-House Conference Committee a compromise was reached, which received the support of Eisenhower, that gave the judge the right to decide on a jury trial and provided that if there were no jury trial, the maximum penalty could total no more than ninety days and three hundred dollars.[54]

The Civil Rights Act of 1957 provided no meaningful way to hasten the speed of school desegregation. It is historically important because it was the first civil rights legislation since 1885 and marked the beginning of the Second Reconstruction. The Civil Rights Act of 1957 provided for the establishment of a Civil Rights Commission and a Civil Rights Division to the Department of Justice. It gave the attorney general the power to seek an injunction against any individual deprived of the right to vote, and it included the trial-by-jury compromise.

Weaknesses of the 1957 Civil Rights Act were evident from the beginning. The only area authorized for action by the attorney general's office was in the area of voting rights. King had argued in his civil rights strategy that this was the key to effectively bringing about the end of segregated schooling. But in 1959, after the civil rights statute had been in effect over one year, only one insignificant case had been brought into the courts.[55] In 1959 Eisenhower called for another civil rights bill but failed to mention expanding the power of the attorney general's office to include bringing court action against violation of civil rights outside the area of voting rights. In 1960 Eisenhower again pressed for civil rights legislation in a special message to Congress.

One of the striking things about Eisenhower's civil rights message on February 5, 1960, was its underlying concern about violence. There was a great fear that the civil rights movement would unleash a reign of terror and violent confrontation and possible civil war. It should be remembered that even in the NAACP brief in the school desegregation cases, there had been an argument that segregation bred a violent and criminal personality. Race relations in the history of the United States had been marked by a continual cycle of race riots, brutality, and violence. One effect of the nonviolent technique advocated and used by black leaders was to place the image of violence on the shoulders of the southern white. This issue of violence and civil strife primarily concerned Eisenhower in 1960. He warned Congress in 1960, "There have been instances where extremists have attempted by mob violence and other concerted threats of violence to obstruct the accomplishment of the objectives of the school decrees." He went on to recommend additional legislative authority for the FBI "in the cases involving the destruction or attempted destruction of schools or churches, by making flight from one State to another to avoid detention or prosecution for such a crime a Federal offense." [56]

The Civil Rights Act of 1960 did not contain any provisions for involvement of the attorney general in the area of school desegregation. All it did was contain two provisions for actions against forms of violence occurring from attempts at desegregation and implementation of court orders. However, this provided no aid in getting school desegregation suits into the courts. In addition, the civil rights act attempted to strengthen voting rights. But as Thurgood Marshall, the leading lawyer in the NAACP school desegregation cases, stated, "The Civil Rights Act of 1960 isn't worth the paper it's written on." [57]

While black leaders were condemning the federal government for failing to enforce court decisions, the civil rights movement in the South was moving toward greater activism. On February 1, 1960, four black students, after reading a comic book on *Martin Luther King and the Montgomery Story,* left their dormitory at North Carolina A&T College in Greensboro and walked into the local Woolworth store. They took seats at the "whites only" lunch counter. Refused service, they began to return on a daily basis. With the power of the media to spread this incident, sit-ins began to occur around the South. Within two weeks, there were sit-ins in eleven more cities in four different states. Within three months, seventy-eight southern communities had experienced sit-ins, and two thousand youths had been arrested.[58]

The student sit-ins provided the springboard for the formation of the Student Non-Violent Coordinating Committee (SNCC) at a civil rights student conference held in Raleigh, North Carolina, on April 15–17. The organization had the backing of CORE and SCLC. Martin Luther King presented at the meeting three major points of action for the new group. These included a continuation of the struggle, a national campaign of selective buying to be used as a weapon against segregated businesses, and a call for volunteers prepared to accept prison sentences. One of the things that became clear during the Raleigh meeting was that many new members of the civil rights movement considered King not radical enough and viewed nonviolence as a technique rather than as Christian love building a brotherhood of humanity.[59]

SNCC, CORE, and the SCLC provided a crescendo of activity throughout the South. Freedom rides, sit-ins, and arrests became daily occurrences. Many of the attempts at trying to get local communities to comply with civil rights decisions were defeated. In Albany, Georgia, Martin Luther King and SNCC entered the community after failure by local officials to comply with

an Interstate Commerce Commission ruling banning
segregated buses and station facilities. After a long period of harassment, arrests, and violence, the civil rights
activists had to admit defeat.

Civil rights activity also began to move into the
North. In Chicago, 22,500 schoolchildren boycotted
classes in protest over school segregation. The protest in
Chicago introduced a new and important element in the
civil rights dialogue. Chicago did not have laws requiring
segregation of schools, but longstanding practices and
policies of the board of education and its conservative
superintendent, Benjamin C. Willis, had resulted in a
segregated school system based on district boundaries.
As civil rights activity moved into the North it was to
concentrate on de facto segregation existing in schools,
housing, and employment.[60]

Two major, well-planned civil rights activities of this
period were to provide the final push toward the enactment of a strong civil rights law which would give the
federal government the potential leverage needed to end
desegregation in the schools. These two events were
staged in Birmingham, Alabama, and in a march on
Washington in 1963. The civil rights movement was to
make Birmingham and its director of safety, Bull Connor, symbols of the oppression of black people in the
United States. President John F. Kennedy was quoted
as saying, "Our judgment of Bull Connor should not be
too harsh. After all, in his way, he has done a good deal
for civil rights legislation this year." [61] The March on
Washington symbolized to Congress and the American
people the growing strength of the civil rights movement
and provided the stage for mass television coverage of
speeches by leading civil rights leaders.

The advance planning that went into both activities
provided the opportunity to alert the media to the
coming events and to assure that all the drama could be

carried into the homes of millions of television viewers. In 1962 SCLC and Martin Luther King decided to make Birmingham the next theater of nonviolent action. The feeling among SCLC leaders was that Kennedy was following the same route of inaction as his predecessor, Dwight D. Eisenhower, and dramatic events were needed to force his hand.[62]

At the end of 1962, SCLC after a three-day retreat agreed to launch Project C in Birmingham in early March as a method to hinder Easter sales and apply pressure to the business community to bring about changes. The major targets in Project C were voting rights, employment, and segregation in public facilities. In 1963 there were only 10,000 registered black voters in Birmingham. In the steel mills and the industrial complex surrounding Birmingham, blacks were hired for the most menial tasks. Commercial areas of Birmingham still had segregated drinking fountains and public facilities.[63]

Following the decision on Project C, SCLC set about getting funds for the campaign. Their major financial supporters turned out to be black entertainers, particularly singer Harry Belafonte. Black entertainers provided not only free talent at rallies to raise money for civil rights, but their presence at civil rights demonstrations also proved attractive to the television people. SCLC planned a budget of $475,000 for the Birmingham campaign. The actual planning took place through a series of confidential letters that were circulated through SCLC, CORE, SNCC, and the NAACP.

The actual beginning of Project C was changed from March to April so as not to interfere with local elections. On April 2 Project C began with the issuance of the *Birmingham Manifesto* demanding an end to all city ordinances requiring segregation and the institution of merit hiring. From that date national television viewers were treated to scenes of mass arrests, the knocking down of demonstrators by fire hoses, and open brutality by Bull Connor's safety forces. Religious leaders, black students, and white students around the country flocked to join the civil rights forces. When Martin Luther King was arrested and placed in solitary confinement in the Birmingham jail, President Kennedy was embarrassed into action. Through the actions of his brother, Attorney General Robert Kennedy, he was at least able to gain King the right to call his family. By early May over two thousand persons had been arrested in Birmingham, and a final agreement was reached with the city to end desegregation and increase employment opportunities.

The second stage of the events in 1963 took place on August 28 when two hundred thousand citizens marched on Washington protesting the oppression of black people. The march was well organized and staged with considerable funding from a variety of religious, civil rights, and labor groups. It was planned to avoid any confrontation or violence. Speeches were even censored so that while civil rights would be demanded, nothing offensive to the Kennedy administration would be stated. The major goal was to provide support for civil rights legislation. Entertainers, blacks and whites, were utilized to attract the crowds and provide glamour for national television and marchers. In many ways the march was brilliant in its execution and effectively struck at the national conscience. The high point of the march was Martin Luther King's speech "I Have a Dream." [64] The speech became a classic of American oratory.

Of the two events, Birmingham had the most powerful effect. The march on Washington provided the image of a calmed civil rights movement if effective legislation were passed by Congress. There seems little doubt that the events in Birmingham sent a ripple of fear through the hearts of white Americans. Martin Luther King was later to state, "It is a harsh indictment but an inescapable conclusion, that Congress is horrified not at the conditions of Negro life but at the product of these conditions—the Negro himself." [65]

Kennedy proposed the passage of a five-point civil rights program. The first part of the program was in answer to the sit-ins at lunch counters and public facilities. Kennedy proposed to end segregation in these areas and provide for equal access to hotels, restaurants, places of amusement, and retail establishments. The second proposal was directed toward enforcing the *Brown* decision by giving the attorney general the authority to initiate court cases against local school districts and institutions of higher learning. The third proposal was aimed at creating a permanent Committee on Equal Employment Opportunity that would step up efforts to end discrimination in employment. The final proposal was one which in its final form would have the greatest effect on American education. Kennedy argued that programs and institutions receiving federal assistance should be required to end all discriminatory practices.

Kennedy's civil rights program made very little headway through Congress in 1963 and became trapped within congressional committees. Even the August march on Washington failed to provide enough leverage for action. But on November 22 President Kennedy was assassinated, and his funeral became one of the major dramas of modern television. Kennedy's successor, Lyndon B. Johnson, appeared before Congress five days after the assassination and declared, "No memorial oration or eulogy could more eloquently honor President Kennedy's memory than the earliest possible passage of the civil rights bill for which he fought so long." [66]

President Johnson, a master of congressional strategy, was able to move the civil rights legislation through Congress.[67] On January 31, 1964, congressional debate began in the House of Representatives in the Committee of the Whole House under a rule limiting debate with final action required by February. On February 10, the House voted in favor of the bill by 290 to 130. The bill then went to the Senate where motion was introduced to bypass hearings in the Judiciary Committee and send the bill directly to the floor of the Senate for debate and consideration. The controversial nature of the legislation and the fact that there were no committee hearings resulted in one of the longest filibusters in the history of the Senate. The Senate debated for seventy-four days before voting passage of the bill on June 19 by 73 to 27.[68]

The Civil Rights Act of 1964

The Civil Rights Act of 1964 was one of the most significant pieces of social legislation in the United States in the twentieth century. Under eleven different titles the power of federal regulation was extended in the areas of voting rights, public accommodations, education, and employment. Title IV and Title VI of the legislation were directed toward ending school segregation and providing authority for implementing the *Brown* decision. In terms of federal control of American education, Title VI was the most important section because it established the precedent for using the disbursal of government money as a means of controlling educational policy.

Originally, Kennedy had merely proposed requiring institutions receiving federal funds to end discriminatory practices. In its final form Title VI required mandatory withholding of federal funds. Title VI stated that no person, because of race, color, or national origin, could be excluded from or denied the benefits of any program receiving federal financial assistance. It required all federal agencies to establish guidelines to implement this policy. Refusal by institutions or projects to follow these guidelines was to result in the "termination of or refusal to grant or to continue assistance under such program or activity."

The strength of Title VI was in the fact that the government had already extended its activities into many educational institutions around the country. The activities of the National Science Foundation and the various Titles of the National Defense Education Act had spread federal spending into most of the educational institutions in the United States. A large number of institutions of higher learning were receiving federal funds for NSF institutes and research projects. In addition, research funds flowed into universities from other government agencies including the Department of Defense. Many institutions around the country received funds for Reserve Officers Training Programs. The National Defense Education Act had provided money for the purchase of equipment, guidance, fellowship and student loans. The South was particularly affected by the 1950 laws providing funds to federally assisted schools. This program was extremely important to the South because of its large number of military bases and government installations. By the early 1960s the federal government under this program had allocated $2.5 billion to help build over 50,000 classrooms and provided aid for operating expenses to school systems enrolling over one-third of all elementary and secondary school pupils in the United States.[69] Title VI announced that all aid to institutions and school districts that failed to comply with federal guidelines would end. This was certainly a powerful government weapon. The most extreme concern about Title VI was voiced by Senator Sam Ervin of North Carolina who claimed, "No dictator could ask for more power than Title VI confers on the President." [70]

It is interesting to note that during the congressional debates on education bills in the 1950s there was a continuous argument that none of these programs would involve government regulation. Title VI reversed these arguments. Title VI represented one of those many contradictions that appear in American history. In order to protect the constitutional rights of black citizens, the government had been forced to adopt a measure which involved a major step toward the regulation of American education. In defense of civil rights, the power of the central government had been increased.

The administrative justification for Title VI was given by Senator Hubert Humphrey. Since debate was limited in the House of Representatives and committee hearings were bypassed in the Senate, the major arguments for and against the legislation were given in the lengthy Senate floor debate. Senator Humphrey, as majority whip and floor manager of the legislation, presented the administration's arguments in support of the bill. Humphrey gave the following facts to the Senate. In 1962, under the provisions of the 1950 laws on federally affected schools, Alabama, Georgia, Mississippi, South Carolina, and Virginia received $35,282,048. Yet, Humphrey told the Senate, "for the school year 1962–63 Alabama, Mississippi, and South Carolina had no Negroes and white together in any type of school. Georgia has only 44 Negroes in integrated schools, and only about one-half of 1 percent of Virginia's Negro children were in desegregated schools." [71] In addition, Humphrey cited incidents of segregation in other federally funded programs in hospitals and institutions of higher learning. Humphrey argued that Title VI was not designed to be punitive, but designed to make sure that funds were not used to support segregated programs. He also claimed that Title VI did not create any new government authority. "Most agencies," he stated, "now have authority to refuse or terminate assistance for failure to comply with a variety of requirements imposed by statute or by administrative action."

Humphrey's concluding arguments on the federal authority involved in Title VI were reminiscent of arguments given by white citizens in southern states. Southern whites often stated that if blacks did not like segregation laws, they could move to another state. Humphrey argued that Title VI represented an unquestioned power of the federal government to establish the terms under which funds shall be disbursed. He also remarked, "No recipient is required to accept Federal aid."

Humphrey's claim of no new federal authority might have been theoretically correct, but it was completely contradicted by the revolution caused by Title VI in the Office of Education. The Office of Education had traditionally defined its constituency as local and state school officials. The doctrine of local control and opposition to federal control had resulted in most money being disbursed by the Office of Education with minimum requirements and regulation. Staff members of the Office of Education had tended to be recruited from elderly specialists who had spent most of their careers in local and state school systems.[72]

Title VI completely reversed the situation where the Office of Education was viewed as public servant of each local and state educational system. With Title VI, the Office of Education was forced to embark upon a path that would put it in an adversary position with many school systems. School systems would now be required to show proof of compliance with civil rights guidelines, and the Office of Education would be placed in the position of judging the adequacy of the actions of local school systems. The Office of Education was also given the responsibility of drafting the guidelines that would be used in enforcing the provisions of Title VI in government educational programs. This meant the Office of Education was placed in the position of being both interpreter and enforcer of the law. An agency that had always avoided any hint of federal control was suddenly handed the problem of protecting the constitutional rights of children around the country.

The powerful authority of Title VI was also evidenced by the increased rate of desegregation that began to occur after the passage of the Civil Rights Act of 1964. In April 1965 the Department of Health, Education, and Welfare announced that all public schools should plan to eliminate segregation by 1967 and show evidence of a good-faith start or face the possibility of losing all federal funds. The guidelines that were first established were considered very conservative by groups like the NAACP.[73] But even with conservative guidelines Title VI was able to achieve results far beyond anything achieved under the enforcement decision of the Supreme Court. By the fall of 1965, about 89 percent of the schools in the border states and the South had integrated at least four classes, and black attendance at integrated schools had increased 56 percent over the previous year. Also in the fall of 1965, the Office of Education announced that sixty-five school districts in Mississippi, Georgia, Arkansas, Louisiana, Alabama, and South Carolina faced possible loss of funds for noncompliance with the guidelines. By late 1965, the Office of Education was able to announce that 97 percent of the southern school districts had submitted acceptable desegregation plans. Ninety-seven school districts had submitted unacceptable plans and sixty-nine had not submitted any plans.[74]

There was, of course, a major difference between submitting a plan and actual desegregation of a school system. One of the reasons southern districts tended to react more quickly to HEW guidelines than the Supreme Court decision was not only the possibility of losing federal money but also the double-edged sword contained in the 1964 civil rights legislation. Title VI of the act gave the attorney general the authority, upon complaint from a parent or parents, to initiate legal action against school systems that failed to comply with the *Brown* decision. Local school districts were faced with the possibility that if they did not comply with the Office of Education guidelines and refused federal aid, they could still be taken into court by the attorney general. Given this situation, most school districts were willing to comply with the first set of guidelines.

The enforcement of Title VI resulted in another paradox in the accomplishments of the civil rights movement. Many southern school districts, in an effort to maintain segregated schooling but still submit a plan for desegregation, adoped the method of "freedom of choice." This would have allowed the students in any school system using the plan to choose any school to attend within the system. Critics of American education in the 1950s would have viewed this as an important step forward, breaking the power of the local educational bureaucracy and introducing an element of competition between schools. But in the South, with its traditions of white control and harassment, it meant continuation of segregation under the name of freedom. In 1966 the Commission on Civil Rights issued a report which declared that freedom-of-choice plans were allowing dual school systems to continue because of the fear of reprisal among blacks if they transferred to a white school.[75]

To counter the situation growing out of the freedom-of-choice plans, a new set of guidelines was issued in 1966 which stated that freedom-of-choice programs would be acceptable only if at least 8 to 9 percent of the students transferred from segregated schools, with at least twice that amount being required in 1966–67. Other quotas were established for school systems with lower percentages of initial transfers. This plan placed the Office of Education in the position of establishing racial quotas which were quickly recognized and protested by southern congressional leaders. The reaction in the South was so strong that by April 1966 only about 60 percent of the southern school districts had filed compliance forms. After extending deadlines and constant work, this percentage was increased to almost 100 percent with about 77 percent submitting acceptable plans.[76]

The rate of desegregation was more rapid after the 1964 Civil Rights Act than before, but abundant evidence by the end of the 1960s showed that segregated education continued in the South. One political scientist argued that school desegregation in the South by 1968 looked massive compared to the level in the early 1960s. But compared to an ideal of total integration the actual results could be labeled as token. In using a standard that defined a desegregated school as one where blacks attend and more than 20 percent of the school population is white, he found that in a sample of 894 counties in the South 5 percent or less of the black pupils "were attending integrated schools in 25 percent of the counties, 10 percent or less in 40 percent of the counties. At a level approaching genuine integration, 90 percent or more of the black pupils were reported to be attending integrated schools in 20 percent of the counties. For all southern counties, the median attending integrated schools was 15.6 percent." [77]

One of the reasons for the tokenism that resulted from Title VI was the problem of de facto segregation. On the one hand, it was clearly unconstitutional for state or local communities to have laws that required or allowed for segregation. On the other hand, segregation could result not from actual laws but from other sources, such as community pressure, residential patterns, and the methods used in determining the line of local school districts. One of the problems occurring under Title VI was to determine whether de facto segregation fell within the jurisdiction of the law. The policy toward the South tended to be that if integration did not occur, then planned segregation was occurring and action could be taken under Title VI. This meant using a method of quotas and broadly interpreting Title VI, a policy that was sharply curtailed when President Johnson began to need southern support for his Vietnam policies.[78] Without a continuing direct attack on de facto segregation, hopes for complete integration in the South were dim.

In addition, the question of de facto segregation in the North and West raised a difficult problem with regard to Title VI. The civil rights legislation obviously had been passed in reaction to conditions in the South, but there were well-documented cases of de facto segregation in Chicago and Boston. In addition, federal courts had ruled in 1961 that the racial gerrymandering of school boundaries was unconstitutional. In September 1965, the Office of Education decided to take its first action by announcing $32 million was being withheld from the Chicago public school system pending investigation. Chicago at this time had one of the best known and greatest struggles over school desegregation in the country. Black students in Chicago attended segregated, overcrowded schools on a double-shift basis. As a result, black students spent less time in school than white students. In one west side district of Chicago, black students were forced to attend schools on a double-shift basis, while nearby white schools had empty classrooms. The superintendent, Benjamin C. Willis, refused to cooperate with local civil rights groups and maintained a continuing policy of segregation.[80]

The attempt to apply Title VI to Chicago resulted in failure and sharply limited future attempts at applying the provisions in the North. The one factor that the Office of Education did not weigh carefully was the tremendous political power of the Chicago political machine headed by Mayor Richard J. Daley. Daley represented one of the major political powers in the Democratic party and could strongly influence presidential power. After the announcement by the Office of Education, Mayor Daley and Congressional leaders from Illinois placed immediate pressure on President Johnson. Johnson quickly let it be known that he wanted the funds to begin flowing to Chicago. After Chicago, the major thrust of Title VI would be directed at the South.[81]

The failure of Title VI to be applied effectively in the North occurred at a time when racial segregation was actually increasing in northern metropolitan areas. The United States Commission on Civil Rights reported in 1967 that the level of racial separation in city schools was increasing. It found 75 percent of the black elementary students in cities attended schools that were nearly all black, while 83 percent of the white students attended all-white schools. This situation was increasing as the white population moved from the city into suburban areas. The report noted that by 1960 four of every five black children in metropolitan areas lived in the central cities, while three of every four white children lived in the suburbs.[82]

Title VI and Title IV had been the result of the hopes of civil rights leaders for full implementation of the *Brown* decision. In practice, it had little effect outside the South and provided only token integration within the South. It did accomplish more in the South than the implementation decision of the Supreme Court.

The major consequence of Title VI was the breaching of the barriers against federal control of education. The government, of course, had always had the power to tax and the power to spend. Implied in this right was the power to determine how money would be spent. In the area of education this right had been exercised primarily in terms of categorical appropriations, where money was appropriated to be used for specific programs. Institutions or school districts were required to use the money for designated programs, but this had no direct effect on other policies and programs except where they might be influenced by the federally funded programs. Title VI reversed this situation by establishing the precedent that all programs and policies of an educational institution or school system had to meet federal requirements before receiving funds for a specific program. Title VI created the precedent for direct regulation of institutions of higher learning and local public schools.

As Humphrey pointed out, schools did not have to accept federal aid. But in the long run this was to prove unrealistic because of financial dependence on federal money. It was also true that the purpose of Title VI and the social climate which produced it were primarily related to the denial of constitutional rights of black people. But the actual results of the application of Title VI were token when compared to the actual increase in school segregation around the country. What Title VI did accomplish was the precedent for future national regulation of education to implement other policies.

THE WAR
ON POVERTY

5 The rhetoric of manpower planning of the 1950s was based on the assumption that all Americans would have equal opportunity to begin the social race at the same starting line. The schools and selective service were to function as democratic social-sorting devices if all participants were given equal chances to move ahead in the social system. The civil rights movement highlighted the fact that not all Americans were given this opportunity. Chronic poverty and unemployment also seemed to suggest that the social system was not functioning in an equitable manner. Discrimination and poverty were recognized as the two basic problems in using the schools as a means of discovering and classifying talent for the national economy and national defense.

The response of the federal government to this situation was the declaration of a war on poverty and the passage of the Economic Opportunity Act of 1964 and the Elementary and Secondary Education Act of 1965. Two of the most important programs of the Economic

Opportunity Act of 1964 were the Job Corps for occupational training and Head Start. Head Start was to provide an opportunity for children of the poor to enter the social-sorting process of education on equal terms with children from more affluent backgrounds. The Elementary and Scondary Education Act of 1965 contained major provisions for improving educational programs for children from low-income families, to provide equality of opportunity.

Three major related areas of concern went into the war on poverty. One was for unemployed and delinquent youth. Work in this area in the 1950s and early 1960s provided some of the basic ideas that went into the Economic Opportunity Act. Another area was the disadvantaged student for whom education did not provide equality of opportunity. The disadvantaged student became one of the central targets of the Elementary and Secondary Education Act. The third concern, which embraced the other two, was the cycle or circle of poverty. This conceptual approach to the problem of proverty was described in chapter 4 in terms of Gunnar Myrdal's 1944 study, *An American Dilemma*. Myrdal's model of the circle of poverty continued its intellectual influence into the 1960s and provided the rationale for the programs in the war on poverty.

The Culture of Poverty

The major theoretical arguments that supported the war on poverty assumed an integrated set of social and psychological conditions existed among the poor that could be directly attacked by a set of comprehensive government programs. Myrdal's 1940 study of poor blacks had described this situation as an interrelated set of causal factors which were mutually interdependent. For instance, a poor education restricted employment opportunities which caused a low standard of living and consequently poor medical care, diet, housing, and education for the next generation. This model of poverty suggested that one could begin at any point in the set of causal relationships and move around the circle of poverty. One important part of Myrdal's argument had been that within this cycle of poverty there developed a certain set of psychological characteristics which helped to maintain the circle. These psychological characteristics included a sense of defeatism and subservience, and a lack of belief in the possibility of upward mobility in the social system. These factors contributed to the existence and perpetuation of the circle of poverty.

This model of poverty was the one that captured the imagination of the Kennedy administration in the early 1960s. A major problem Kennedy faced when he entered the White House was unemployment in the national labor force, particularly among nonwhites and the young. In 1960, 1961, and 1962 the unemployment rate for white males was, respectively, 4.8, 5.7, and 4.6; and among white females it was 5.3, 6.5, and 5.5 In contrast to these figures the unemployment rate for nonwhite males for these three years was 10.7, 12.8, and 10.9; and for nonwhite females it was 9.4, 11.8, and 11.2. The unemployment figures for the young were even grimmer. For white males between the ages of 18 and 19 for these three years, it was 13.5, 15.1, and 12.7 For nonwhite males in this age category, it was 25.1, 23.9, and 21.8.[1]

The story is told that the idea of launching a massive federal program against unemployment and poverty came directly from President Kennedy in 1962 when he told Walter Heller, chairman of the Council of Economic Advisers, to gather all the figures on the poverty problem in the United States. At the time Kennedy also requested copies of Michael Harrington's recently published *The Other America: Poverty in the United States*.[2] By 1963, it was claimed, President Kennedy had decided to launch a war on poverty that would not be piecemeal but would attack the very structure of poverty. This meant an acceptance of the idea that poverty involved an interrelated set of causal factors and that a comprehensive government program aimed at each one of these factors was needed.

Historically, it is difficult to pinpoint directly sources of intellectual influence. For instance, it is impossible to determine how much influence Harrington's *The Other America* had on the thinking of Kennedy and his advisers.[3] But one thing is certain: the basic arguments given by Harrington were reflected in the final report on poverty written by the Council of Economic Advisers and presented to Congress as the basic program for the Economic Opportunity Act of 1964. If not a direct influence, Harrington's book at least summarized an increasingly popular approach to the problem of poverty that would pervade government actions. It also widened the scope of Myrdal's model from just black poverty to all poverty and called the circle of poverty a culture of poverty.

Harrington saw the circle of poverty becoming a culture of poverty that would divide America into two parts because of increased insulation of the poor from the rest of society. He claimed to have begun his study originally out of a desire to give meaning to the cold statistics of 40 to 50 million poor people in the United States. The study presented a bleak picture of the different types of poverty existing around the country. There were the workers who lived in the economic underworld of the city and factory. These were the people who either lived on fly-by-night jobs as dishwashers or day workers or worked in factories and hospitals that were not unionized or covered by minimum wage laws. There were the poor rural farmers who had been unable to compete with large corporate farming and the migrant farm workers who moved from job to job. There were the minority groups, such as blacks, who continued to live in grinding poverty under the burden of discrimination. In the city there were the alcholic poor who populated skid row and an expanding number of rural poor in urban slums. In apartments, rooming houses, and nursing homes, the aged lived a meager and lonely existence on inadequate social security benefits and medical care.

One of the tragedies Harrington thought was occurring was that the poor were becoming increasingly invisible to the rest of society. The rise of suburbia had reduced the contact between the poor, who increasingly inhabited the inner city, and the middle and upper classes. Modern highways rushed the suburban dweller past the pockets of rural poor and the migrant worker in the field. The mass production of clothing had made the poor unidentifiable by dress. Harrington argued that it was easier to be decently dressed in the United States than it was to have decent housing, food, and medical care. In addition, Harrington argued that many of the poor were the wrong age to be seen. The aged poor are often trapped in their roominghouses and nursing homes. While the young were more visible than the aged, they stayed close to their neighborhoods. And finally, Harrington argued, the poor were politically invisible because they lacked representation in unions, fraternal organizations, or political parties.

All these groups, Harrington believed, lived within the "vicious circle." The poor got sick more often because of unhealthy living conditions in slums and inadequate nutrition. Because of inadequate medical care, their sicknesses lasted longer and they lost wages and work. Because of lost wages, they could not afford adequate housing, education, and medical care. Harrington argued that there was a much richer way of describing this circle and that was as a *culture*. The vicious circle of poverty had created its own cultural patterns. The family structure was different from the rest of society with more homes without fathers, early pregnancy, different attitudes toward sex, and less marriage. Millions of children of the poor, he claimed, did not know affection or stability. The culture of poverty was also defined by the actions of other institutions in society. For instance, there was a marked difference between the way the police treated the poor and how they acted toward the middle class.

The culture of poverty, Harrington argued, was beginning to perpetuate itself under the pressures of modern technology. As technology increased, so did the educational requirements for occupations. As technological progress swept through the rest of society, the poor were increasingly left behind, and it became more difficult to move up in the social structure. Poverty was passed on from generation to generation because of the increasing difficulty of children to receive adequate education and job training. The price of more complex technology was the growing existence of a culture that could not participate in its benefits.

The culture of poverty was also different from previous forms of poverty. The new poverty, as Harrington referred to it, was different from the poverty that existed in previous generations of ethnic groups in urban slums. While these ethnic poor lived without decent housing or medical care, and suffered poverty, they were not impoverished. They had aspirations to get ahead and believed in the possibility of upward mobility. They lived at a time when technological complexities did not block entrance into the labor market. In contrast, the new poor had developed a culture that was without aspiration or hope of ever escaping their conditions.

For Harrington, the only solution was a total assault on all the factors related to the culture of poverty. This would include housing, employment, education, and medical care. The purpose would be totally to uproot the environment surrounding the poor and to change their patterns of existence. The war on poverty, in these terms, was to be an assault on an entire culture. Family and living patterns were to change, and with these changes improved education and job training would result. For instance, in reference to the civil rights movement, Harrington argued, true freedom for the black could not be achieved unless there was a full-scale attack on the culture of poverty that would change entire patterns of existence.

The attack on the culture of poverty became one of the central focuses of government plans. In October 1963, Walter Heller began to draw together various plans for an invasion of the culture of poverty. A memorandum from Heller was sent to government agencies requesting plans that would be directed toward the prevention of entry into poverty and providing means of escape.[4] In November 1963, while responses to this memorandum were being reviewed, President Kennedy was assassinated. Almost immediately, President Johnson announced his intentions of supporting the program and directed Heller to complete his task. In January 1964, Heller's report was included in *The Annual Report of the Council of Economic Advisers* as "The Problem of Poverty in America."[5]

One of the important emphases of the report of the Council of Economic Advisers was on the role of education in uprooting the culture of poverty. Certainly social scientists, like Myrdal and Harrington, had considered education a link in the circle of poverty and one of the areas of attack. But the Heller report gave education the central role in the battle strategy. The report proclaimed in its opening section, "Equality of opportunity is the American dream, and universal education our noblest pledge to realize it. But, for the children of the poor, education is a handicap race; many are too ill motivated at home to learn at school." In these words were the recognition of education as a social "race" and the proclamation of a desire to give all an equal chance in the "race" by providing equality of opportunity.

The report defined poverty in terms of income levels. Using figures provided by the Social Security Administration, a family income of $3000 or less was considered to be at a poverty level. This meant that in terms of all families in the United States, 20 percent were living in a state of poverty. The report argued that poverty was not peculiar to any one group in the United States but pervaded the entire social system. But certain groups had a higher incidence of poverty than other groups. The report argued that by looking at the special characteristics of the groups that had a higher than 20 percent incidence of poverty, the roots of poverty could be highlighted. Using this method, the report defined the most important links in the chain of poverty as being families with no earners, low rates of pay, and little education.

According to figures presented by the report, the highest incidence of poverty occurred in families with no wage earners. The rate for these families was 76 percent, or 56 percent above the national average. Of course, these figures reflected general unemployment and restated the obvious fact that if no one is working in a family, there is probably poverty. The report stressed the other factors of "age, disability, premature death of the principal earner, need to care for children or disabled family members, lack of any salable skill, lack of motivation." One of the things suggested by these figures was providing some method by which potential wage earners could be freed from certain types of family responsibilities. The method proposed in the report was for the establishment of day-care centers.

The high incidence of poverty caused by low incomes was directly linked to education. The report stated, "The chief reason for low rates of pay is low productivity, which in turn can reflect lack of education or training, physical or mental disability, or poor motivation." This argument placed the responsiblity for low incomes directly on the shoulders of the wage earners and not on the economic system which paid so little for certain types of occupation. "The importance of education," the report continued, "as a factor in poverty is suggested by the fact that families headed by persons with no more than 8 years of education have an incidence rate of 37 percent." These figures varied according to patterns of discrimination with nonwhites earning less than whites with the same level of education.

The importance of education in the war on poverty was underlined with the claim, "The severely handicapping influence of lack of education is clear. The incidence of poverty drops as educational attainments rise for nonwhites as well as white families at all ages." Education was also given prominence in the vicious circle of poverty argument in the report. It should be noted that in the report "the vicious circle" was no longer treated as a hypothesis but as a social law. One section of the report was labeled "The Vicious Circle" and began with the straightforward statement, "Poverty breeds poverty." The report defined the role of education in this circle, "It is difficult for children to find and follow avenues leading out of poverty in environments where education is deprecated and hope is smothered." The report cited a number of studies to support its contention. A Michigan study was used to show that inadequate education was perpetuated from generation to generation. The study found that in the families identified as poor, 64 percent had family heads with less than an eighth-grade education. Sixty-seven percent of these had fathers with the same low level of formal schooling. Figures were also presented in the report to show the high level of school dropouts in poor families and the relationship between dropping out of school and low incomes.

One argument given by social scientists such as Harrington, and contained in the report of the Council of Economic Advisers, was that increased productivity and earnings in the economic system would not eliminate proverty. This argument was crucial to the whole idea that a war should be launched on poverty. For instance, one could have argued that continued economic growth would be the ultimate cure of poverty and that programs directed at the social structure of poverty would have little effect until the economic system improved. In fact, the figures presented by the Council of Economic Advisers seemed to support this argument. The percentage of families with less than $3000 incomes at 1962 prices had declined from 32 percent in 1947 to 20 percent in 1962. The council projected that by 1980 this figure would be reduced to 13 percent if economic growth continued. But the council rejected the idea of allowing economic growth alone to war away at poverty. It argued, "Rising productivity and earnings, improved education, and the structure of social security have permitted many families or their children to escape; but they have left behind many families who have one or more special handicaps." It was these families that were trapped in the culture of poverty. The conclusion reached in the report was that "future economic growth alone will provide relatively fewer escapes from poverty. Policy will have to be more sharply focused on the handicaps that deny the poor fair access to the expanding incomes of a growing economy."

The battle strategy offered in the report contained several items that were listed as part of the war on poverty but were considered as separate legislative items from what would become the Economic Opportunity Act. When President Johnson assumed office, his most pressing legislative items were a tax reduction to stimulate the economy and the civil rights legislation proposed by President Kennedy. Both these items were considered to have a direct relationship to overall planning against poverty. The inclusion of support for civil rights legislation in the report of the Council of Economic Advisers as a method for improving the economy and eliminating proverty highlighted the general acceptance of the culture-of-poverty argument. Civil rights legislation could have been viewed as just a method to extend constitutional guarantees to the entire population. But in the context of the war on poverty, as it had been stated in Myrdal's writings, ending discrimination was considered part of economic strategy.

The major emphasis given in the strategy against poverty was education. The report flatly stated, "Universal education has been perhaps the greatest single force, contributing both to social mobility and to general economic growth." No data were presented to support this statement nor was there any discussion of the complexities involved in linking mobility and economic growth to education. The only data offered in the report were the previously mentioned studies on levels of schooling being passed on from generation to generation. Without supporting data, the statement must be viewed as one of belief and not fact. And it was this belief that was incorporated into the battle plan.

Following this statement of belief was the argument that if the children of poor families could be given skills and motivation, they would not become poor adults. The current problem, the report maintained, was that many young people were condemned to inadequate schools and instruction, and many school systems concentrated their efforts on children from higher income groups.

Effective education for the children at the bottom of the economic ladder required special methods and greater expenses. The report stated, "The school must play a larger role in the development of poor youngsters if they are to have, in fact, 'equal opportunity.' " And in language that pointed the direction toward the eventual plans for Head Start, the report continued, "This often means that schooling must start on a pre-school basis and include a broad range of more intensive services." In addition, the report urged the development of a Youth Conservation Corps, adult education programs, day-care centers for working mothers, improved health programs, and increased assistance to the aged. Here was the total package designed to uproot and destroy the environment and culture of poverty.

The final writing of the report of the Council of Economic Advisers had been completed with the close cooperation of President Johnson at his ranch in Texas during the last week of December 1963. Walter Heller and Kermit Gordon, director of the Bureau of the Budget, spent long hours over the Christmas holiday discussing with Johnson the evolving outlines of the poverty program. Johnson invited to the meeting friends who had worked with him in public service during the 1930 depression. During the depression, President Johnson had served as Texas director of the National Youth Administration and had worked closely with the development of training and education programs for youth. He later claimed that this experience had convinced him of the importance of schooling in breaking the cycle of poverty.[6] This could be one reason why the final report placed such strong emphasis on education.

President Johnson accepted the argument that the problem of poverty in the 1960s was different from that of the depression. He wrote about his meeting with Heller that, "the most significant aspects of this new poverty, once the spotlight of attention was thrown on it, were the dismaying nature of its stubborn entrench- ment and total entrapment of its victims from one gen- eration to the next." [7] While accepting the idea of the new nature of poverty, he did claim to rely upon his depression experiences for guidance. This experience, he insisted, convinced him that any successful plan would require programs that provided opportunites for people to escape the cycle of poverty. His depression expe- riences also led him to state, "I wanted to place heavy emphasis on efforts to help children and youth. They offered the best hope of breaking the poverty cycle." [8]

President Johnson announced the plans for a war on poverty in his State of the Union message to Congress on January 8, 1964. He told Congress it was their responsi- bility to replace despair with opportunity and declared "this Administration today, here and now, declares un- conditional war on poverty in America." [9] He said that the chief weapons of the battle would be better schools, better health, better homes, and better training and job opportunities. This was to be a battle to help Americans escape squalor, misery, and the unemployment rolls.

Delinquent and Unemployed Youth

One proposal in the report of the Council of Economic Advisers was for a Youth Conservation Corps. In the final legislative action this proposal emerged as the Job Corps. The idea of a Youth Conservation Corps or Job Corps could certainly be traced back to the depression years; the model, of course, was the Civilian Conserva- tion Corps.[10] As noted in previous chapters, this idea continued after World War II in the form of pleas for universal military training. During the latter part of the 1950s this idea began to receive more attention as un- employment rates among youth were at a high level and national concern about the problem of juvenile delinquency increased. In 1961, the National Committee for Children and Youth issued a report which warned that the high unemployment rates of teen-agers were "social dynamite." [11] In 1959 and 1963, Senator Hubert Humphrey had introduced legislation for a Youth Employment Bill which contained the youth corps idea.[12]

A concern about delinquent and unemployed youth was one of the major factors in shaping the organization of the war on poverty. As mentioned, one problem facing President Kennedy when he entered the White House was the high unemployment rate among youth. A startling fact about this rate was its rapid increase since World War II. In 1948 the unemployment rate for white youth was 8.3 percent and for nonwhite youth, 7.6 percent. But during the 1950s the unemployment rate for nonwhite youth quadrupled while that for white youth doubled. Adding to this problem was the increasing proportion of the population which fell into the category of youth. During the 1950s the percentage of the population under eighteen increased by 37 percent.[13]

In 1961 President Kennedy established the President's Committee on Juvenile Delinquency under the chairmanship of Attorney General Robert F. Kennedy. One of Robert Kennedy's close friends, David Hackett, was asked to organize the efforts against juvenile delinquency. A program that attracted Hackett's interest was the gray-areas projects of the Ford Foundation. Gray areas referred to the zone of deterioration that existed within cities between the downtown area and suburban communities. During the early 1950s the Ford Foundation had used two approaches in granting aid to city problems. One of these was the establishment of metropolitan governments that would reintegrate the central cities with the suburbs. The other was urban renewal, which was designed to attract prosperous residents and businesses back to the central city.

By 1957 the Ford Foundation became dissatisfied

with the workings of these projects and began to shift its attention to projects designed to attack social problems directly. One of the first grants under what was to be called the "gray areas projects" was to seven city school systems to develop special programs and schools for the education of inner-city children. As the Ford Foundation expanded its program, it turned more and more to the concept of community action as an effective approach to solving social problems. One program that attracted the attention and financial support of the Ford Foundation was the Mobilization for Youth program which had originated at the Henry Street settlement house in New York City. In 1958 social workers Richard Cloward and Lloyd Ohlin at Columbia University were asked to help prepare a research design for requesting a grant from the National Institute of Mental Health. This program began the Mobilization for Youth which received support from the Ford Foundation. By 1963 its budget was $5.25 million with funding from the Ford Foundation, the National Institute of Mental Health, New York City, and the President's Committee on Juvenile Delinquency.[14]

The work of the Mobilization for Youth had a powerful influence on the thinking of the Committee on Juvenile Delinquency. In 1960, while David Hackett was making plans for the formation of the President's committee, he invited a number of experts to discuss the problem of juvenile delinquency. Among these was Lloyd Ohlin. Hackett could not achieve a consensus of agreement among the experts and so decided to rely on one expert. He chose Ohlin.[15] It was also in 1960 that a full statement of Cloward's and Ohlin's theories on juvenile delinquency were published in book form as *Delinquency and Opportunity*.[16] One observer later remarked that the President's Committee on Juvenile Delinquency became "a $30 million test of Ohlin's 'opportunity theory.' "[17]

The Cloward and Ohlin approach to the problem of juvenile delinquency fit into the more general concept of a culture of poverty. Their basic argument was that juvenile delinquency occurred and persisted because of the need of youth to conform and achieve within some form of social system. Juvenile delinquency was identified as existing within subcultures of the more general culture in the United States. These subcultures provided delinquent youth with the opportunity to achieve status and identity. Cloward and Ohlin argued that youth entered these delinquent subcultures because of the limited possibilities of achievement in the greater social system. Youth, particularly among the poor, were faced with the tension between the high aspirations they were taught by society and the lack of opportunity to achieve those aspirations. The delinquent subculture provided one opportunity for some form of social opportunity. It was also argued that the existence of a delinquent subculture often attracted youth who might never have adopted a delinquent style of life. They were attracted to the delinquent subculture by the possibilities of exciting friendships and activities.

Like the idea that poverty in the 1950s and '60s was different from poverty in the past, it was argued that delinquent subcultures were facing new conditions. Cloward and Ohlin argued that in the past delinquent subcultures among ethnic slum neighborhoods provided a center for community integration and economic opportunity. They identified two stages in the evolution of delinquent subcultures. The first was one of violent gang strife that occurred in unorganized and unintegrated slum neighborhoods. But over a period of time these delinquent subcultures became integrated into a community social organization where possibilities of economic mobility existed through organized crime and the urban political machines. The delinquent subculture at this stage of development became a training ground for entry into crime or politics. The money gained through these activities provided opportunity for investment in legal businesses and an escape to the suburbs.

What was different about the existing juvenile subcultures was the closing off of avenues by which juvenile subcultures could be integrated into community life and could provide the means of upward economic mobility. The causes of this situation were identified as the decline of the urban political machine, the development of highly organized crime, and the welfare system. All three items caused new delinquent subcultures to remain at the level of gang violence and not evolve to the more stable stage organized around social and economic mobility. Cloward and Ohlin felt this was particularly true of southern blacks who migrated to northern urban areas like New York. Urban political reform in the twentieth century had eliminated the political machine as a means of opportunity and already existing syndicate crime limited access to large criminal profits. In addition, the modern welfare state provided social benefits through a system of bureaucrats and therefore limited the possibilities of local community patronage. Based on this analysis, Ohlin and Cloward warned that juvenile subcultures would remain at the first stage of development and would become increasingly violent in their actions.

Their solution to the existing problem of delinquency was, like the war on poverty, directed toward changing cultural patterns. They defined as the target area of action the social setting that produced delinquent subcultures. This meant that major effort at eliminating delinquency should be directed at the reorganization of slum communities. The progressive deterioration of modern slums, they argued, was closing off the traditional paths of social ascent. What needed to be done was the development of functional substitutes for these traditional structures and the opening of new paths of opportunity. Only this approach, they maintained, would end the trend toward violence by adolescents in urban slums.

One of the characteristics of the Mobilization for Youth and the gray-areas projects of the Ford Foundation was the belief in community action. This approach to social change was to be a unique feature of the Equal Opportunity Act of 1964. The basic assumptions of community action were the existence of the poverty cycle and the lack of opportunity for the poor. Part of the problem was seen as being located in social service agencies such as education, medical, and welfare. These institutions, as Ohlin and Cloward had argued, had made the poor depend upon them rather than make the poor independent and self-reliant. This in turn reinforced one of the elements in the circle-of-poverty hypothesis. The general argument given in the projects sponsored by the Ford Foundation was that the culture of poverty bred apathy and lack of motivation which in turn was reinforced by social agencies. One reason for this, it was argued, was that social agencies had become bureaucratic and dependent on middle-class approval. The bureaucratic nature of social agencies and the decline of the urban political machine had made the poor powerless before these agencies and provided no means for influencing policy. In addition, the middle-class bias of agencies such as the schools failed to meet the needs of the poor and provide a focal point for opportunity.[18]

The goal of the theory of community action was to transform existing social agencies and create new ones that would improve the opportunity structure and attack the feelings of dependence and apathy among the poor. To obtain this goal it was considered desirable to have the poor participate more fully in the policy making and operation of social agencies. This would make these organizations more responsive to the needs of the poor and provide for integration into an opportunity structure. It would also decrease the sense of power- lessness and dependency among the poor and provide for the development of self-motivation and social confidence.

Community action, therefore, provided an added di- mension to the general cry for a war on poverty. It suggested that if a comprehensive program which at- tacked all the links in the chain of poverty were to be developed, it would have to include an attack on lack of motivation and apathy. This could be accomplished by combining the community-action idea with an attack on a specific item in the circle of poverty. For instance, if the attempt was to improve education among the poor, this might be approached by just improving school fa- cilities and instruction. But according to the idea of community action, this would not do anything about the bureaucratic structure and middle-class bias of the school. Community-action theory dictated that im- proved educational facilities had to be accompanied with greater participation and control by the poor.

The Economic Opportunity Act of 1964

Community action, the theory of the culture of pov- erty, and the desire to create an opportunity structure for youth became major elements of the Economic Op- portunity Act. Immediately after announcing a war on poverty in his State of the Union message, President Johnson began to search for the means of putting to- gether specific legislative proposals. He decided not to use any of the existing government agencies and made Sargent Shriver director of the poverty program on February 1, 1964. When the Economic Opportunity Act was finally signed on August 20, Shriver's staff and functions became the Office of Economic Opportunity. After his appointment, Shriver quickly assembled a task force to hammer out the specific proposals that were to be included in the legislation. Included in the team of Shriver's advisers were Michael Harrington, Walter Heller, and the head of the public affairs program of the Ford Foundation. In addition, to developing a plan of attack, Shriver had to deal with the interests of other government agencies. The Agriculture Department wanted a small loan and grant program for rural farmers and businessmen. It was considered politically wise to include this as a means of gaining legislative support from congressmen representing rural areas. The Labor Department wanted a youth-employment program which was accepted by Shriver as part of the war on poverty concept. In addition, a proposed National Service Corps, which had been blocked in Congress in 1963, was included and became Volunteers in Service to America, or VISTA.[19]

In less than a month and a half Shriver assembled a legislative package that was approved by President Johnson on March 16 and submitted to Congress. On March 17, Shriver and Heller appeared before a subcommittee of the Committee on Education and Labor of the House of Representatives to testify in support of the proposed legislation. Shriver opened his testimony by saying, "The objective of this program is an all-out war on poverty. We believe this is a program which, if effectively and intelligently carried forward, will eliminate grinding poverty in the United States." [20] In terms of numbers, Shriver proposed to raise 30 to 35 million people, from the culture of poverty. A focal point of the program, Shriver told the congressmen, was community-action programs which he described as relying on local initiative and leadership. Shriver also claimed that the legislative package placed a new emphasis on youth. In words that reflected the opportunity theory of Cloward and Ohlin and the more general culture-of-poverty argument, Shriver stated to the committee, "We want to give young people a chance to escape from the cycle of poverty and to break out of the ruthless pattern of poor housing, poor homes, and poor education. We want to give them a way out." [21] Walter Heller followed Shriver's opening statement with a description of the dimensions of poverty and submitted the report of the Council of Economic Advisers and its description of the cycle of poverty.[22]

The legislative proposals quickly worked their way through Congress with only minor changes occurring before President Johnson signed them into law in August. There were heated congressional disputes over the loans and grants program for rural poverty under Title III and for small businesses under Title IV of the law. Title V of the law established work-experience programs, and Title VI established the Office of Economic Opportunity and VISTA. The most important elements in the new law were the Youth Programs in Title I and the Urban and Rural Community Action Programs in Title II.

Part A of Title I established the Job Corps. This was to be a unique combination of approaches to the youth problem. First, it attacked unemployment among youth by providing urban and rural residential training centers. Youth enrolled in these centers would essentially be removed from the labor market. One of the activities of the Job Corps in rural residential centers was to be "conserving, developing and managing the public natural resources of the Nation." [23] This idea was a carry over from the Civilian Conservation Corps of the 1930s and had been the major thrust for solving youth unemployment in the bills for a Youth Conservation

Corps submitted to Congress by Hubert Humphrey in 1959, 1961, and 1963.[24] The Conservation Corps was retained within the Job Corps as a means of winning support for the legislation from conservationists in Congress. Title I specifically stated that at least 40 percent of the Job Corps enrollees had to be assigned to camps doing conservation work.

In a sense the Job Corps could be viewed as one section of a three-part national attempt to provide activity for youth. One part was higher education while the other was selective service. For those who could not make it to college or were rejected by the armed forces, there was the Job Corps. In fact, major support for the youth programs of the Economic Opportunity Act came from a report issued in 1964 by the President's Task Force on Manpower Legislation which claimed that the high rejection rate of draftees by the armed forces was due to causes related to poverty.[25] While there was certainly no specifically stated intention written into the law that the Job Corps was to be part of a national manpower channeling process, it certainly did fit into such a scheme.

Besides aiding the problem of youth unemployment, the Job Corps was to attack the poverty cycle by providing residential centers, vocational training, and remedial education. One of the basic assumptions in the establishment of residential centers was that the poverty cycle could be attacked by taking youth away from their home environment.[26] At the residential centers Job Corps enrollees were to be given vocational training and remedial education. As plans were developed after the passage of the legislation, these activities were divided between rural and urban centers. At rural camps one-half the time of the enrollees was spent in conservation activities while the other half was spent in education and job training. The curriculum of the conservation camps provided for the teaching of reading, writing, and arithmetic skills to the eighth-grade level. After attaining this level of educational skill, the enrollee could qualify for an urban residential center for more specific job training.[27] The legislation defined the age range to be included in the Job Corps as between 16 and 21. One congressional change in the legislation was the inclusion of women in the program. During its first year the Job Corps planned to enroll 40,000 members with an increase to 100,000 the next year.

Parts B and C of the Title I Youth Programs were for Work-Training Programs and Work-Study Programs. The Work-Training Programs were to be an extension of the public-service-employment approach to solving unemployment among youth. The training projects were to be conducted by local public institutions or nonprofit organizations. The law stated that the purpose of the programs was "to provide useful work experience opportunities for unemployed young men and young women . . . so that their employability may be increased or their education resumed." The purpose of the work itself would be to perform some "service in the public interest that would not otherwise be provided." [28] Like the Jobs Corps, this section of the law reflected the continuing idea of youth being mobilized for some form of national service. Part C of Title I was a provision for part-time employment of students in institutions of higher education who were from low-income families.

In its final form the youth program of the war on poverty provided a combination of attacks on youth unemployment and the cycle of poverty. Opportunity was to be increased through education and vocational training. The opportunity structure was to be maintained at the college level through part-time employment. Both the educational and vocational training provisions were to attack elements in the cycle of poverty. The problem of the poverty environment was to be attacked through residential centers. The youth unemployment problem was to be attacked through public-service occupations. In many ways the approach was similar to that advocated by President Truman's Commission on Universal Military Training in the 1940s. The major differences between the two programs were that the youth programs of the Economic Opportunity Act were not under military control and were not universal but were directed toward the poor and unemployed. The armed forces and educational institutions were to assume the custodial care of the rest of youth.

Title II of the Economic Opportunity Act provided for Urban and Rural Community Action Programs. Community action programs were defined in the legislation as a mobilization and utilization of public and private resources in rural and urban communities "in an attack on poverty." These endeavors had to provide services and assistance to eliminate poverty "through developing employment opportunities, improving human performance, motivation, and productivity, or bettering the conditions under which people live, learn and work." And in keeping with the general philosophy of community action, the legislation stated that the programs were to be "conducted and administered with the maximum feasible participation of residents of the areas and members of the groups served." [29] While this definition was in keeping with the community-action philosophy, it became one of the most controversial statements in the legislation.

After the passage of the Economic Opportunity Act, the requirement of "maximum feasible participation" created tensions between local political structures and locally initiated community-action programs and between national programs of the Office of Economic Opportunity and local programs. On the one hand, programs initiated at the local level through community agencies were open to charges that they were bypassing the power of locally elected government officials. This occurred because the money went directly from the federal government to these agencies and in turn these agencies sought local participation in the program through community elections and appointments. Local political officials often wondered if they weren't representative of the people since they had been elected in popular elections. But according to the philosophy of community action, these local political structures were viewed as representing the establishment and were not responsive to the poor. As events developed, local public officials often charged that the Office of Economic Opportunity was providing money to support militant radicals to organize the poor to attack the institutions of local democracy. When the Office of Economic Opportunity did rely on mayors and local officials, they were charged by local representatives of the poor as selling out to the establishment.[30]

On the other hand, programs developed at the national level were charged by local community-action people with violating the concept of local initiative and maximum participation. During the first four years of Title II's community-action programs, 40 percent of the projects funded were from local initiative while 60 percent were national projects. Locally initiated projects ranged over a variety of areas including neighborhood service systems, manpower, education, housing, social services, and consumer action. National programs were planned in the Office of Economic Opportunity and contracted out through local agencies. By 1968 these national emphases projects included Head Start, Upward Bound, Comprehensive Health Services, Family Planning, Senior Opportunity Services, and Legal Services.[31]

During the first year of operation, all community-action programs were local initiative programs except for Head Start. Head Start was the first and probably the most popular of the national emphases community-action programs. There had been no specific mention of the education of younger children as a component in the war on poverty in the Economic Opportunity Act of 1964. One reason for this was the highly explosive issues of race and church-state relationships that had hindered federal education bills in the past. Plans for the educational component of the war on poverty were postponed for the Elementary and Secondary Education Act of 1965 which will be discussed later in this chapter. A congressional amendment for a preschool program had been attached to the original Economic Opportunity Act but was withdrawn when assurances were given that the Office of Economic Opportunity would support such a program.[32] In January 1965, President Johnson announced the decision to fund a preschool program named Head Start under the antipoverty program. In February, Sargent Shriver announced that the program would be launched during the summer of 1965. The response to the announcement was immediate and enthusiastic, and during the first summer 560,000 children entered the Head Start program.[33]

The Disadvantaged

The underlying assumption of Head Start and the Elementary and Secondary Education Act of 1965 was that children living in the cycle of poverty were at a disadvantage in the educational race when compared to children from middle- and upper-income families. The Head Start program (as the name suggests) was to give the children of the poor a head start in the educational race so that they might compete on equal terms with other children. Once in school, the equal chances of the children of the poor were to be maintained through compensatory education. In a sense, compensatory education was a form of social compensation for being born into a culture of poverty.

During the early 1960s a wealth of educational literature began to appear which used interchangeably terms such as "culturally deprived," "educationally deprived," "culturally disadvantaged," and "educationally disadvantaged." [34] All these terms were related to the education of lower socioeconomic groups in the United States. This, of course, was not the first time since World War II that American educators had directed their attention to the problems of the American lower class, but this time there was a major shift in the approach to the problem.

In the late 1940s a classic sociological study, *Elmstown's Youth,* had explored the relationship between social class and education in a small Midwestern town.[35] The study had found that teachers and administrators identified with the middle- and upper-middle-class groups in the community. This identification was reflected in the actions of teachers and administrators toward the youth from different socioeconomic backgrounds. Children from upper-class families received preferential treatment in the schools while children from the lower class received discriminatory treatment. This was found in the academic tracking system where the majority of the children in the college preparatory track were from upper-income families while the majority of children in the vocational track were from lower-income families. It was also found in extracurricular activities where the amount of participation followed the pattern of social-class lines, and it was found in the discipline of the students. Children from lower-class families received harsher punishments for the same offense than children from upper-income families. This pattern was found in the counseling program where, even though children from the lower class received on the average lower academic grades and were more likely to fail subjects, their parents were more often called to school for behavior problems and not learning problems than were the middle- and upper-class parents. The picture painted by *Elmstown's Youth* was that of an educational system reflecting a social-class bias and, consequently, reinforcing the social-class structure of the community.

The major difference in the approach of a study like *Elmstown's Youth* in the 1940s and the literature on the disadvantaged of the 1960s was that the focus of the problem was a shift from the school to the culture of the lower class. True, the literature of the early 1960s did identify the social-class bias of the school as a problem but only in the sense that the school had to recognize the values of the lower-class culture and use those values as a steppingstone for changing lower-class cultural patterns. Like the more general war on poverty, the education of the disadvantaged was to be an educational attack on the culture of poverty. It was designed to change the culture of the poor into a culture that would support the process of schooling. If one believed the educational literature which identified school as a middle-class institution, this meant changing cultural patterns to something called middle class.

The general goal of this educational attack on the disadvantaged was to improve the manpower channeling function of the school by equalizing the opportunity structure. President Johnson most clearly stated this idea in a speech dealing with black poverty given at Howard University in 1965. President Johnson told his predominantly black audience that civil rights legislation was not enough to erase the legacy of years of discrimination. "You do not take a man," President Johnson stated, "who, for years, has been hobbled by chains, liberate him, bring him to the starting line of a race, saying 'you are free to compete with all the others,' and still justly believe you have been completely fair." President Johnson went on in language reflecting the educational attack on the disadvantaged to say, "Thus it is not enough to open the gates of opportunity. All our citizens must have the ability to walk through those gates." [36]

Educators recognized that the concern about the disadvantaged represented a shift in emphasis from the 1950s. The 1950s were marked with a concern about identifying talent in the social-sorting process of the school with the ultimate goal of increasing scientific manpower in the cold-war competition with the Soviet Union. The early 1960s shifted the major concern from the talented to the disadvantaged but still kept within the framework of the social-sorting process. For instance, James Conant, who in his report on the *American High School Today* in the late 1950s expressed primary interest in the selection and education of the academically talented, shifted his attention in the early 1960s to the culturally deprived in what was called the second "Conant report," *Slums and Suburbs*. Conant maintained his major argument that the primary function of schooling was selectivity and training for the labor market. He warned that not enough emphasis had been given to this process in terms of the education of the poor and "social dynamite" was accumulating in the slum neighborhoods of large cities in the form of unemployed lower-class youth. In keeping with his general philosophy of education he argued that the primary function of education should be to relate the educational experiences of youth to their subsequent employment. This meant not only improved vocational education for youth in slum areas but also improved vocational guidance. Vocational guidance, of course, had always been viewed by Conant as one of the most important functions of the schools. In *Slums and Suburbs,* Conant expanded his idea of the role of vocational guidance to include aiding youth after they left school. He recommended that guidance officers follow post-high school careers of youth from the time they left school until they reached twenty-one years of age.[37]

This shift in emphasis in the selective function of the school from the talented to the disadvantaged was clearly recognized at a national conference on Education and Cultural Deprivation at the University of Chicago in 1964. The conference was attended by thirty-two leading educators in the area of what was now called "education for the disadvantaged" and by observers from the Rockefeller Foundation, the Ford Foundation, the Russell Sage Foundation, the Carnegie Foundation and the U.S Office of Education.[38] Financial support for the conference came from the U.S. Office of Education. The conference report, written by Benjamin Bloom, Allison Davis, and Robert Hess, argued that as long as there was opportunity in the labor market for unskilled workers with a minimum education "the thought and energy of educators could be directed to the continual weeding out of the scholastically less able and the selection of the more able to get more education and specialization. The lives and careers adversely affected by this selection process have not been a central concern of school people." [39] But, it was argued, basic social changes, which the report labeled as a "revolution," were requiring new approaches.

These basic social changes were identified as a rapidly developing industrial society which required a high degree of education for the labor market and a rising level of expectation among groups living in a state of poverty. The report argued that the major change in education in response to these social changes "will be a shift in the conception of education from a status-giving and selective system to a system that develops each individual to his highest potential." [40] This did not mean that the school should abandon the social-sorting process but that all members of the school population, besides the talented, should be brought into the process. To raise "each individual to his highest potential" meant finding all students a place in the labor market. Or as the report stated, "A central factor in the entire problem of education and cultural deprivation is the rapidly changing economy and job-distribution system which requires more and better education for the entire population." [41]

Basic to the whole discussion of giving all students equal opportunity in the educational race was defining and giving meaning to the term *educationally disadvantaged*. The meaning of the term was often difficult to determine. On the one hand, it could mean that children of certain groups began the educational race on unequal terms with children from other social groups. On the other hand, it could mean that certain children received unequal education when compared to other children, and this might be related to the nature of the school and not the socioeconomic background of the students.

These problems of definition were best illustrated by an exchange that took place between Senator Robert Kennedy and Commissioner of Education Francis Keppel at the Senate hearings on the 1965 Elementary and Secondary Education Act. Senator Kennedy asked for a definition of an educationally deprived child. Commissioner Keppel responded by saying that the definition being used was devised by the superintendents of fifteen of the biggest city school systems and it meant "children whose home backgrounds do not include the encouragement for study that is normal . . . in the sense that there are books at home, there is encouragement to learn to read as a child . . . educational deprivation for children from low-income families involves the lack in all too many cases of preschools to get them ready for the first grade." Senator Kennedy then asked, "Is the child an educationally deprived child if it receives an education which is substantially inferior to the average U.S. education at that grade level?" Keppel responded with a yes. Kennedy followed with, "Is an educationally deprived child, necessarily, therefore, from a family of low income—a low-income family?" Commissioner Keppel answered, "No, sir. Clearly there can be deprivations and are in our society for a host of tragic family reasons." In Keppel's response the burden of responsibility for deprivation was again placed on the family and culture, but with the admission that these were not just characteristics of low-income families. Kennedy accepted the idea that family and home background might cause difficulty in school, but asked, "I think also would you agree that it is not restricted to that, that from your experience of studying the school systems around the United States, that the school system itself has created an educationally deprived system?" Commissioner Keppel replied, "I am sorry to say that is true." [42]

The exchange between Kennedy and Keppel showed that a broad definition of educational deprivation would include all family backgrounds that did not provide preparation for school and all schools that did not provide adequate education. But as the term was used by most educators it had a definite social-class meaning. For instance, in 1962 a report of the Educational Policies Commission of the National Education Association and American Association of School Administrators defined the disadvantaged as those who were left in isolation from the rest of society by technological changes and class structure. In particular, they identified the agrarian cultures of the South, Southwest, and Puerto Rico which because of economic displacement had moved to the large urban centers of the North.[43] Frank Riessman in his popular book, *The Culturally Deprived Child,* published in 1962, simply defined the disadvantaged as those members of lower socioeconomic groups who had limited access to education.[44] The National Conference on Education and Cultural Deprivation held in Chicago in 1964 defined as the disadvantaged one-third of the high school entrants who did not complete secondary school. The majority of these were identified as Puerto Ricans, Mexicans, and southern Negroes and whites who had moved to urban areas. Also included were the poor born in the cities and rural communities. But even in this report there was difficulty in clearly defining cultural deprivation. The report of the conference stated in reference to social and economic changes, "In light of the vast changes taking place, we are all culturally deprived." [45]

Most discussions of the disadvantaged in the early 1960s relied upon descriptions and figures provided by the Great Cities School Improvement Studies funded by the Ford Foundation. These studies were responsible for the often quoted figure that one-third of the students in urban school systems were disadvantaged. These studies also provided the basic information for the testimony of the secretary of HEW and the commissioner of education on educational deprivation before congressional hearings on aid to education in 1965. These studies identified the disadvantaged youth as "newcomers to the city who have had limited opportunities for intellectual, social, aesthetic and physical development. Not-so-new residents of the city who are oblivious to the opportunities which surround them." In addition, the studies included, "Residents of the city who have rejected these opportunities because of feelings of insecurity, an inadequate or distorted sense of values, lack of familial encouragement, or limited aspirations." [46] As Senator Kennedy pointed out, some of these characteristics might have nothing to do with low income and might be characteristics found throughout the socioeconomic structure. But for most educators and for the report of the Great Cities School Improvement Studies, these were characteristics of "disadvantaged youth concentrated in the impacted, economically depressed areas of our cities." [47]

What made children of these groups disadvantaged was often identified as the family and home background. The emphasis of Head Start and early childhood education programs was to provide an education that would counteract what were believed to be the negative effects of families living in a culture of poverty. On a national level this theme was stated by President Johnson in his Howard University speech in 1965 when he proclaimed, "The family is the cornerstone of our society. More than any other force it shapes the attitude, the hopes, the ambitions, and the values of the child. When the family collapses the child is usually damaged. When it happens on a massive scale the community itself is crippled." [48] The first draft of President Johnson's speech had been written by Daniel Patrick Moynihan, who had been urging government officials to adopt a national family policy and who believed that broken families, dominated by women, were the source of crime, violence, unrest, and community disorder. [49]

But the problem of broken families among the poor was considered only one aspect of the problem. The other part of the problem was the type of intellectual influence families of the poor had on their children. For instance, Frank Riessman, in *The Culturally Deprived*

Child, argued that most families of the poor prized education highly but for different reasons than the middle class. The poor, it was argued, emphasized education as a means of getting a job but were basically antiintellectual. This antiintellectualism, Riessman claimed, was a result of a childhood upbringing that was physical and nonsymbolic. Families of the poor had fewer books and other reading material in the homes as compared to the middle class and less frequently engaged in abstract discussions. Riessman argued that children from poor families were not deprived in the sense of wanting an education but were deprived in terms of what they valued in education. The culturally deprived child, he stated, was interested in the three Rs and the sciences, but not in social studies, literature, and the arts. It was the duty of the school to begin working with these children at a concrete level and to expand their interests to more intellectual levels.[50]

Most educators of the period tended to agree with Riessman that the problem was lack of intellectual stimulation in families of the poor and lack of opportunity to "learn how to learn." Basically, it was argued, poor children were at a disadvantage because they did not have the advantage of middle-class families. These disadvantages were considered to be not only the lack of books and verbal stimulation but also the lack of a stimulating environment rich in toys, games, and objects for manipulation. The lack of these was considered to retard intellectual and linguistic development and place the child of the poor at a disadvantage when entering school with the child of the middle class.[51]

One of the things frequently discussed in the literature on the disadvantaged in the early 1960s was the nature of the IQ and how much it was determined by the environment and how much by the biological nature of the individual. By the end of the 1960s this issue would provide one of the most heated educational discussions

about the value of programs such as Head Start.
Throughout the twentieth century, debate has continued as to whether IQ or the level of intelligence was fixed
at birth or influenced by the environment. One reason
for the controversy has been that IQ tests have tended to
show that lower socioeconomic groups have lower
levels of intelligence than upper groups and there exists
major differences in IQ between racial groups.[52] If this
measure were accurate and intelligence was determined
by heredity, then special education for the disadvantaged might be meaningless. In other words, the children of the poor have difficulty in school because they
are simply not intelligent.

In the early 1960s the pendulum of the IQ debate had
swung in favor of the environment. It was argued that
children from poor families received low IQ scores
because they were not motivated to achieve on the tests
and because the tests contained questions that were not
meaningful to children from a culture of poverty. In
addition, family and neighborhood life did not provide
enough stimulation for intellectual growth. What was
needed, it was argued, was an IQ test that was free of
cultural bias and an enriched educational environment.
These factors would eliminate the social-class bias of IQ
scores.[53]

Head Start was believed to be a unique preschool
program designed to attack the problem of the disadvantaged child and provide one educational focus of the
war on poverty. At Senate hearings on the Economic
Opportunity Act in 1966, Sargent Shriver explained to
Congress, "Head Start is not a typical pre-school education program. . . . Educators have talked about pre-
school programs for years. . . . But Head Start is not a
kindergarten or a government-paid-for babysitting
service adorned with crayons, stuffed animals and
pictures." [54]

What was supposedly unique about Head Start was its

five components of action. The first of these was provision for medical and dental services for impoverished
children. In terms of both the cycle-of-poverty hypothesis and the literature of the disadvantaged, health
problems were viewed as a major link in the circle of
poverty and in poor educational achievement. By 1967,
20 percent of money allocated for Head Start was devoted to nutrition and health services.[55] The second
component of Head Start was social services for the
child's home environment and education of the parents.
Since in the discussions of the disadvantaged, the home
and family were considered the major causes of educational deprivation, it was only logical to gear part of the
program toward family intervention. Supposedly the
introduction of intellectually stimulating toys and objects into the home plus training and education of the
parent would be one major step in the direction of
changing family life. In keeping with the philosophy of
community action, some parents were trained and utilized at Head Start centers. By 1967, 6 percent of the
Head Start budget was devoted to parent services.[56] Two
other components of the program were psychological
services for the child and school-readiness programs.
School readiness was, of course, the heart of the program
with emphasis on preparing the child to enter school on
equal terms with children of more privileged members of
society. The fifth component was the utilization of volunteer help.

In keeping with the philosophy of community action,
involvement of the poor in the planning and development of Head Start programs was essential. Shriver told
the Senate committee in 1966, "One of the operating
principles of Head Start, as is true throughout the
Community Action Program, is the involvement of the
poor. Parents help plan and develop Head Start centers;
representatives of residents of the areas sit on policy

boards; and the poor fill 45,000 non-professional jobs in Head Start classrooms." [57] Shriver went on to claim "our evidence shows that we were effective in getting the parents and the professionals engaged together in carrying out local Head Start programs." Head Start centers were also organized through local private and public institutions. Approximately two-thirds of the summer Head Start programs were operated by public schools and about 10 percent by private schools with the remainder being operated by private nonprofit agencies, including community-action agencies. One-third of the full-year programs of Head Start were operated by public school systems and 10 percent by private schools; 29 percent were operated by community-action agencies and 25 percent by private nonprofit agencies.[58]

The Elementary and Secondary Education Act of 1965

The major focus of government action toward the disadvantaged child came in the Elementary and Secondary Education Act of 1965. In fact, the emphasis on the disadvantaged child made possible the development of an aid formula that overcame one of the traditional obstacles to federal aid to education. Traditionally, the major obstacles to federal aid had been the issue of segregated schools, the problem of church-state relations, and fears of federal control. Essentially the issue of segregated schools had been taken care of by 1965 in the form of Title VI in the 1964 Civil Rights Act. The issue of church-state relations had been the major obstacle in President Kennedy's attempts to get legislation enacted providing federal aid to education. Parochial school leaders, of course, wanted federal aid to provide their schools with some sort of benefits. On the other hand, there was strong Congressional and public opposition to supplying this type of aid.

The solution to the problem of federal control fit neatly into the overall strategy of the war on poverty. As President Johnson was later to write, "Throughout the government we began to search for the formula that would both override the church-state issue and minimize the fear of federal control. We found it in a simple equation: $A/2 \times B = P$." [59] Within this formula, A represented a state's average expenditure per pupil, and B represented the number of poor children in a school district. In its final legislative form the level of poverty was set at a family income of $2000. In addition, it was proposed to include special services and library support in the legislation that would go to both public and private schools. It was felt this could be done without raising the problem of church-state relations because of a Supreme Court ruling in 1947 that busing of parochial students was aid to the pupils and not to the Catholic church. When the church-state issue was raised in legislative hearings, the problem was resolved under this child-benefit theory. Added to the legislation was a provision that title to all library resources and instructional materials would be vested in a public agency. In turn these materials were to be lent to teachers and pupils in any public or private educational agency approved by the state. What this meant was that the aid would go directly to the teachers and children in parochial schools and not to the school. [60]

President Johnson established a very strong coalition of support before submitting the legislation to Congress. The coalition included public and religious educational organizations and Catholic and Protestant congressional leaders. In addition, he achieved general congressional agreement that attempts to amend the act would be blocked. He also achieved agreement among committee members charged with the responsibility of holding hearings on the legislation to avoid discussions and issues that might shatter the coalition that had been established. President Johnson's legislative strategy worked so effectively that Republican opponents referred to the legislation as the "Railroad Act of 1965."[61] President Johnson submitted the legislation to Congress on January 12, 1965, and House committee hearings began on January 22. By April 11 President Johnson was able to sign the bill into law. He selected as the site for the final signing a one-room schoolhouse near Stonewall, Texas, where his own education had begun. For the occasion, his first schoolteacher was flown in from retirement in California, to stand at his side.

The most important section of the Elementary and Secondary Education Act was Title I which received approximately 78 percent of the $1.25 billion initially appropriated for the legislation. The money was distributed on the basis of 50 percent of the average state pupil expenditure multiplied by the number of children from families with less than $2000 annual income. The purpose of Title I was to provide improved educational programs for children designated as educationally deprived. Title I specifically stated, "the Congress hereby declares it to be the policy of the United States to provide financial assistance . . . to expand and improve . . . educational programs by various means . . . which contribute particularly to meeting the special educational needs of educationally deprived children."[62]

In essence, Title I was the major educational component of the war on poverty. At the opening congressional hearings on the bill before the House Committee on Education and Labor in January 1965, Anthony J. Celebrezze, secretary of HEW, and Commissioner of

Education Francis Keppel provided the President's justification and rationale for special educational assistance to the educationally deprived. In his opening statement to the committee, Celebrezze quoted President Johnson's statement, "Just as ignorance breeds poverty, poverty all too often breeds ignorance in the next generation." Celebrezze went on to claim, "The President's program . . . is designed to break this cycle which has been running on from generation to generation in this most affluent period of our history." He stated that here was a clear link between "high educational and high economic attainment" and warned that lack of adequate educational facilities for the children of the poor was resulting in high rates of youth unemployment, delinquency, and crime.[63]

Commissioner Keppel gave his statement immediately after Celebrezze. Keppel also drew upon the rhetoric and arguments that had come to characterize the whole approach to the problem of poverty. But in this case, as it had in the report of the Council of Economic Advisers, education was viewed as the major element in the cycle of poverty that had to be attacked. Keppel told the House committee, "Archimedes . . . told us many centuries ago: 'Give me a lever long enough and a fulcrum strong enough and I can move the world.' Today, at last, we have the prospect of a lever long enough and supported strongly enough to do something for our children of poverty." [64] The lever, of course, was education, and the fulcrum was federal financial assistance.

The other sections of the legislation covered a variety of special purposes which in many cases were included to assure passage of Title I. Title II provided financial assistance for school library resources, textbooks, and other instructional materials. As mentioned previously, one of the primary reasons for including this title was to win support from private school interests. In addition, Keppel supported Title II during congressional hearings with statistics showing that the quality of the school library was one of the four most important factors associated with student performance. Title III provided funds for the establishment of supplementary educational centers to promote local educational innovations. Educators who had helped President Johnson draft the legislation hoped that this could be one method for stimulating creativity in local school systems. Title IV provided money for educational research and for the establishment of Research and Development Centers at universities and in different regions of the country. Title IV was included in the legislation because it was believed that if it were submitted as a separate bill, it would receive minimal legislative support. In a sense the concept of research and development in education was to ride in on the coattails of Title I. Funds for strengthening state departments of education were designated under Title V. The purpose in this case was to allay the fears of those concerned about federal control of education by giving direct support to the state and to provide the money by which the state departments of education could administer the funds provided in other sections of the legislation. Title VI provided a statement of definitions used in the act and contained a clause prohibiting federal control over the operations of local school systems.

In general, the Elementary and Secondary Education Act followed in the tradition of federal involvement in education that had been evolving since World War II. The basic thread of this tradition was manpower planning for the national economy. In the 1950s, under pressure from the technological and scientific race with the Soviet Union, the emphasis had been on channeling talented youth into higher education. In the early 1960s the emphasis was shifted to the proper utilization of the manpower of the poor through equality of opportunity. President Johnson, who had chaired the Senate hearings on Selective Service in the early 1950s, clearly reiterated this theme in his educational message to Congress that had accompanied the proposals for the Elementary and Secondary Education Act. He declared a national goal of full educational opportunity for every child in the land. He warned, "Nothing matters more to the future of our country; not our military preparedness, for armed might is worthless if we lack the brainpower to build a world of peace; not our productive economy, for we cannot sustain growth without trained manpower." [65]

But unlike the manpower policies of the 1950s, the approach of the 1960s was essentially a war on a culture. Within the theoretical framework of the war on poverty, it was not the social and economic system that had created poverty and allowed for its continued existence that was considered the problem; but the problem was the culture of the poor. Indeed, the overall strategy was to integrate the poor into the social and economic system that was responsible for poverty. Special educational programs for the children of the poor had as a purpose the replacement of something called a "disadvantaged culture" with a more advantaged environment. While educators were often vague about the nature of what this advantaged environment was, it seems clear that it had something to do with the ability to function well in school. In essence this meant that the disadvantaged child was to be rescued from the culture of poverty by being trained for the culture of the school.

The rhetoric of the war on poverty with its strong educational emphasis also served as a means of conservatively dealing with the issue of social-class differences. On the one hand, social-class differences can be viewed as creating an inevitable social conflict. The rich and the middle class have a particular set of economic interests which depend on controlling and repressing the poor.

The poor also have a set of economic interests which depend for their realization on changing the social and economic structure which supports the rich and the middle class. This means an inevitable conflict between these groups. On the other hand, the approach of the war on poverty was that no basic conflict existed between the interests of social classes. The poor were poor because they had been left behind by social and economic developments. The major economic interest of the poor was to enter the middle class and not to change the economic and social system. The interest of the middle class was not in repression of the poor but in solving such problems as crime, delinquency, and unemployment by bringing the poor into the main stream of society. Education comes to play a major role in this particular analysis of social-class differences because it supposedly would provide the bridge for the poor to enter the opportunity structure of society. In the rhetoric of the war on poverty, education was considered the hope of the poor and the method of the middle class.

CAREER EDUCATION AND EQUALITY OF EDUCATIONAL OPPORTUNITY

6 In the middle of the 1960s the national educational policy began to encounter a series of explosive problems. The major theme of educational policy since World War II had been the channeling and sorting of the national labor force. During the 1950s the focus had been on the discovery and education of the talented for national defense and for a highly technological society. In the early 1960s, under pressure from the civil rights movement, concern had been broadened to include the children of the poor and provide for equality of opportunity. Both these elements of educational policy carried with them seeds of controversy.

During the 1950s the primary concern had been with channeling talented youth into institutions of higher education. The methods for accomplishing this goal had been the student deferments of the Selective Service System and government loans and scholarships. These policies resulted in a rapid expansion in the enrollment of youth between eighteen and twenty-one in institutions of higher education. In 1946 the percentage of this age group in colleges and universities, was 17.6. In 1956 the figure had increased to 31.2, and by 1965 it was 43.9.[1] The policies that had sparked this rapid increase in enrollment had centered around American foreign policy and concern about maintaining American military strength. Even though the Selective Service System provided student deferments, it also provided for draft into military service after graduation. The maintenance of this educational policy depended on acceptance and support of American foreign policy.

Actually it was the unpopular nature of American involvement in Vietnam which resulted in the sharpest protest against American educational policy in the late 1960s. College and high school campuses around the United States had sit-ins, protest marches, bombings, and demonstrations which in a variety of ways protested American foreign policy. Accompanying these protests were criticisms of the educational policies that had received original support because of foreign policy considerations. University and college involvement in military research and projects conducted by the Agency for International Development became one focus of protest. Another criticism was leveled at the close links between the universities and large corporations. And, of course, the Selective Service System, which brought the reality of war into every household and campus, became a bitter target of attack.

In addition to campus protests, a movement developed for alternative schools and free universities to provide an education that would supposedly be free of the corrupting influences of national educational policy. While alternative schools varied in terms of method and curriculum, there was one thing they seemed to have in common: rejection of the type of manpower policies that had been ingrained in the traditional American public school system.[2] Most alternative schools abandoned academic tracking, standardized intelligence and achievement testing, ability grouping, and vocational guidance. One leader of the alternative school movement, Ivan Illich, called for the deschooling of society and the complete elimination of the school as a controlling device for a modern technological society.[3]

The student protest movement and alternative schools reflected only one side of the turmoil of the late 1960s and early 1970s. On the other side was the civil rights movement and the demand for equality of opportunity in schooling. In 1965 a riot in the Watts area of Los Angeles signaled the beginning of black urban riots that would spread across the country.[4] Accompanying the riots were increasing demands by civil rights leaders to end de facto segregation in urban areas of the North. A school boycott in protest over de facto segregation in Chicago in February 1964 was followed by similar massive demonstrations in Cleveland, Boston, and New York. Out of these demands emerged the explosive issue of busing children to achieve racial integration. By 1972, the issue of busing was to become a major element in the presidential campaign. Involved in the concern about integration was the meaning of equality of opportunity in relationship to American education.

The Vietnam war, student demonstrations, and the turmoil in the civil rights movement all became contributing factors in President Johnson's decision to not seek reelection in 1968.[5] A combination of national educational policy and foreign policy had resulted in the ending of a political career. In 1969, Johnson's successor, President Richard M. Nixon, entered the White House after waging a campaign calling for law and order and an end to demonstrations and riots. One of the things that occurred during Nixon's early years was an attempt to establish a volunteer army to reduce protests centered around the draft.[6] Another thing was an attempt to heighten the manpower-channeling emphasis of American public schooling by more closely linking the academic programs of the schools to the labor market. President Nixon attempted to achieve this goal by appointing Sidney P. Marland as U.S. commissioner of education. Marland's solution to student protests and turmoil in the educational system was "career education."

Career Education

The career education movement, like the new mathematics and science programs of the late 1950s, was an example of the power of the federal government to affect school curriculums around the country. In 1971 and 1972, Marland began to earmark the discretionary funds provided by Congress to the Office of Education for the development of career education models. Projects using these funds were initiated in Arizona, California, Georgia, Michigan, and New Jersey. In addition, funds were made available through the Office of Education to finance states for the development and operation of career education programs.[7] As money started to flow from the federal coffers, educators began to jump on the bandwagon of career education. During the first two years $100 million in discretionary funds went into the program. Marland was able to announce that in 1972–73, one year after the beginning of the program, 750,000 young people participated in career education demonstrations and models supported by funds from the U.S. Office of Education and that five state legislatures had been persuaded to approve funds to launch career education. He also reported that the Dallas public school system had been completely restructured around the concept of career education.[8]

Marland believed career education was the answer to

student rebellion, delinquency, and unemployment. In his first annual report to Congress in 1971, he argued that disenchantment among youth existed because education did not lead to career opportunities. For Marland, the villain was general education programs that lacked specific goals and were not linked to the job market. Marland argued that education should be meaningful, and by "meaningful" he meant related to a career objective. He stated, "When we use the word 'meaningful,' we imply a strong obligation that our young people complete the first 12 grades in such a fashion that they are ready either to enter into some form of higher education or to proceed immediately into satisfying and appropriate employment." [9] This, of course, was a restatement of the traditional goal of the comprehensive high school and followed the arguments given by James Conant in his report on the high school in the late 1950s. Marland claimed allegiance to the concept of the comprehensive high school but considered its primary weakness to be its general education programs not directly related to entry into the job market or into higher education. He argued, "The emergence of the comprehensive high school, properly defined and implemented, carries the ultimate solution." [10]

Therefore, Marland believed, students and schools were in a state of turmoil because the schools had never completely achieved the goal of sorting students for the labor market. In his first report to Congress he stated, "We must eliminate anything in our curriculum that is unresponsive to either of these goals [higher education and employment], particularly the high school anachronism called 'the general curriculum,' a false compromise between college preparatory curriculum and realistic career development." [11] For Marland, all elements of school life had to be justified in terms of career development. Or as Marland's associate commissioner stated, "The fundamental concept of career education is that all educational experiences, curriculum, instruction, and counseling should be geared to preparing each individual for a life of economic independence, personal fulfillment, and an appreciation for the dignity of work." [12] This meant complete alignment between the job market and the public school. Marland believed career education would be one solution "to some of our more serious social and economic problems, including high unemployment and the attendant problems of disaffection and drug excess among the young." [13]

What was unique about career education was the attempt to make vocational guidance a part of the academic program of the school and to begin the program in the early grades of school. During the elementary and junior high school years, career education was to be a subject-matter field that would acquaint students with the world of work and the varieties of occupations available. After studying and preparing for an occupational choice in these early grades, the student upon entering high school was to begin preparing either for entry directly into an occupational career or entry into higher education. It was also believed that higher education had to begin to organize upon a career education model. For Commissioner Marland, the real hope in this regard was the community college. Marland argued that the community college should not be viewed as merely a "large anteroom for the four year-institutions." It was a unique institution of higher learning, Marland claimed, whose developing philosophy centered around the concept of career education. Close ties with local businesses made it possible for the community college to gear its programs to the needs of the labor market. [14]

Support for career education even found its way into

the 1972 amendments to the Elementary and Secondary Education Act. The original legislation passed in 1965 had undergone a number of changes by the 1970s, primarily the addition of programs for specific groups labeled as disadvantaged. In 1966 the Elementary and Secondary Education Act had been amended to include special programs for Indian children, migratory agricultural workers, delinquents, and the handicapped. Amendments in 1967 designated Title VII of the Act for Bilingual Education Programs directed mainly at the educational problems of children from Spanish-speaking and Indian-speaking homes. The 1972 amendments focused on career education and the importance of these programs for the disadvantaged. One amendment stated that "equal consideration shall be given to the needs of elementary and secondary schools for library resources, textbooks, and other printed and published materials utilized for instruction, orientation, or guidance and counseling in occupational education." [15]

In addition, the 1972 amendments called for the development of career education programs that would be treated as academic subjects and be given equal status with other educational programs. An amendment provided for "programs designed to encourage the development in elementary and secondary schools of occupational information and counseling and guidance, and instruction in occupational education on an equal footing with traditional academic subjects." [16] In one sense, these amendments were not in conflict with the original purpose of the legislation. What they did was to state more specifically that the major purpose of education for the disadvantaged was to solve the manpower problems of the United States. In a broader framework, career education was the solution of President Nixon's administration to the problem of educating the disadvantaged and ending the rebellion and turmoil in the schools.

Equality of Educational Opportunity

The other major educational problem that confronted President Nixon was the issue of busing children to achieve integration of the schools. During the 1972 presidential campaign busing became a major political issue. The whole idea of busing was entangled in the variety of meanings given to the phrase "equality of educational opportunity." On the one hand, equality of educational opportunity could mean equal access to educational institutions, that is, no children should be denied the right to attend equal educational institutions. According to the 1954 Supreme Court decision ending school segregation, this meant the racial integration of public schools. On the other hand, equality of educational opportunity could mean special educational programs that would provide equal chances in school for children from backgrounds labeled as disadvantaged. This had been the major goal of the compensatory education programs of the war on poverty. President Nixon used the rhetoric of equality of educational opportunity to justify his opposition to busing. He did this by deemphasizing the integration of educational facilities and by emphasizing compensatory education.

To understand the debate that occurred during the Nixon administration over busing and equality of educational opportunity, one must go back to the 1964 Civil Rights Act. Title IV of this Act gave the commissioner of education the responsibility to "conduct a survey and make a report to the President and the Congress, within two years of the enactment of this title, concerning the lack of availability of equal educational opportunities for individuals by reason of race, color, religion, or national origin in public educational institutions at all levels." It seems clear from the original context of the provision and legislative debate that the congressional intent of this survey was to provide information on the

degree of segregation in educational facilities.[17] The final
survey that was issued as Equality of Educational Opportunity went far beyond the intent of Congress and
tried to determine what factors in schooling contributed
to equality of educational achievement. This report,
along with the compensatory education programs of the
war on poverty, opened a continuing debate over the
meaning of equality of educational opportunity.

When the Civil Rights Act of 1964 was passed, the
commissioner of education selected James Coleman of
Johns Hopkins University to assume major responsibility for the design, administration, and analysis of the
survey. The steps that led to the survey going beyond the
intention of Congress occurred when Coleman and his
staff tried to define the concept of equality of educational opportunity. They outlined five major approaches
to the problem. One approach defined the concept in
terms of the degree of racial segregation that existed in
school systems. The second approach thought in terms
of inequality of resource inputs from the school system.
This meant items such as books, school facilities, and
student-teacher ratios. The third method was in terms of
inequality of intangible resources, such as teacher
morale. These three definitions fell clearly into the intent of Congress, but the fourth and fifth definitions
went beyond this intention. The fourth approach mea-
sured inequality of inputs in terms of their effectiveness
for educational achievment; and the fifth considered
inequality of output as evidence of inequality of opportunity. The survey, or as it was later called, "The Coleman Report," attempted to measure all five of these
approaches to the problem of equality of educational
opportunity.[18]

It was later charged that Coleman and his staff attempted to do too much in too short of a time. The
national survey was conducted with blinding speed and
submitted to Congress in 1966. One criticism of the re-

port was that it should have done well the very minimum task of carefully measuring the resources in schools attended by blacks and those attended by whites, to determine the kind and degree of discrimination. Coleman responded to this criticism that if his staff had concentrated on the question of equality in terms of school resources alone, it would have reinforced that definition. The major virtue in the final report, he felt, was that it shifted policy attention from traditional concerns about resources—per pupil expenditure, class size, teachers salaries and school facilities—to attention on the effectiveness of these school resources on student achievement.[19]

What the Coleman Report found with regard to the basic issue of school segregation was that almost "80 percent of all white pupils in 1st grade and 12th grade" attended schools that were from "90 to 100 percent white." In terms of black students, 65 percent in the first grade attended schools that were between 90 and 100 percent black. This meant that the majority of children in the United States attended segregated schools, with white children being the most segregated. In terms of school resources, white children as compared to minority children attended schools with smaller class sizes, more science and language laboratories, more books in the library, and more opportunities for participating in college preparatory and accelerated academic curriculums.[20] These findings were not particularly startling since most of the nation had become aware of the nature and problem of segregation. These facts merely confirmed current beliefs.

The Coleman Report then tried to compare these differences in resources with student achievement. Student achievement in the report was determined by achievement tests. The report assumed about achievement tests that "what they measure are the skills which are among the most important in our society for getting a good job and moving up to a better one, and for full participation in an increasingly technical world." [21] It certainly was a debatable point whether performance on the school achievement test really reflected future earnings and job abilities, but this was the assumption of the Coleman study. In terms of achievement test scores, the Coleman Report found that, except for Oriental Americans, all other minority groups scored significantly lower than whites and that the differences increased from the first through the twelfth grade. The report stated, "For most minority groups ... schools provide little opportunity for them to overcome ... initial deficiency; in fact they fall farther behind the white majority in the development of several skills which are critical to making a living and participating fully in modern society." [22]

When these differences in achievement were compared to school resources, it was found "differences between schools account for only a small fraction of differences in achievement." [23] There were differences between the effect of school resources between white and minority students. The achievement of white students seemed to be less affected by the strengths or weaknesses of curriculums and school facilities, while these did seem to have some effect on the achievement of minority students. Student achievement was strongly related "to the educational backgrounds and aspirations of the other students in school." There were marked differences between white and minority groups in regard to this factor. The Coleman Report argued that if a white pupil from a family that was strongly supportive of education was put in a school with pupils who did not come from this type of background, the pupil's achievement would "be little different than if he were in a school composed of others like himself." On the other hand, if "a minority pupil from a home without much educational strength is put with schoolmates with strong educational backgrounds, his achievement is likely to increase." [24]

The conclusions of the Coleman Report opened a complex set of questions. It should be noted that the report did give strong support to the policy of school integration. Since the most important factor affecting achievement was pupil backgrounds, the report could conclude "the analysis of school factors described ... suggests that in the long run, integration should be expected to have a positive effect on Negro achievement." [25] In general, the conclusions of the report seemed to suggest that the quality of school curriculums and facilities had little relationship to the question of equality of educational opportunity.

In fact, other studies began to appear in the late 1960s which suggested that compensatory education could not have much effect on student achievement. The most famous and controversial of these studies was Arthur Jensen's "How Much Can We Boost I.Q. and Scholastic Achievement?" which appeared in a 1969 issue of the *Harvard Educational Review*.[26] Jensen argued that compensatory education programs such as Head Start could not produce any lasting effect on a child's IQ. He maintained that environmental factors were not as important in determining intelligence as were genetic factors. This conclusion suggested that minority students did poorly in school because of low levels of intelligence and that improving school facilities and providing compensatory education programs would have little effect on IQ and, consequently, on student achievement. It should be noted that the findings of the Coleman study and Jensen were in fact duplications of studies in the 1920s and represented a continuing debate on the value of schooling and the meaning of IQ.[27] The difference was that in the 1960s there was a major national concern about the value of integration and the meaning of equality of educational opportunity.

While the Coleman Report found little relationship between the quality of school facilities and curriculums and student achievement, it did find differences in the availability of school resources. On one level it could be argued that these differences were meaningless since there was no apparent relationship to student achievement. Why worry about differences in class sizes, per pupil expenditures, and other school resources? On another level it could be argued that all children should have access to equal educational facilities regardless of the question of academic achievement. Parents as citizens had the right to expect equal treatment by public institutions. School facilities should be equal for all students. Within this context, equality of educational opportunity meant equality of educational institutions.

The tactic of the Nixon administration in its opposition to busing was to define equality of educational opportunity in terms of compensatory education programs and in terms of equality of educational facilities. For this reason, President Nixon gave strong support to a complete overhauling of the method for financing public education. Commissioner Marland reported to Congress in 1972 that the Office of Education and other divisions of the executive branch were working closely on designing alternative financing methods for public education. The background for this move was a California State Supreme Court decision in 1971, *Serrano* v. *Priest,* which found that the California method of financing schools was unconstitutional. In this decision the California court extended the meaning of the Fourteenth Amendment of the Constitution to include equality of school resources. The decision centered around the fact that children in wealthy communities had better educational facilities than children in poor communities.[28] As Commissioner Marland told Congress, "The Court noted that affluent districts have their cake and eat it too, they can provide a high quality education for their children while paying lower taxes. Poor districts, by contrast, have no cake at all. Grotesque variations in financial ability exist among as well as within States." [29] The decision of the California court required a new method of financing that would equalize per pupil spending or equalize the quality of educational programs.

The *Serrano* v. *Priest* decision stressed that side of the equality of educational opportunity argument which was most appealing to those who opposed school integration. In addition, it won support from educational bureaucrats such as the Office of Education because it would centralize the financing of public education on a state level and reduce the control of local citizens over the public schools. It could be argued that the last vestige of local control of education in the United States by the early 1970s was the control of the local school purse.

The major book that contributed to the legal arguments in *Serrano* v. *Priest* was *Private Wealth and Public Education* published in 1970.[30] The first part of the book presented a critical treatment of existing state aid to education plans and persuasively argued that existing attempts to equalize educational expenditures either had failed or had actually created greater inequalities. As a substitute for existing educational financing plans, the book offered a power-equalization formula that would equalize spending between school districts and between states. The formula supposedly would have ended inequality of educational resources between school districts. The study presented a plan for implementing the power-equalization formula through the judicial process by arguing in court that the education of children should be considered under the equal protection clause of the Fourteenth Amendment. One of the judicial techniques that was suggested was to compare the inequality of educational spending with the reapportionment decisions of the Supreme Court which led to the one-man, one-vote doctrine. In the minds of the authors of the book, schooling should be considered the equal of voting in importance to a democratic society.

The rationale given in the study for the need to support a power-equalization formula centered around the arguments for equality of educational opportunity. The book argued that the United States was a competitive democracy in which a marketplace of talent was the prime determiner of individual success. Like other arguments about equality of opportunity, the primary concern was with assuring equal competition. The book stated that "the sine qua non of a fair contest system . . . is equality of training. And that training is what public education is primarily about." The authors also recognized that the primary purpose of American education was preparation for a competitive job market. They stated, "There are, we hope, loftier views of education that coexist, but in a competitive democracy those views represent dependent goals that can be realized only upon a foundation of training for basic competence in the market." Providing for equality in the financing of public education was to make the operations of the marketplace fair and provide for the social mobility of the poor. The authors restated their faith in American education, "Social mobility as a value plays a potent role here, and public education must be seen in its special relation to the underclasses to whom it is the strongest hope for rising in the social scale." [31]

It was understandable why the Nixon administration could support both the plans for new methods of financing education and career education. Both ideas supported the concept of education as training for the labor market. New financing plans were to assure equality of opportunity for training for the labor market. Career education was to provide the actual training.

While the Nixon administration poured money into the development of new financing plans, a major setback occurred in the legal struggles. In 1973 the Supreme

Court ruled in one of the school financing cases, *Rodriguez* v. *San Antonio Independent School District,* that the right to an education was not implicitly protected by the Fourteenth Amendment and was not entitled to constitutional protection. The Court declared, "The consideration and initiation of fundamental reforms with respect to state taxation and education are matters reserved for the legislative processes of the various states." [32] This decision meant that the school financing cases would have to be argued within the courts of each state in terms of state constitutions. The Court essentially refused to make the refinancing of schools a national policy.

Busing and Equality of Opportunity

The issue of busing hit the national scene with full force in 1971 when the Supreme Court in *Swann* v. *Charlotte-Mecklenburg Board of Education* supported busing as a legitimate tool for bringing about the desegregation of school districts. The Court warned that "schools all or predominantly of one race in a district of mixed population will require close scrutiny to determine that school assignments are not part of state-enforced segregation." [33] The implications of this decision were that de facto segregation in northern urban school districts would come under close scrutiny of the courts and that busing would be considered a legitimate tool for implementing desegregation plans. Traditional arguments about the value of neighborhood schools could no longer be used to avoid integration. Also, school districts would be viewed as unitary systems, and wherever possible, racial integration within those districts must be achieved.

In March 1972 President Nixon sent a special message to the Congress requesting a moratorium on student

busing.[34] Nixon's arguments were couched in the rhetoric of equality of opportunity. Nixon declared, "Conscience and the Constitution both require that no child
should be denied equal educational opportunity." He
went on to argue that the purpose of the *Brown* v.
Board of Education decision in 1954 was to eliminate
the dual school system of the South. This purpose, he
maintained, had been achieved. President Nixon
claimed the present problem was the maze of differing
court orders that had developed to end segregation.
Many of these plans, including busing, had resulted in
violence and community disruption and had imposed
hardships on children. He argued there were wrong
reasons and right reasons for opposing busing. The
wrong reason was racial prejudice. The right reasons
were a dislike of "wrenching of children away from their
families, and from the schools their families may have
moved to be near, and sending them arbitrarily to others
far distant."

President Nixon went on to argue that since the dual
school system had been substantially dismantled there
should be a greater balance of "emphasis on improving
schools, on convenience, on the chance for parental involvement." This meant, for Nixon, that the argument
for equality of educational opportunity should concentrate "much more specifically on education: on assuring
that the opportunity is not only equal, but adequate."
He stated that the legitimate concerns in the busing
issue were quality of education, transportation of children to distant schools, and equality of educational resources. The reforms he proposed were:

—*To give practical meaning to the concept of equal
educational opportunity.*
—*To apply the experience gained in the process of desegregation, and also in efforts to give special help to
the educationally disadvantaged.*

—*To ensure the continuing vitality of the principles laid down in* Brown v. Board of Education.

—*To downgrade busing as a tool for achieving equal educational opportunity.*

—*To sustain the rights and responsibilities vested by the States in local school boards.*

The more specific details of President Nixon's proposed reforms were presented to a Senate subcommittee seven days after his special message to Congress by Secretary of Health, Education, and Welfare Elliot Richardson. As mentioned, the strategy of the Nixon administration was to deemphasize the integration part of the argument for equality of educational opportunity and emphasize equality of resources and compensatory education. Richardson repeated before the Senate subcommittee the basic arguments Nixon had given that the dual school system had been abolished and that busing was occurring without regard for rational educational values. Busing must be downgraded, he reiterated, and there must be a "reestablishment of the primacy of educational objectives." [35] The Nixon strategy called for a moratorium on busing and the targeting of funds for compensatory education projects.

One of Secretary Richardson's more difficult tasks in presenting Nixon's proposals was justifying the targeting of money for compensatory education programs. The Coleman Report and studies of compensatory education programs had suggested the ultimate failure of this strategy. Richardson admitted, "The findings of the Coleman Report have been a keystone for many of the arguments that compensatory education cannot work." He recognized that a clear finding of the report was that differences in school spending did not seem to be a significant factor in explaining differences in the achievement of children and that the social and economic status of children was an important factor in explaining achievement. But, he argued, it was a misinterpretation of the Coleman Report to conclude that no matter what is done, school will have no effect on achievement. The reason for this was that the Coleman Report dealt with current educational practices and not possible changes in those practices. Richardson told the senators, "The Coleman Report analyzed the then existing range of school conditions and had nothing to say about situations in which very substantial additional resources above normal school expenditures were provided for basic learning problems." [36] The Nixon proposals were to provide money for specific basic learning programs.

The failure of many compensatory education programs supported by the 1965 Elementary and Secondary Education Act, Richardson stated, was because the grant formula hindered the ability of the federal government to concentrate on schools and school districts with the greatest need. Richardson claimed the major problem was actual misuse of Title I funds provided by the 1965 act. He told the senators, "The most prevalent failing has been the use by local school districts of Title I funds as general revenue. Out of 40 States audited between 1966 and 1970, local school districts in 14 were found to have spent Title I funds as general revenue." In these cases the funds were diffused through the educational system and did not reach the educationally deprived child. He announced that the Office of Education had recently asked eight states to return $6,249,915 in misused funds and would shortly take action against approximately fifteen additional states for another $23 million. "The recovery of misspent funds," he warned, "is hardly easy to explain, since scarce State and local education resources must be depleted to finance the recovery. Thus our efforts at recovery can be interpreted as efforts to take money from the very children we are all trying to help." [37]

Richardson also argued that national evaluations

of Title I's compensatory education programs had found little relationship between the programs and achievement for low-income children because the money had been spread very thinly with, for instance, the average child receiving Title I services having only one or two hours of help with reading per month. One reason for the money being spread thinly was that it was often viewed as a substitute for funds normally spent rather than extra dollars for special programs.

President Nixon's plan called for targeting three hundred dollars of compensatory service per poor pupil with an additional amount going to the school based on the percentage of poor children. The compensatory supplement was to be provided over and above the normal educational expenditures in a school district. Approximately 75 percent of the funds were to be used for what were called basic learning programs and the rest for counseling, nutrition, and health. Secretary Richardson justified this approach by citing statistics from Title I evaluations of compensatory education programs that did seem to work. The focus of these statistics was on seven states where there had been improvement in achievement through compensatory education programs.

The major study cited by Richardson was conducted by an educational economist, Herbert Kiesling, who analyzed forty-two California compensatory education projects. Richardson told the Senate subcommittee, "His study concluded that significant achievement gains occurred in every situation where well managed programs using diagnostic reading specialists provided learning assistance costing between $200 and $300 per child." [38] Richardson concluded his testimony by claiming there was no need for a choice between desegregation and compensatory education to achieve equality of educational opportunity. Desegregation must be viewed in terms of its contribution to improving education. For

President Nixon, it should be remembered, busing had distorted the goal of desegregation for improved education. Richardson stated, "Any local school district which genuinely seeks to solve its problems of educational deprivation will, I trust, achieve that part of the solution which desegregation can achieve by desegregating and achieve that part which will persist, because of poverty and environment, through good, compensatory Government programs." [39]

President Nixon's attempt to stem the tide of busing was defeated. By 1974, major community violence occurred as Boston began to use busing as a tool for racial integration of the public schools. By the mid-1970s, the emphasis on career education and basic educational programs seemed to be advancing through the public schools. How much of an impact on public education they would have was difficult to determine at the time of writing this volume. One thing was clear by the 1970s: the power of the federal government to influence educational policy in school districts throughout the United States.

The Great Retreat

The Nixon administration's support of targeting money for compensatory education was only a means of presenting its opposition to busing in the language of equality of opportunity. Other actions of the Nixon administration evidenced a general retreat from the support of federal educational programs. Between 1970 and 1973, Nixon vetoed three of six appropriation bills for Health, Education, and Welfare and vetoed and pocket-vetoed the 1973 appropriations bill. [40] On the one hand, Nixon justified the vetoes in terms of the need to reduce the federal budget. On the other hand, they were justified in terms of the lack of evidence that improved schooling resulted in any significant social change.

The individual responsible for formulating the latter reasons for reduced federal spending in education was White House counselor and Nixon confidant Daniel Patrick Moynihan. As mentioned in chapter 5, Moynihan had played a significant role in formulating some of the policies for Johnson's war on poverty. Of particular importance was his argument that there needed to be a national policy for support of the family.[41] These ideas were to be incorporated into President Nixon's attempts to establish a guaranteed family income that would supposedly result in the stabilization of the family unit and be an important step toward breaking the cycle of poverty. In addition, Moynihan had also led the opposition to the community-action philosophy in the war on poverty.[42] One could argue that the attempt to achieve maximum feasible participation of the poor in community agencies was one of the most democratic aspects of the war on poverty. It was also one of the most controversial because it appeared to be organizing the poor into class warfare against established interests. Both Nixon and Moynihan shared an opposition to the community-action programs of the Office of Economic Opportunity.

Moynihan was strongly influenced by the Coleman Report in his thinking about the proper role of federal involvement in education. In 1966, the same year as the publication of the report, the Carnegie Foundation provided funds for Moynihan and Fredrick Mosteller to conduct a faculty seminar at Harvard on the findings of the report.[43] One of the things that impressed Moynihan about the Coleman Report was its contradiction of what he called "conventional wisdom." The Coleman Report seemed to show that things people assumed were important in improving achievement in the schools had in fact little relationship to achievement. This supposed contradiction with conventional wisdom provided Moynihan with the ammunition to attack social scientists as a group and federal educational programs.

In 1967, in a paper on "The Education of the Urban Poor," Moynihan accused social scientists of attempting to shape opinions on public issues on the basis of their personal views and not by what he called "professional findings." He argued that social scientists were deeply committed to social change and tended to be at odds with the forces of personal wealth and political power. Social scientists tended to be either liberal or radical in their political persuasion, which resulted in the poor and minority groups in America assuming that the social scientists would always be on their side. Moynihan argued that social scientists should not take sides on social issues but should rely upon the facts of their findings. In terms of the federal educational efforts, Moynihan felt programs such as compensatory education had not been supported on the basis of research findings but by the general persuasion of educators and social scientists to want to do something for the poor.[44]

In addition, Moynihan argued for a clear recognition of the differences between programs and policies. On one level, the government might have programs; but on another level, none of these programs might be related to an overall policy. The government might have a program for building highways, but the implications of that program might not be understood unless there was a federal policy with regard to suburban and urban development that could evaluate the impact of highway building. Involved in the development of policy was the translation of the findings of social science into terms that could be used in a public debate. In this regard, Moynihan called for the development of a new journalism and political leadership that would be capable of fulfilling this function.[45] One can only assume that this was the role

Moynihan assumed for himself in his relationship to President Nixon.

Within the framework of the above reasoning, Moynihan could in the 1970s support increased spending for educational research but not increased spending for educational programs. Writing in the *New York Times* in 1972, he gave support to recent legislation for a National Institute of Education to conduct basic research in education. The research findings of this institution were to provide the basic facts for the development of a federal educational policy and programs designed to achieve that policy. Moynihan felt that past educational programs had failed to achieve objectives because basic research had not been conducted before their implementation. The National Institute of Education had been proposed by President Nixon to Congress in 1970 with the objective, as stated by Moynihan, "to bring 'big' science to bear on education, especially the problem of low achievement among students from low-income families." [46]

Moynihan believed that the results of educational research would support the Nixon administration's general retreat from the funding of federal educational programs. He wrote, "I for one would be willing to bet that the more we learn about formal schooling the less we will come to value it." He even suggested that research findings would show the need for a greater stress on the placement of the school graduate in the job market. Moynihan argued, "Rather than spending more money on early education, for example, we are likely to conclude that the transition we manage least well in our society is that of the young person leaving the world of school for the world of work, and that accordingly much more resources should be applied to this period in individual development rather than the much earlier one." [47]

One of the significant things about Moynihan's statement was that it represented an abandonment of the attempt to make the system of social selection in the schools work fairly by some provision for equality of opportunity. Moynihan's attitude was essentially that educational research had shown that nothing could be done in the schools to increase achievement in the lower class and, therefore, such efforts were not worth the spending of federal dollars. This, of course, did not mean that the role of the school in sorting the population for the labor market should be abandoned. What it meant was continuing this purpose of schooling in the more rigid form of career education and accepting social-class discrimination as inevitable.

The Social Forces Shaping National Educational Policy

The more general motivation for the Nixon administration's retreat from the support of federal educational programs must be understood against the background of the social forces shaping national educational policy since the end of World War II. Daniel Moynihan's arguments only provided justification for the retreat.

As mentioned in earlier chapters, the major concern following World War II was with increasing U.S. military strength and increasing the numbers of scientists and engineers. Both these elements were related to the protection and expansion of U.S. economic interests in foreign countries. The military was to protect these interests from communist competition, hence requiring more scientists and engineers to produce military weapons and to staff expanding corporations. Corporations with a stake in overseas economic expansion played an important role in shaping educational policy in the 1950s. The Conservation of Human Resources Project (see chapter 2) was sponsored by some of the major corporate interests in the United States. This organization provided the springboard for the founding of the National Manpower Council. Among the sponsoring corporations were Continental Can, E. I. DuPont de Nemours, General Dynamics, General Electric, Standard Oil (New Jersey), and Coca-Cola. A mere listing of these corporations does not convey the full impact of their involvement in military and foreign expansion, relationships to other corporations, and support of members of the scientific establishment.

For instance, the Du Pont family not only controlled E. I. Du Pont de Nemours but also had controlling interest in General Motors, U.S. Rubber, North American Aviation, and Boeing Aircraft, and had major holdings in Continental Can and Coca-Cola. The Du Pont fortune had been built on supplying military weapons from the time of the War of 1812. During World War II, Du Pont built all the facilities and supplied scientists and engineers for the production of the atomic bomb. The Manhattan project has been called by one writer the "Du Pont project." [48] This led to an obvious alliance between scientists such as Vannevar Bush and James Conant and corporate involvement in military research. In 1950 the Du Pont corporation was given the government contract for the development and production of the hydrogen bomb. Between 1950 and 1952, Du Pont controlled General Motors, received $5.5 billion in war contracts, and had annual profits that reached a high of 13.3 percent. President Eisenhower confirmed his support of this corporate expansion when he appointed the president of General Motors, Charles Wilson, as secretary of defense. Wilson announced, "What is good for America is good for General Motors, and vice versa." [49]

In addition to corporate concerns about profits from the military race with the Soviet Union was concern for the protection of overseas investments. President Eisenhower declared a need for overseas corporate expansion in his first inaugural address. He told the nation, "For all our material might even we need the markets in the world for the surpluses of our farms and factories. Equally we need for these same farms and factories vital materials and products of distant lands." [50]

President Eisenhower's friendship with James Conant and his appointment of Conant as high commissioner for Germany were all within the context of support for American economic expansion. It should be remembered that Conant's political rise was a result of his chairmanship of the Committee on Present Danger which gave support to military overseas expansion and the manpower-channeling features of Selective Service. This was also a natural outgrowth of his involvement in military research and the Manhattan project. Conant's involvement in the development of the National Science Foundation and his national study of the American high school in the late 1950s were both directed toward getting the American educational system to produce more scientists and engineers for military and corporate expansion.

Within the context of this argument one can conclude that the major factors shaping national educational policy in the 1950s were the expansion of corporate interests abroad and the military expansion required to protect those interests. The Universal Military Training and Service Act of 1951, the National Science Foundation, the National Defense Education Act, and the new curriculums in science and mathematics were all related to those goals. While it is true that all scientists and educators involved in these federal programs did not necessarily understand their relationship to these factors, they did all function as servants of power.

In the 1960s national educational policy began to shift toward an interest in the problem of poverty. The major force precipitating this shift was the civil rights movement which not only enlisted the concern of

Americans about racial justice but also created a fear of class conflict. Martin Luther King was not only a Christian pacifist but also a critic of American capitalism, and in the latter part of his life a critic of American foreign policy. In the early 1960s the civil rights movement became a poor people's campaign. Federal response in the form of the war on poverty was based on a philosophy that denied class conflict and sought a solution in using education to bring the lower class into the middle class. The primary purpose of the war on poverty was to maintain social order by holding out the promise that poverty could be eliminated through community-action programs and education.

It should also be remembered that the primary source of ideas for the war on poverty came from private foundations. The work of the Ford Foundation in the gray-areas projects provided the sociological theory that supported the rationale of the attack on poverty. Historically, the major function of organizations such as the Carnegie and Ford Foundations has been to support social policies that will maintain social order and protect the interests of their corporate donors.[51] It would be hard to imagine these organizations functioning in any other manner, given the source of their financial support.

The Economic Opportunity Act and the Elementary and Secondary Education Act were attempts to maintain social order by stemming the tide of potential class conflict as it was emerging from the civil rights movement. Again it should be stated that the social scientists and educators involved in these projects were not necessarily conscious of their role, but it is worth remembering that when they became too radical in the community-action programs they were quickly slapped down. Social scientists and educators have an amazing way of shifting their interests and research with the shifting tides of available money. Educators in the 1950s tended to concentrate on the issue of the academically talented but quickly shifted to the disadvantaged child as the flow of educational money shifted in that direction. One could say that where the money is, one will find the educators following quickly behind.

The urban riots and student rebellions of the late 1960s seemed to contradict the argument that education could maintain social order and serve economic interests. As stated earlier in this chapter, the Nixon administration's response to this issue was to define more rigidly the manpower-sorting function of the schools in terms of career education. But more importantly, the Nixon administration retreated from the support of federal educational programs because they no longer seemed to be serving the interests of economic power as they had in the 1950s and '60s.

CONCLUSION

7 One of the questions that has not been directly disussed so far is whether or not a national educational policy has in fact existed. It seems clear after the history given in the previous chapters that a national educational policy since 1945 has not been formulated and executed as a single, coherent plan. Our national educational policy, if there has been one, has been a product of a number of different historical events, government actions, and national public organizations. The two significant events that increased federal government involvement in education were the cold war and the civil rights movement. The cold war set the stage for federal involvement in manpower planning and curriculum development which led to the use of the Selective Service System as a channeling device, the National Defense Education Act, and the new mathematics and science curriculums sponsored by the National Science Foundation. The civil rights movement set the stage for the important battle over integration and the educational programs of the war on poverty. The story of all these events has been discussed in previous chapters.

The important question at this point is whether these actions constituted a national educational policy. In answering this, one should first recognize that elements of a national educational system exist which have a direct effect upon local educational units. The elements of this system are national in the sense that they have a national constituency and influence. The most obvious examples are organizations of professional educators, such as the National Education Association and the American Federation of Teachers. The Council for Basic Education represents another type of organization that had its origin not among professional educators but from the winds of debate that were stirred in the 1950s. In addition, magazines, television, radio, and books provide another forum for national debate. The importance of public organizations in developing and stimulating educational programs and changes is clearly represented by the civil rights movement. The NAACP fought the court battles for the *Brown* decision; and SCLC, CORE, and SNCC along with the NAACP provided the pressures for civil rights legislation and the war on poverty.

Another element that contributes to a national system of schooling is the major role of publishing companies. One of the important things learned in the development of new science and mathematics curriculums in the late 1950s was that textbooks had the most direct effect on the curriculum of local public school systems. In addition, national testing programs extend their power into local schools. The most important program in terms of a working relationship with the federal government and almost monopolistic influence over college admissions and entrance into professional schools is the Educational Testing Service.

These organizations and their influence on the federal

government and courts have already been discussed, and it should by now be recognized that they do not represent a formally organized educational system but discrete elements that provide a variety of influences on educational systems. The two most powerful groups directly formulating educational policy and providing monetary influence on the actions of local school districts are the private foundations and the federal government. It was the Carnegie Foundation which sponsored the work leading to the publication of the *American Dilemma* and Conant's study of the American high school. The Ford Foundation sponsored the early programs that were to provide the outlines of the war on poverty.

The federal government, of course, is the focal point of any discussion of the existence of a national educational policy. But even in this case, no single organization within the government has assumed sole responsibility. The courts have led the battle for school desegregation, and the Congress has followed with the passage of civil rights legislation. The U.S. Office of Education since the 1950s has emerged as the major policing agent in education as it has written and administered guidelines based on legislation passed by Congress. The executive branch has sponsored a variety of educational bills which have either died in the morass of congressional debate or have been passed as major instruments in developing a national educational policy.

Given all these different public and private organizations—which sometimes compete and sometimes work together on educational issues—there would appear to be no such thing as a single national educational policy. This would be true except for one important fact. When all the major federal legislation and actions in the area of education since 1945 are studied, and the major educational changes on a national level are considered in terms of historical development, a coherent and clear national educational policy emerges. In other words, the sum total of historical events has created a national educational policy that exists but has not been formally stated by any single individual, national organization, or government body.

This national educational policy, which is the sum of major events discussed in this volume, has been directed toward the creation of a rationalized and controlled labor market through the sorting function of the public schools and the control of social conflict arising from racial discrimination and inequalities in the distribution of income. Ideally the schools were to provide for efficient distribution of human resources to meet the needs of an increasingly stratified and organized economic system. This has been the goal of national programs such as Selective Service, the National Defense Education Act, parts of the war on poverty, and career education. In terms of controlling social conflict, the war on poverty was an attempt to institutionalize social conflict caused by the pursuit of upward social and economic mobility. Belief in the power of the school to provide economic mobility was to replace the bitterness caused by discrimination and inequalities in the social system. Disruptions in the social system caused by the pursuit of social advancement were to be curbed by focusing the American dream of opportunity within the walls of the schoolhouse and rationalizing it into competition for grades, test scores, and diplomas. This has been the statement of national educational policy which emerged from the pattern of events studied in this book.

At the conclusion of chapter 6, it was argued that this national educational policy served the interests and philosophy of American corporate expansion in the 1950s and protected corporate interests in the 1960s and '70s. On the surface this conclusion is a gross oversimplification because it suggests a picture of a conspiratorial group manipulating the educational system. As the preceding chapters have shown, important decisions about educational policy have evolved from a complex set of social and historical circumstances. What is important is that while no single individual or group determined educational policy, certain groups and individuals did emerge and played important roles in education decision making at each crucial phase of the evolution of national educational policy. These groups and individuals reflected a philosophy that was in the interest of American corporate expansion. James Conant and Vannevar Bush were directly tied to these interests, as reflected in their participation in the Committee on Present Danger. The Committee on the Conservation of Human Resources and the National Manpower Council were sponsored by a group of international corporations. The Carnegie and Ford Foundations appear at crucial times to support programs such as Conant's study of the high school and the early programs of the war on poverty. Again it should be emphasized that what is being argued is not that there was a conspiracy, but that certain types of educational philosophy received support because they reflected the interests of major economic groups.

Another way of looking at this argument is to consider possible alternative routes that were available for national educational policy and speculate on why they did not receive support. For instance, the establishment of a National Peace Foundation rather than a National Science Foundation was never given consideration or support. One would think that at a time of global tensions and potential nuclear war this would be considered a quite viable approach to the problem. Instead, American leadership concentrated on the need for increasing the supply of scientists and engineers to feed and expand the military and corporate establishments. The Selective Service System could have been organized so that there were no discriminatory deferments. It is interesting that, suddenly, class rank and test scores provided deferment from military duty in what was called the most democratic nation in the world. It should be remembered that this system of deferments was in many ways a compromise. Bush and Conant wanted only scientists and engineers to be deferred. American colleges might have witnessed the scene of large numbers of students marching around campuses dressed in the uniform of a national scientific corps.

There was also an educational philosophy in the 1950s which received some public support and could have been an alternative to the sorting-machine concept of American education. The Council for Basic Education and its leaders received a wide readership for their books and magazine articles. This philosophy argued that education should concentrate on teaching intellectual skills that would produce free individuals who would be able to understand and control their social environment. Their argument was that sorting students was not democratic because it did not provide everyone with a maximum set of intellectual skills. In fact, its leaders were so bold as to suggest that public education had begun to resemble universal military training and that individuals were being trained to serve the state and not their own freedom. What is important about the growth of the Council for Basic Education in the 1950s was that the Carnegie Foundation did not rush to their aid with financial support; instead, it supported the cold warrior James Conant in a counterattack against this libertarian philosophy.

It should also be remembered that there were alternatives to the National Defense Education Act. The National Education Association did not originally support this legislation because of its emphasis on producing scientists, engineers, and language specialists. In fact, the NEA continued its support of federal financial aid to education that would have left the determination of educational policy and decision making at the state and local level. Funding given to the National Defense Education Act and the National Science Foundation helped to guide the public schools down one particular path of development.

There were, of course, alternatives to President Johnson's war on poverty. The civil rights movement seemed always to serve as a constant source of embarrassment to American leaders and to create the fear of potential insurrection. When the NAACP won the important *Brown* decision in the 1950s, President Eisenhower avoided any public statement on the decision and expressed concern about communists in the civil rights movement ruining his chances of election. The Carnegie and Ford Foundations and the federal government could have given complete support to the activities of groups such as those led by Martin Luther King, and used them as the main force to achieve racial and economic justice. Instead, the war on poverty evolved with its army of social scientists who were to engineer community participation and tell the poor that the public schools were the answer to all major social and economic problems.

The importance for history of all these potential routes is not whether they would have been better in some fashion but that they were not taken in favor of some other path. Choices and conflicts existed, but in the end the major decisions added up to a national educational policy that sought to turn the schools into major instruments of social sorting and control for the national state. What should the future be in the formulation of a national educational policy? At one level it could be argued that there should not be a national educational policy because of the potential inherent conflict between individual needs and desires and the power of a national state. This position would argue that there should be no federal involvement in education. But at this point in time it is probably too late to cut all ties between the national government and education. Court decisions, government legislation, and the Office of Education have left an indelible pattern on American education. In addition, private national educational groups would continue to exist and exert tremendous influence over the functioning of local schools. The power of national testing organizations would probably continue. No program or blueprint for future action can be given until the American people become aware that education can be used for either liberation or social enslavement and that education is not good in and of itself. It is hoped that this book will aid in an understanding of this issue and that we might begin to formulate a national educational philosophy based on individual liberty, not on service to the state and corporate interests.

NOTES

Chapter 1.
THE NATIONAL BATTLE OF THE
SCHOOLS

1. A large number of historical works are available on the variety of arguments given for the support of public schooling. The best introduction for arguments dealing with the necessity of public schooling for building a political community is Rush Welter, *Popular Education and Democratic Thought in America* (New York: Columbia University Press, 1962). An introduction to the arguments given for schooling as a means of reducing crime and producing social training for an industrial society is Michael B. Katz, *The Irony of Early School Reform* (Boston: Beacon Press, 1972). The concern about Americanization and social reform is detailed in Marvin Lazerson, *Origins of the Urban School: Public Education in Massachusetts, 1870–1915* (Cambridge, Mass.: Harvard University Press, 1971).

2. Edward Krug, *The Shaping of the American High School* (New York: Harper & Row, 1964), shows how these arguments influenced the development of the high school. Joel Spring, *Education and the Rise of the Cor-*

porate State (Boston: Beacon Press, 1972), shows how these arguments reflected the ideological changes in American liberalism at the beginning of the twentieth century. *American Education and Vocationalism* (New York: Teachers College Press, 1974), edited by Marvin Lazerson and W. Norton Grubb, provides an introduction into how these arguments were reflected in the development of vocational education. Articles on the testing movement can be found in *Roots of Crisis* by Clarence Karier, Paul Violas, and Joel Spring (Chicago: Rand McNally, 1973).

3.   Richard Barnes Kennan, "No Ivory Tower for You," *NEA Journal* 40 (May 1951): 317–18.

4.   Richard Hofstadter, *Anti-Intellectualism in American Life* (New York: Random House, 1962), pp. 3–55.

5.   David Hulburd, *This Happened in Pasadena* (New York: Macmillan, 1951); James B. Boyle, "Pasadena, Calif.," *Saturday Review of Literature,* 8 September 1951, pp. 7–8. Some authors have sought to play down the role of anticommunism in the Pasadena school controversy. For an interpretation of this, see Mortimer Smith's *The Diminished Mind* (Chicago: Henry Regnery, 1954), pp. 114–29.

6.   Mary Anne Raywid, *The Ax-Grinders* (New York: Macmillan, 1963).

7.   Ibid., p. 50.

8.   Lawrence Martin, "Denver, Colo."; August J. Wiesner, Jr., "Englewood, N.J."; Louis Engel, "Port Washington, N.Y." All these articles can be found in the *Saturday Review of Literature,* 8 September 1951, pp. 6-13.

9.   Hulburd, *This Happened in Pasadena,* pp. 90–91.

10.   Ibid., pp. 107–8.

11.   See Spring, *Education and the Rise of the Corporate State,* pp. 62–125.

12.   See Joel Spring, "Education and Progressivism," *History of Education Quarterly* 10 (Spring 1970): 53–71.

13.   Lawrence Cremin, *The Transformation of the School* (New York: Random House, 1961), pp. 240–74.

14.   Martin, "Denver," pp. 9–10.

15.   Hulburd, *This Happened in Pasadena,* p. 109.

16.   Ibid., p. 106.

17.   Robert Shaplen, "Scarsdale's Battle of the Books," *Commentary* (December 1950): 530–40.

18.   Jack Nelson and Gene Roberts, Jr., *The Censors and the Schools* (Boston: Little, Brown, 1963), pp. 40–53.

19.   *Official Statement by The American Textbook Publishers Institute,* April 1953. This statement can be found in C. Winfield Scott and Clyde M. Hill, *Public Education Under Criticism* (New York: Prentice-Hall, 1954), pp. 337–38.

20.   Arthur Bestor, "Proposals for a Permanent Scientific and Scholarly Commission on Secondary Education," in *Educational Wastelands* (Urbana: University of Illinois Press, 1953), pp. 197–98.

21.   Ibid., p. 203.

22.   Bestor, *Educational Wastelands,* p. 3.

23.   See Lawrence Cremin, ed., *The Republic and the School* (New York: Teachers College Press, 1957).

24.   See Lazerson, *Origins of the Urban School.*

25.   Krug, *Shaping the American High School,* chaps. 1–4.

26.   Franklin R. Zeran, "Life Adjustment in Action,

1944–1952," in *Life Adjustment Education in Action,* ed. Franklin R. Zeran (New York: Chartwell House, 1953), pp. 33–53.

27.　Ibid., p. 36.

28.　Ibid., pp. 37–52.

29.　Bestor, *Educational Wastelands,* p. 86.

30.　Ibid., pp. 36-38.

31.　Ibid., pp. 36-38.

32.　Ibid., pp. 101-121.

33.　Ibid., p. 120.

34.　Albert Lynd, *Quackery in the Public Schools* (Boston: Little, Brown, 1953), p. 73.

35.　Ibid., p. 136.

36.　Ibid., p. 225.

37.　Bestor, *Educational Wastelands,* pp. 204–5.

38.　Original statement of purpose of Council for Basic Education can be found in Raywid, *Ax-Grinders,* pp. 89–90.

39.　Harold Clapp, "The Stranglehold on Education," *Bulletin of the American Association of University Professors* 35, no. 2 (Summer 1949).

40.　Harry J. Fuller, "The Emperor's New Clothes, or Primus Dementat," *Scientific Monthly* 72 (January 1951): 32–41.

41.　Mortimer Smith, *And Madly Teach: A Layman Looks at Public School Education* (Chicago: Henry Regnery, 1949), p. 86.

42.　Ibid., p. 30.

43. Ibid., p. 35.

44. Ibid., pp. 91–93.

45. Ibid., pp. 21–25.

46. Ibid., pp. 59–60.

47. James D. Koerner, ed. *The Case for Basic Education* (Boston: Little, Brown, 1959).

48. James D. Koerner, *The Miseducation of American Teachers* (Baltimore: Penguin Books, 1965) and *Who Controls American Education?* (Boston: Beacon Press, 1968).

49. Koerner, *Who Controls American Education?*, p. 155.

50. Quoted by Edward R. Murrow in foreword to Hyman G. Rickover's *Education and Freedom* (New York: E. P. Dutton, 1959), pp. 5–7.

51. Ibid., pp. 39–52.

52. Ibid., p. 45.

53. Ibid., p. 33.

54. Ibid., p. 192.

55. Edgar Gumbert and Joel Spring, *The Superschool and the Superstate* (New York: John Wiley & Sons, 1974), pp. 87–115.

56. Rickover, *Education and Freedom,* pp. 111–30.

57. James B. Conant, *My Several Lives*: *Memoirs of a Social Inventor* (New York: Harper & Row, 1970), p. 621.

58. James B. Conant, *The American High School Today* (New York: McGraw-Hill, 1959), p. 38.

59. Ibid., p. 43.

60.   Conant, *My Several Lives,* pp. 621–22.

61.   C. Wright Mills, *The Power Elite* (New York: Oxford University Press, 1956).

62.   Conant, *My Several Lives,* pp. 234–304.

63.   Ibid., p. 515.

64.   Ibid., p. 533.

65.   Ibid., pp. 613–16.

66.   C. C. Brigham, *A Study of American Intelligence* (Princeton, N.J.: Princeton University, 1923).

67.   Conant, *My Several Lives,* pp. 417–32.

68.   Conant, *American High School,* p. 20.

69.   See Thomas Grissom, "Education and the Cold War: The Role of James B. Conant," in Karier, Violas, and Spring, *Roots of Crisis,* pp. 177–98.

70.   James B. Conant, *The Child, The Parent and The States* (Cambridge, Mass.: Harvard University Press, 1959), p. 39.

71.   Ibid., pp. 42–43.

72.   Conant, *American High School,* p, 49.

73.   Ibid., p. 50.

74.   Ibid., p. 52.

75.   Ibid., p. 74.

76.   Ibid., pp. 75–76.

Chapter 2.
THE CHANNELING OF MANPOWER IN A DEMOCRATIC SOCIETY

1. Dael Wolfle, "America's Intellectual Resources," *National Association of Secondary-School Principals* (January 1952): 125–35.

2. Tom C. Clark, "Letter From the Attorney General Concerning the Constitutionality of a Universal Training Program," in *A Program For National Security: Report of the President's Advisory Commission on Universal Training* (Washington, D.C.: Government Printing Office, 1947), pp. 155–60.

3. "Staff Study on: Universal Military Training in the United States: A Brief Historical Summary," in ibid., p. 397.

4. Ibid., p. 409.

5. Joel Spring, *Education and the Rise of the Corporate State* (Boston: Beacon Press, 1972), pp. 91–107.

6. Ibid., pp. 108–26.

7. Joel Spring, "Youth Culture in the United States," in *Roots of Crisis,* ed. Clarence Karier, Paul Violas, and Joel Spring (Chicago: Rand McNally, 1973), pp. 198–215.

8. Edward Krug, *The Shaping of the American High School 1920–1941,* vol. 2 (Madison: University of Wisconsin Press, 1972).

9. Merle Borrowman and Charles Burgess, *What Doctrines to Embrace* (Glenview, Ill.: Scott, Foresman, 1969), pp. 113-43.

10. George C. Marshall, "War Department Circular 347," reprinted in *A Program For National Security,* pp. 397–99.

11. "Staff Study," pp. 401–6.

12. Ibid., p. 408.

13. *A Program for National Security,* p. 63.

14. Ibid., p. 39.

15. Ibid., p. 63.

16. Ibid., p. 62.

17. "The Status of the Health, Education and Well-Being of Children in Relation to National Security," in ibid., pp. 185–209.

18. Ibid., p. 71.

19. Ibid., p. 81.

20. Russell F. Weigley, *History of the United States Army* (New York: Macmillan, 1967), pp. 496–500.

21. *Universal Military Training and Service Act of 1951—Hearings before the Preparedness Subcommittee of the Committee on Armed Services, United States Senate, Eighty-second Congress, First Session, January 10-February 2* (Washington, D.C.: Government Printing Office, 1951), p. 21.

22. Ibid., p. 52.

23. Ibid., pp. 37–53.

24. Ibid., pp. 54–57.

25. Ibid., pp. 444–63.

26. Ibid., p. 817.

27. Ibid., pp. 820–21.

28. Ibid., pp. 819, 825–35.

29. Ibid., pp. 1081–91.

30.   Vannevar Bush, *Pieces of the Action* (New York: William Morrow, 1970), pp. 1–25.

31.   Vannevar Bush, *Science—The Endless Frontier: A Report to the President* (Washington, D.C.: Government Printing Office, 1945); Dorothy Schaffter, *The National Science Foundation* (New York: Frederick Praeger, 1969).

32.   Bush, *Science—The Endless Frontier,* pp. 20–21.

33.   Bush, *Pieces of the Action,* pp. 65–66.

34.   *Universal Military Training and Service Act of 1951,* pp. 1082–83.

35.   *Hearings before the Committee on Interstate and Foreign Commerce, Eightieth Congress, First Session on Bills Relating to the National Science Foundation, March 6 and 7, 1947* (Washington, D.C.: Government Printing Office, 1947), p. 147.

36.   Ibid., pp. 155–57.

37.   *Universal Military Training and Service Act of 1951,* p. 833.

38.   Ibid., pp. 838–60.

39.   National Manpower Council, *Student Deferment and National Manpower Policy* (New York: Columbia University Press, 1951), pp. 30–32.

40.   Henry David, *Manpower Policies for a Democratic Society* (New York: Columbia University Press, 1965), p. vi.

41.   Howard Snyder, "Foreword," in Eli Ginzberg's *The Lost Divisions* (New York: Columbia University Press, 1959), pp. xvi–xx.

42.   Ibid., pp. 151–66.

43.   National Manpower Council, *Student Deferment,* pp. 8–9.

44.   Ibid., pp. 11–13.

45.   Ibid., p. 63; *Statistical Studies of Selective Service Testing 1951–1953* (Princeton, N.J.: Educational Testing Service, 1955).

46.   National Manpower Council, *Student Deferment,* pp. 62–63.

47.   Ibid., pp. 68–69.

48.   National Manpower Council, *A Policy for Scientific and Professional Manpower* (New York: Columbia University Press, 1953), pp. vii–xvi.

49.   Ibid., p. 255.

50.   National Manpower Council, *A Policy for Skilled Manpower* (New York: Columbia University Press, 1954), p. 138.

51.   Ibid., p. 139.

52.   Michael Katz, *The Irony of Early School Reform* (Boston: Beacon Press, 1972).

53.   Spring, *Education and Rise of Corporate State,* pp. 44–61.

54.   National Manpower Council, *A Policy for Skilled Manpower,* pp. 139–40.

55.   Ibid., pp. 275–78.

56.   National Manpower Council, *Womanpower* (New York: Columbia University Press, 1957), p. 5.

57.   Quoted in David, *Manpower Policies,* p. 7.

58.   Ibid., pp. 9–16.

Chapter 3.
THE DEVELOPMENT OF A NATIONAL CURRICULUM

1.   See Paul E. Marsh and Ross A. Gortner, *Federal Aid to Science Education: Two Programs* (Syracuse: Syracuse University Press, 1963), pp. 9–14.

2.   Ibid., p. 11.

3.   Dwight D. Eisenhower, "Our Future Security," reprinted in *Science and Education for National Defense: Hearings before the Committee on Labor and Public Welfare United States Senate Eighty-fifth Congress Second Session* (Washington, D.C.: Government Printing Office, 1958), pp. 1357–59.

4.   Ibid., p. 1360.

5.   Dwight D. Eisenhower, "Message from the President of the United States Transmitting Recommendations Relative to Our Educational System," reprinted in *Science and Education for National Defense,* pp. 195–96. Also see Dwight D. Eisenhower, *Waging Peace 1956–1961* (New York: Doubleday, 1965), pp. 239–62.

6.   Ibid., pp. 196–97.

7.   A reprint of the 1958 NDEA can be found in Raymond F. McCoy, *American School Administration* (New York: McGraw-Hill, 1961), pp. 421–52.

8.   "Statement of William G. Carr, Executive Secretary, National Education Association," *Science and Education for National Defense,* p. 475.

9.   For a study concentrating on the federal aid issue during the 1950s, see Frank J. Munger and Richard F. Fenno, Jr., *National Politics and Federal Aid to Education* (Syracuse: Syracuse University Press, 1962).

10.   Ibid., pp. 19–76.

11.   "Statement of William G. Carr," pp. 479–80.

12.   Ibid., p. 481.

13.   Ibid., pp. 482–95.

14.   Ibid., pp. 502–10.

15.   "Statement of Doctor Detlev A. Bronk, President of the National Academy of Sciences and National Research Council," *Science and Education for National Defense,* p. 6.

16.   Ibid., p. 7.

17.   Ibid., p. 8.

18.   Ibid., pp. 5–9.

19.   Ibid., pp. 11–15.

20.   "Statement of M. H. Trytten, Director, Office of Scientific Personnel," *Science and Education for National Defense,* pp. 575–82.

21.   "Statement of Wernher Von Braun, Director, Development Operations Division, Army Ballistic Missile Agency, Huntsville, Alabama," *Science and Education for National Defense,* pp. 64–84.

22.   "Statement of Dr. Edward Teller, Physicist at the Radiation Laboratory, University of California," *Science and Education for National Defense,* pp. 130–39.

23.   "Statement of Dr. Lee A. DuBridge, President of California Institute of Technology," *Science and Education for National Defense,* pp. 36–55.

24.   Jerrold R. Zacharias and Stephen White, "The Requirements for Major Curriculum Revision," in *New*

Curricula, ed. Robert W. Heath (New York: Harper & Row, 1964), p. 80.

25. Ibid.

26. Reprinted in Marsh and Gortner, *Federal Aid to Science Education,* p. 20.

27. A history of the development of PSSC can be found in "The Requirements for Major Curriculum Revision," pp. 78–81, and Marsh and Gortner, *Federal Aid to Science Education,* pp. 15–58.

28. Zacharias and White, "Requirements for Major Curriculum Revision," p. 79.

29. Marsh and Gortner, *Federal Aid to Science Education,* pp. 43–51.

30. Ibid., pp. 45–47.

31. Ibid., p. 62.

32. Ibid., pp. 58–63.

33. William Wooton, *SMSG: The Making of a Curriculum* (New Haven: Yale University Press, 1965), pp. 13–14.

34. Ibid., p. 20.

35. See "Imagination + X = Learning," *Carnegie Corporation of New York Quarterly* 5, no. 4 (October 1957), reprinted in *Science and Education for National Defense,* pp. 1466–70; and Max Beberman, "An Emerging Program of Secondary School Mathematics," in Heath, *New Curricula,* pp. 9–35.

36. "Imagination + X = Learning," pp. 1470–71.

37. Wooton, *SMSG,* PP. 7–9.

38. Ibid., pp. 17–43.

39. Ibid., pp. 61–81.

40. Ibid., pp. 82–104.

41. Ibid., pp. 124–25.

42. Ibid., pp. 133–34.

43. See Bentley Glass, "Renascent Biology: A Report of the AIBS Biological Sciences Curriculum," in Heath, *New Curricula,* pp. 94–120.

44. See J. A. Campbell, "CHEM Study—An Approach to Chemistry Based on Experiments," in ibid., pp. 82–94.

45. Gordon B. Turner, "The American Council of Learned Societies and Curriculum Revision," in ibid., p. 147.

46. Jerome S. Bruner, *The Process of Education* (New York: Vintage Books, 1960), pp. vii–xvi.

47. Ibid., p. 1.

48. Jerome S. Bruner, Jacqueline J. Goodnow, and George A. Austin, *A Study of Thinking* (New York: John Wiley & Sons, 1956), pp. vii–x.

49. Ibid., pp. 1–24, 231–46.

50. Bruner, *The Process of Education,* p. 17.

51. Ibid., p. 24.

52. Ibid., pp. 23–24.

53. Ibid., pp. 33–54.

54. Ibid., p. 38.

55. Ibid., p. 9.

56. Ibid., p. 73.

57. Ibid., pp. 76–77.

58.   Ibid., p. 77.

59.   Jerome S. Bruner, *On Knowing: Essays for the Left Hand* (New York: Atheneum, 1962), p. 118.

60.   Ibid., p. 121.

Chapter 4.
THE CIVIL RIGHTS MOVEMENT

1. See Bernard Schwartz, ed., *Statutory History of the United States, Civil Rights, Part II* (New York: McGraw-Hill, 1970), p. 1160.

2. "A. Philip Randolph's Call to the March on Washington of 1941," *Black Worker,* May 1941, p. 4, reprinted in *The Afro-Americans: Selected Documents,* ed. John H. Bracey, Jr., August Meier, and Elliott Rudwick (Boston: Allyn & Bacon, 1972), pp. 611–14.

3. See Louis Coleridge Kesselman, *The Social Politics of FEPC: A Study in Reform Pressure Movements* (Chapel Hill: University of North Carolina Press, 1948), pp. 3–24.

4. *The Statistical History of the United States from Colonial Times to the Present* (Stamford, Conn.: Fairfield Publishers, 1965), p. 218.

5. *To Secure These Rights: The Report of the President's Committee on Civil Rights* (New York: Simon & Schuster, 1947), p. 139.

6. Ibid., pp. 141–46.

7. Ibid., pp. 146–48.

8. Monroe Billington, "Civil Rights, President Truman and the South," *Journal of Negro History* 58, no. 2 (April 1973): 127–39.

9. For a description of this conflict, see Harry Truman, *Memoirs, Volume Two, Years of Trial and Hope* (New York: Doubleday, 1956), pp. 170–87.

10. *To Secure These Rights,* pp. 112–14.

11. *Plessy* v. *Ferguson,* 163 U.S. 537 (1896). For a discussion of the case, see Albert P. Blaustein and Clarence

Clyde Ferguson, Jr., *Desegregation and the Law: The Meaning and Effect of the School Segregation Cases* (New Brunswick, N.J.: Rutgers University Press, 1957), pp. 95–113.

12.   *To Secure These Rights,* p. 113.

13.   See Blaustein and Ferguson, *Desegregation and the Law,* pp. 15–38.

14.   Ibid., pp. 39–53.

15.   Ibid., pp. 11–14.

16.   Ibid., pp. 126–37.

17.   *Brown et al.* v. *Board of Education of Topeka et al.* Reprinted in Blaustein and Ferguson, *Desegregation and the Law,* pp. 273–82.

18.   Kenneth Clark, "The Background: The Role of Social Scientists," *Journal of Social Issues* 10, no. 4 (1953): 2–8.

19.   Kenneth Clark, "The Effects of Prejudice and Discrimination," in *Personality in the Making: The Fact-Finding Report of the Midcentury White House Conference on Children and Youth* ed. Helen Witmer and Ruth Kotinsky (New York: Harper & Brothers, 1952), pp. 135–59.

20.   "The Effects of Segregation and the Consequences of Desegregation: A Social Science Statement," Appendix to Appellants' Brief filed in the *School Segregation Cases,* in the Supreme Court of the United States, October term, 1952. Reprinted in Bracey, Meier, and Rudwick, *Afro-American,* pp. 661–71.

21.   Ibid., pp. 663–65.

22.   Gunnar Myrdal, *An American Dilemma: The Negro Problem and Modern Democracy* (New York: Harper & Brothers, 1944), p. lx.

23. Ibid., pp. li–lxvii.

24. Ibid., p. lxxi.

25. Ibid., pp. lxxii–lxxiii.

26. Ibid., pp. 75–80, 207–19.

27. Ibid., p. 208.

28. Ibid.

29. Ibid., p. 1067.

30. Ibid., pp. 1060–65.

31. "Effects of Segregation and Consequences of Desegregation," pp. 668–71.

32. Enforcement decree reprinted in Blaustein and Ferguson, *Desegregation and the Law,* pp. 273–82.

33. Gary Orfield, *The Reconstruction of Southern Education: The Schools and the 1964 Civil Rights Act* (New York: Wiley-Interscience, 1969), pp. 15–32; and Blaustein and Ferguson, *Desegregation and the Law,* pp. 240–73.

34. Henry Allen Bullock, *A History of Negro Education in the South from 1619 to the Present* (New York: Praeger, 1970), pp. 231–62.

35. Dwight D. Eisenhower, *Waging Peace, 1956–1961* (New York: Doubleday, 1965), p. 150.

36. Ibid., pp. 151–52.

37. Ibid., p. 152.

38. Ibid., 162.

39. Ibid., p. 168.

40. "Eisenhower's Address on the Situation in Little Rock, September 24, 1957," *New York Times,* 25 Sep-

tember 1957, p. 14. Reprinted in *Civil Rights and the American Negro* ed. Albert Blaustein and Robert Zangrando (New York: Trident Press, 1968), pp. 456–58.

41.   The history of the development of CORE can be found in August Meier and Elliot Rudwick, *CORE: A Study in the Civil Rights Movement 1942–1968* (New York: Oxford University Press, 1973). The story of A. J. Muste's early involvement in school reform can be found in Joel Spring's *Education and the Rise of the Corporate State* (Boston: Beacon Press, 1972), pp. 143–48.

42.   Quoted in Meier and Rudwick, *CORE,* p. 5.

43.   Ibid., pp. 3–39.

44.   For a summary of the intellectual influences on Martin Luther King's early development, see David L. Lewis, *King: A Critical Biography* (New York: Praeger, 1970); and Martin Luther King, Jr., *Stride Toward Freedom: The Montgomery Story* (New York: Harper & Brothers, 1958), pp. 90–107.

45.   King, *Stride Toward Freedom,* p. 91.

46.   Ibid.

47.   Ibid., pp. 94–95.

48.   Ibid., pp. 96–97.

49.   A description of events in Montgomery is in King's *Stride Toward Freedom* and Lewis's, *King,* p. 84. A detailed account, including map, can be found in William Robert Miller, *Martin Luther King, Jr.: His Life, Martyrdom and Meaning for the World* (New York: Weybright & Talley, 1968), pp. 30–56.

50.   Lewis, *King,* pp. 87–89.

51.   Ibid., pp. 91–93.

52.   See Eisenhower, *Waging Peace,* pp. 153–62.

53. Quoted in ibid, p. 160.

54. The origins of the Civil Rights Act of 1957 including reprints of major speeches and congressional debate can be found in Schwartz, *Statutory History of the United States,* pp. 837–935.

55. Ibid., p. 935.

56. "Special Message to Congress by the President, February 5, 1960," reprinted in ibid., pp. 947–49.

57. Quoted in ibid. p. 938.

58. Meier and Rudwick, *CORE,* pp. 101–31; Lewis, *King,* pp. 112–39.

59. Lewis, *King,* pp. 115–17.

60. For details of school controversy in Chicago, see Orfield, *Reconstruction of Southern Education,* pp. 151–208.

61. Quoted in Lewis, *King,* p. 171.

62. See James C. Harvey, *Civil Rights During the Kennedy Administration* (Jackson: University and College Press of Mississippi, 1971).

63. A description of events at Birmingham can be found in Benjamin Muse, *American Negro Revolution: From Nonviolence to Black Power, 1963–1967* (Bloomington: Indiana University Press), pp. 26–39; and Lewis, *King,* pp. 171–209.

64. Details on the March on Washington can be found in Muse, *American Negro Revolution,* pp. 1-17; and Lewis, *King,* pp. 220–31.

65. "Special Message to Congress by the President, June 19, 1963," reprinted in Schwartz, *Statutory History of the United States,* pp. 1055–63.

66.   Ibid., pp. 1017–20.

67.   See James C. Harvey, *Black Civil Rights During the Johnson Administration* (Jackson: University and College Press of Mississippi, 1973), pp. 3–26.

68.   Reprint of major parts of congressional debate can be found in Schwartz, *Statutory History of the United States,* pp. 1080–453.

69.   See I.M. Labovitz, *Aid for Federally Affected Public Schools* (Syracuse: Syracuse University Press, 1963).

70.   As quoted in Orfield, *Reconstruction of Southern Education,* p. 36.

71.   In reprint of House and Senate debates, in Schwartz, *Statutory History of the United States,* p. 1212.

72.   See Orfield, *Reconstruction of Southern Education,* pp. 47–101.

73.   See Harvey, *Black Civil Rights During the Johnson Administration,* p. 171.

74.   Congressional Quarterly Almanac 21, p. 568. "Desegregation," *Southern Education Report* 1 (November-December 1965): 30, 32.

75.   U.S. Commission on Civil Rights, *Southern School Desegregation 1966–67* (Washington D.C.: Government Printing Office, 1967), pp. 141–45.

76.   Martin L. Cooper, "The New School Desegregation Guidelines," *Harvard Civil Rights—Civil Liberties Review* 2 (Fall 1966): 89–90.

77.   James W. Prothro, "Stateways Versus Folkways Revisited: An Error in Prediction," *Journal of Politics* 34 (May 1972): 356–57.

78.   See Harvey, *Black Civil Rights During the Johnson Administration,* p. 206.

79.   Orfield, *Reconstruction of Southern Education,* p. 151.

80.   Ibid., pp. 152–59.

81.   Ibid., pp. 159–207.

82.   U.S. Commission on Civil Rights, *Racial Isolation in the Public Schools* (Washington, D.C.: Government Printing Office, 1967), 1: 199–200.

Chapter 5.
THE WAR ON POVERTY

1. U.S. Department of Labor, *Statistics on Manpower: A Supplement to the Manpower Report to the President* (Washington, D.C.: Government Printing Office, 1969), p. 15.

2. This story was told by Walter Heller in a speech at Indiana State College, Indiana, Pennsylvania, 26 March 1965. See James L. Sundquist, "Origins of the War on Poverty," in *On Fighting Poverty,* ed. James L. Sundquist (New York: Basic Books, 1969), p. 7.

3. Michael Harrington, *The Other America: Poverty in the United States* (New York: Macmillan, 1962).

4. See Sundquist, *On Fighting Poverty,* pp. 21–25.

5. "The Problem of Poverty in America," *The Annual Report of the Council of Economic Advisers* (Washington, D.C.: Government Printing Office, 1964).

6. A description of this meeting is given by Lyndon Baines Johnson in *The Vantage Point: Perspectives of the Presidency 1963–1969* (New York: Holt, Rinehart & Winston, 1971), pp. 72–73.

7. Ibid., p. 72.

8. Ibid., p. 73.

9. Lyndon B. Johnson, "The State of the Union Message to Congress, 8 January 1964," reprinted in *A Time for Action: A Selection from the Speeches and Writings of Lyndon B. Johnson 1953–1964* (New York:Atheneum, 1964), pp. 164–79.

10. A comparison of the CCC with the Job Corps can be found in John Gilbert Herlihy's "A Comparison of the Educational Purposes of Two Federal Youth Programs:

The Civilian Conservation Corps and the Job Corps of the Economic Opportunity Act of 1964" (Ph.D. dissertation, University of Connecticut, 1966).

11.   National Committee for Children and Youth, *Social Dynamite* (Washington, D.C.: The Committee, 1961).

12.   See Herlihy, "Two Federal Youth Programs," pp. 104–6; and Garth L. Mangum, *MDTA: Foundation of Federal Manpower Policy* (Baltimore: Johns Hopkins Press, 1968), pp. 9–26.

13.   Peter Marris and Martin Rein, *Dilemmas of Social Reform: Poverty and Community Action in the United States* (Chicago: Aldine, 1973), p. 11.

14.   Ibid., pp. 7–32; Sundquist, *On Fighting Poverty,* pp. 8–14; and Daniel P. Moynihan, *Maximum Feasible Misunderstanding: Community Action in the War on Poverty* (New York: Free Press, 1969), pp. 38–75.

15.   Sundquist, *On Fighting Poverty,* p. 11.

16.   Richard A. Cloward and Lloyd E. Ohlin, *Delinquency and Opportunity: A Theory of Delinquent Gangs* (New York: Free Press, 1960).

17.   Quoted in Sundquist, *On Fighting Poverty,* p. 11.

18.   The best discussion of the theory and assumptions of community action can be found in Marris and Rein, *Dilemmas of Social Reform,* pp. 7–56. A highly critical evaluation of community action theory can be found in Moynihan's *Maximum Feasible Misunderstanding.*

19.   Sundquist. *On Fighting Poverty,* pp. 25–28; and Johnson, *Vantage Point,* pp. 75–87.

20.   *Economic Opportunity Act of 1964, Hearings before the Subcommittee on the War on Poverty Program of the Committee on Education and Labor, House*

of Representatives, Eighty-eighth Congress, Second Session (Washington, D.C.: Government Printing Office, 1964), p. 20.

21.   Ibid., p. 21.

22.   Ibid., pp. 26–93.

23.   *Economic Opportunity Act of 1964, Public Law 88-452—August 20, 1964.*

24.   Herlihy, "Two Federal Youth Programs," pp. 104–6.

25.   President's Task Force on Manpower Conservation, *One-Third of a Nation* (Washington, D.C.: Government Printing Office, 1964).

26.   Herlihy, "Two Federal Youth Programs," p. 118.

27.   Ibid., p. 124.

28.   *Economic Opportunity Act of 1964.*

29.   Ibid.

30.   See Sar A. Levitan, *The Great Society's Poor Law: A New Approach to Poverty* (Baltimore: Johns Hopkins University Press, 1969), pp. 109–31; and Moynihan, *Maximum Feasible Misunderstanding,* pp. 128–67.

31.   Levitan, *Great Society's Poor Law,* p. 123.

32.   Ibid., pp. 135–36.

33.   Ibid., pp. 136–38.

34.   There was a vast amount of literature on the education of the culturally or educationally disadvantaged student during this period. The best guide to the literature available on this topic during the early 1960s is a 112-page annotated bibliography published as part of a national research conference on education and cultural deprivation. This bibliography can be found in Ben-

jamin S. Bloom, Allison Davis, and Robert Hess, *Compensatory Education for Cultural Deprivation* (New York: Holt, Rinehart & Winston, 1965), pp. 67–179.

35.   A. B. Hollingshead, *Elmstown's Youth* (New York: John Wiley & Sons, 1949).

36.   Lyndon B. Johnson, Commencement address, Howard University, Washington, D.C., 4 June 1965. Reprinted in *Civil Rights and the American Negro: A Documentary History,* ed. Albert Blaustein and Robert Zangrando (New York: Trident Press, 1968), pp. 558–66.

37.   James Bryant Conant, *Slums and Suburbs* (New York: McGraw-Hill, 1961).

38.   Bloom, Davis, and Hess, *Compensatory Education,* pp. i–vi.

39.   Ibid., p. 1.

40.   Ibid., p. 2.

41.   Ibid., p. 5.

42.   *Elementary and Secondary Education Act of 1965, Hearings before the Subcommittee on Education of the Committee on Labor and Public Welfare, United States Senate, Eighty-ninth Congress, First Session* (Washington, D.C.: Government Printing Office, 1965), pp. 500–512.

43.   Educational Policies Commission, *Education and the Disadvantaged American* (Washington, D.C.: National Education Association, 1962).

44.   Frank Riessman, *The Culturally Deprived Child* (New York: Harper & Row, 1962), p. 3.

45.   Bloom, Davis, and Hess, *Compensatory Education,* p. 4.

46.   Frederick Bertolaet, "The Education of Disadvan-

taged Youth," reprinted in *Elementary and Secondary Education Act of 1965 Hearings,* pp. 501–10.

47.   Ibid., p. 501.

48.   Johnson, Commencment Address.

49.   Daniel P. Moynihan, "The Case for a Family Policy," in *Coping: Essays on the Practice of Government* (New York: Random House, 1973), pp. 53–69.

50.   Riessman, *Culturally Deprived Child,* pp. 1–16.

51.   Examples of research studies supporting this argument are A. R. Jensen, "Learning in the Pre-School Year," *Journal of Nursery Education* 18, no. 2 (1964): 133–38; J. Mc. V. Hunt, "The Psychological Basis for Using Pre-School Enrichment as an Antidote for Cultural Deprivation," *Merrill-Palmer Quarterly* 10 (1964): 209–34; M. Deutsch, "The Disadvantaged Child and the Learning Process," in *Education in Depressed Areas* ed. A. H. Passow (New York: Teachers College Press, 1963), pp. 163–80. Also see Riessman, *Culturally Deprived Child,* pp. 36–63; Bloom, Davis, and Hess, *Compensatory Education,* pp. 8–19.

52.   A history of the IQ debate in the twentieth century can be found in Edgar Gumbert and Joel Spring, *The Superschool & the Superstate: American Education in the Twentieth Century, 1918–1970* (New York: John Wiley & Sons, 1974), pp. 87–115.

53.   Examples of research supporting the argument that environment had a significant effect on IQ scores are Allison Davis, *Social–Class Influences upon Learning* (Cambridge, Mass.: Harvard University Press, 1948); M. Deutsch, J. Fishman et al., "Guidelines for Testing Minority Group Children," *Journal of Social Issues* 20, no. 2 (1964): 129–45; K. Eells, *Intelligence and Cultural Differences* (Chicago: University of Chicago Press,

1951). Also see Riessman, *Culturally Deprived Child,* pp. 49–63; and Bloom, Davis, and Hess, *Compensatory Education,* pp. 12, 71–72.

54.   *Amendments to the Economic Opportunity Act of 1964, Hearings before the Subcommittee on Employment, Manpower, and Poverty of the Committee on Labor and Public Welfare, United States Senate, Eighty-ninth Congress.* (Washington, D.C.: Government Printing Office, 1966), pp. 44–45.

55.   Ibid., p. 1386.

56.   Ibid., pp. 1386–88.

57.   Ibid., p. 45.

58.   Ibid., p. 1385.

59.   Johnson, *Vantage Point*, p. 207–8.

60.   Ibid., pp. 209–19; and Stephen K. Bailey and Edith K. Mosher, *ESEA: The Office of Education Administers a Law* (Syracuse: Syracuse University Press, 1968), pp. 40-71.

61.   Eugene Eidinberg and Roy D. Morey's *An Act of Congress: The Legislative Process and the Making of Education Policy* (New York: W. W. Norton, 1969) provides a very detailed study of the congressional history of the Elementary and Secondary Education Act of 1965.

62.   *Elementary and Secondary Education Act of 1965, Public Law 89-10,* reprinted in Bailey and Mosher, *ESEA,* pp. 235–66.

63.   *Aid to Elementary and Secondary Education, Hearings before the General Subcommittee on Education of the Committee on Education and Labor House of Representatives, Eighty-ninth Congress, First Session*

(Washington, D.C.: Government Printing Office, 1965), pp. 63–82.

64. Ibid., pp. 82–113.

65. Ibid., p. 63.

Chapter 6.
CAREER EDUCATION AND EQUALITY OF
EDUCATIONAL OPPORTUNITY

1. Census Bureau, *Long-Term Economic Growth: 1860–1965* (Washington, D.C.: Government Printing Office, 1966), 196–97.

2. For a survey of the alternative school movement, see Allen Graubard, *Free the Children* (New York: Pantheon, 1972).

3. Ivan Illich, *Deschooling Society* (New York: Harper & Row, 1972).

4. For a description of urban riots, see Benjamin Muse, *The American Negro Revolution* (Bloomington: Indiana University Press), pp. 111–31, 204–18, 290–326.

5. For a description of this decision, see Lyndon Baines Johnson, *The Vantage Point* (New York: Holt, Rinehart & Winston, 1971), pp. 532–61.

6. For a discussion of the attempts to establish a volunteer armed force, see *Volunteer Armed Force and Selective Service, Hearing before the Subcommittee on the Volunteer Armed Force and Selective Service of the Committee on Armed Services, U.S. Senate, Ninety-second Congress* (Washington, D.C.: Government Printing Office, 1972).

7. Sidney P. Marland, Jr., "The Endless Renaissance," *American Education* 8, no. 3 (April 1972): 9.

8. Sidney P. Marland, Jr., "The School's Role in Career Development," *Educational Leadership* 30, no. 3 (December 1972): 203–5.

9. Sidney P. Marland, Jr., "The Condition of Education in the Nation," *American Education* 7, no. 3 (April 1971): 4.

10. "Quoting Marland," *American Education* 7, no. 1 (January–February 1971): 4.

11. Marland, "Condition of Education," p. 4.

12. Robert M. Worthington, "A Home-Community Based Career Education Model," *Educational Leadership* 30, no. 3 (December 1972): 213.

13. Marland, "School's Role," p. 204.

14. Sidney P. Marland, Jr., "Career Education and the Two-Year Colleges," *American Education* 8, no. 2 (March 1972): 11.

15. "Education Amendments of 1972," *Public Law 318—June 23, 1972.*

16. Ibid.

17. See "Debate—Civil Rights Act of 1964" in Bernard Schwartz, ed., *Statutory History of the United States, Civil Rights, Part II* (New York: McGraw-Hill, 1970), pp. 1089–1453.

18. James S. Coleman, "The Evaluation of Equality of Educational Opportunity," in *On Equality of Educational Opportunity,* ed. Frederick Mosteller and Daniel P. Moynihan (New York: Random House, 1972), p. 147.

19. Ibid., pp. 148–50.

20. James S. Coleman et al., *Equality of Educational Opportunity* (Washington, D.C.: Government Printing Office, 1966), pp. 3–20, 35–217.

21. Ibid., p. 20.

22. Ibid., p. 21.

23. Ibid., p. 22.

24. Ibid.

25.   Ibid., p. 29.

26.   Arthur Jensen, "How Much Can We Boost I.Q. and Scholastic Achievement?" *Harvard Educational Review* 39, no. 1 (Winter 1969): 1–124.

27.   A history of this continuing debate can be found in Edgar Gumbert and Joel Spring, *The Superschool & The Superstate: American Education in the Twentieth Century, 1918–1970* (New York: John Wiley & Sons, 1974), pp. 87–115.

28.   For a discussion of this case, see William N. Greenbaum, "Serrano v. Priest: Implications for Educational Equality," in *Education for Whom?* ed., Charles Tesconi and Emanual Hurwitz (New York: Dodd, Mead, 1974), pp. 188–92.

29.   Marland, "Endless Renaissance," p. 7.

30.   John E. Coons, William H. Cline III, and Stephen D. Sugarman, *Private Wealth and Public Education* (Cambridge, Mass.: Harvard University Press, 1970).

31.   Ibid., pp. 3–5.

32.   See Thomas A. Shannon, "Rodriguez: A Dream Shattered or a Call for Finance Reform?" in Tesconi and Hurwitz, *Education for Whom?* pp. 192–99.

33.   Tesconi and Hurwitz, *Education for Whom?* pp. 34–66, 174–188.

34.   Richard M. Nixon, Message to Congress, 17 March 1972, reprinted in *Controversies in Education*, ed. Dwight W. Allen and Jeffrey C. Hecht (Philadelphia: W. B. Saunders, 1974), pp. 530–34.

35.   "Testimony of Elliot L. Richardson, Secretary, Health, Education, and Welfare, Friday 24 March 1972," *Equal Educational Opportunities Act of 1972, Hearings before the Subcommittee on Education of the Committee*

on Labor and Public Welfare, U.S. Senate, Ninety-second Congress, Second Session, March 24, 28, 30, April 6, 19, 25, 1972 (Washington, D.C.: Government Printing Office, 1972), p. 26.

36. Ibid., p. 32.

37. Ibid., p. 30.

38. Ibid., p. 33.

39. Ibid., p. 34.

40. For a study of the effect of these actions on the Office of Education, see John Merrow's, "The Politics of Federal Educational Policy: The Case of Educational Renewal," *Teachers College Record* 76, no. 1 (September 1974): 19–38.

41. See Daniel P. Moynihan's, *The Politics of a Guaranteed Income: The Nixon Administration and the Family Assistance Plan* (New York: Vintage Books, 1973).

42. Moynihan's attack on the philosophy of community action is given in his book *Maximum Feasible Misunderstanding: Community Action in the War on Poverty* (New York: Free Press, 1969).

43. The final report of this faculty seminar was published as previously noted in *On Equality of Educational Opportunity*.

44. Daniel P. Moynihan, "On the Education of the Urban Poor," in *Coping: Essays on the Practice of Government* (New York: Random House, 1973), pp. 167–194.

45. Daniel P. Moynihan, "Policy vs. Program in the 1970's," in ibid., pp. 272–84.

46. Daniel P. Moynihan, "Can Courts and Money Do It?" *New York Times,* 10 January 1972, reprinted in

Miriam Wasserman's *Demystifying School* (New York: Praeger, 1974), pp. 226–30.

47.   Ibid., p. 229.

48.   Gerard Colby Zilg, *DuPont: Behind the Nylon Curtain* (Englewood Cliffs, N.J.: Prentice-Hall, 1974), pp. 364–67.

49.   Ibid., pp. 377–78.

50.   Ibid., p. 377.

51.   For a historical study of how the interests of private foundations in education have served the needs of economic power, see Clarence Karier's "Testing for Order and Control in the Corporate Liberal State," in Clarence Karier, Paul Violas, and Joel Spring, *Roots of Crisis* (Chicago: Rand McNally, 1973), pp. 108–38.

INDEX

Abernathy, Ralph, 165, 166
Acheson, Dean, 144
Act for Bilingual Education Programs, 236
Adult education, 197
Advisory Commission on Universal Training, 55, 61
Agency for International Development, 231
Air Force Scientific Advisory Committee, 113
Allied High Commission, 41
Allott, Gordon, 107
Alternative school movement, 232
American Assocation for the Advancement of Science, 27, 121
American Association of School Administrators, 8, 15, 217–18
American Can Company, 82
American Coalition of Patriotic Societies, 8
American Council of Christian Laymen, 8
American Council of Education, 24
American Council of Learned Societies, 127
American Dilemma, An, 149, 150, 152–56, 187, 261
American Federation of Teachers, 103, 105, 260
American Government, 14

American High School Today, The, 38, 45, 214
American Historical Association, 15–16, 22, 23, 25, 26
American Institute of Biological Sciences Curriculum (BSCS), 126
American Legion, 59
American Management Association, 85
American Textbook Publishers Institute, 15
And Madly Teach: A Layman Looks at Public School Education, 27
Annual Report of the Council of Economic Advisers, The, 192–97
Anticommunist crusade, 7–15; Pasadena controversy, 7–12; Scarsdale book battle, 12–15
Anti-Communist League of America, 8
Antiintellectualism, 4, 5–7, 109, 113, 127; causes of, 6; in the schools, 15–37
Anti-Intellectualism in American Life, 5
Arkansas National Guard, 159–60
Army Ballistic Missile Agency, 112
Association for American Colleges, 70–71
Atomic Energy Commission, 85, 113

Baxter, James, 71
Beberman, Max, 121–22, 135
Begle, Edward G., 121
Belafonte, Harry, 173
Bell Telephone Laboratories, 85, 121
Bestor, Arthur, 15–18, 20–23, 25, 29, 32, 39, 127
Bill of Rights, 146
Billington, Ray Allen, 31
Birmingham Manifesto, 173
Bloom, Benjamin, 215
Boeing Aircraft Company, 255
Boston, school busing issue in, 250
Boston University, 165
Boulding, Kenneth E., 90
Boycotts, 145, 232
Braun, Wernher von, 112
Brigham, Carl, 43
Bronk, Detlev W., 108, 109, 110, 111
Brotherhood of Sleeping Car Porters, 142, 169
Brown, Oliver, 147
Brown v. *Board of Education of Topeka,* 141, 145–60, 175, 176, 181, 184, 246, 247, 260, 265
Bruner, Jerome S., 109, 128, 129, 130–31, 132, 133, 134, 137–38
Bulletin of the American Association of University Professors, 26–27
Bush, Douglas, 31
Bush, Vannevar, 40, 74–77, 96, 111, 115, 255, 263, 264
Busing. *See* School busing issue

Cairns, Stewart, 31
California   Anti-Communist League, 8
California Institute of Technology, 72, 113
Capitalism, 18, 164
Cardinal Principles Report (National Educational Association), 47, 58
Career education movement, 2, 230–58; beginning of, 233–36; busing issue, 245–50; equality of opportunity, 237–50; reduced federal spending for, 250–54; social forces shaping national policy and, 254–58; support for, 235–36
Carnegie Corporation, 42, 43, 77, 152

Carnegie Foundation, 215, 257, 261, 263, 264
Carnegie Institute of Technology, 40, 72
Carr, William G., 103–8
Case for Basic Education, The, 30–31
Celebrezze, Anthony J., 225–26
Central High School (Little Rock, Ark.), 156–60
Central Intelligence Agency, 34
Chaucer, Geoffrey, 109
Chein, Isidor, 149
Chemical Education Material Study (CHEM Study), 126
Chicago, de facto segregation in, 183–84
Chicago *Sunday Tribune,* 14
Christian Nationalist Crusade, 8
Circular 347 (War Department), 60
Citizenship program, 63
Civil Rights Act of 1957, 145, 169
Civil Rights Act of 1960, 145, 170
Civil Rights Act of 1964, 141, 145, 237, 238; significance of, 176–184
Civil Rights Commission, 169
Civil Rights Division (Department of Justice), 169
Civil rights movement, 2, 3, 140–85, 196, 213–14, 230, 257, 259; Cold War and, 141–45; legislation, 167–85; nonviolent confrontations, 162–67; Supreme Court and, 141, 145–60; use of mass media, 161–62
Civil War, 146
Civilian Conservation Corps, 59, 206
Clapp, Harold, 25, 26–27, 32
Clark, Kenneth, 149, 150–51, 152
Cloward, Richard, 200–4, 206
Coca-Cola Company, 82, 255
Cold war, 1, 2, 50, 53, 93, 259; civil rights and, 141–45; new curriculum and, 127; NDEA of 1958 and, 96–99
Coleman, James, 238
Coleman Report, 238–42, 247, 248, 251–52
College of the City of New York, 149
College   Entrance   Examination Board (CEEB), 43, 122–23
Columbia University, 11, 24, 81–82, 84–86, 96, 200

Commies Are After Your Kids, The, 9

Commission of School Plant Research, 24

Commission on Civil Rights, 145, 181, 184

Commission on Mathematics, 122–23

Commission on Universal Military Training, 209

Committee on the Conservation of Human Resources, 263

Committee on Equal Employment Opportunity, 175

Committee on Fair Employment Practice, 142

Committee on Manpower, 71

Committee on the Present Danger, 41, 77, 256, 263

Committee of Ten (National Education Association), 18

Communism: criticism of schools in U.S. and, 4, 6, 7–15, 33, 34, 36, 37, 45, 46, 47, 50; crusade against, 7–15; and textbook industry, 13–14, 15. *See also* Union of Soviet Socialist Republics (USSR)

Community action, theory of, 203–4, 223, 251

Comprehensive Health Services Project, 210

Conant, James Bryant, 37–51, 77–80, 96, 214–15; 234, 255, 256, 261, 263, 264

Congress of Racial Equality (CORE), 162, 163, 165, 171, 173, 260

Connor, Bull, 172, 174

Conservation of Human Resources Project, 82–83, 96, 254–55

Continental Can Company, 82, 255

Coughlin, Charles, 9

Council for Basic Education, 15, 26–36, 108, 111, 125, 127, 260, 264

Council of Economic Advisers, 188, 189, 192–97, 226

Counseling profession, 56–59

Counts, George, 11

Crain, Lucille Cardin, 13–14

Crozier Theological Seminary, 163

Culturally Deprived Child, The, 218, 219–20

Curriculum Committee, 115

Daley, Richard J., 184

Daughters of the American Revolution, 9, 14

Davis, Allison, 215

Day-care centers, 193

Defenders of American Education, 8–9

Deferment system (Selective Service), 69–70, 71

Delinquency and Opportunity, 200–1

Depression of 1929, 59

Desegregation, 145, 165, 167, 170; enforcement of, 156–160. *See also* Civil rights movement

Dewey, John, 29, 137, 138

Dexter Avenue Baptist Church (Montgomery, Ala.), 165

Diminished Mind, The: A Study of Planned Mediocrity in Our Public Schools, 27

Disadvantaged, the, educational attack on, 211–23

Discrimination, 89–90, 141–42, 143; *see also* Civil rights movement

Du Pont de Nemours and Company (E.I.), 82, 255

DuBridge, Lee A., 113

Dulles, Allen, 34

Dulles, John Foster, 42

Eastland, James O., 168

Ebenezer Baptist Church (Atlanta), 163

Economic discrimination, 143

Economic Opportunity Act of 1964, 186–87, 189, 203, 221, 223, 257; significance of, 204–11

Education and Cultural Deprivation Conference of 1964, 215

Education and Freedom, 33

Education and Manpower, 85

Educational Policies Commission, 39, 44, 217–18

Educational Records Bureau, 43

Educational Reviewer, 13

Educational Services, Inc., 127

Educational Testing Service (ETS), 42–43, 44, 84, 85, 115, 128, 136, 260

Educational Wastelands, 17

Eisenhower, Dwight D., 5, 41, 96–

100, 101, 104, 116, 158-60, 166-70, 173, 255-56, 265
Elementary and Secondary Education Act of 1965, 186, 187, 211, 257; congressional appropriations, 225; 1972 amendments to, 236; Senate hearings on, 216-17; significance of, 223-29
Eliot, Charles, 18
Elmstown's Youth, 212-13
Encyclopedia of Educational Research, 24
Engineering Society of Detroit, 33
Enlisted Reserve Corps, 65
Equalitarianism, philosophy of, 37
Equality of opportunity, 2, 237-50; busing and, 245-50; Coleman Report on, 238-42
Ervin, Sam, 177
Essay on Civil Disobedience, 163
Executive Order No. 8802 (Roosevelt), 141-42

Fadiman, Clifton, 31
Fair Employment Practices Commission, 145
Family Planning Project, 210
Farmer, James, 162
Fast, Howard, 13
Faubus, Orval, 159
Federal Bureau of Investigation (FBI), 170
Fellowship for Reconciliation, 162
Five Year Plan (USSR), 85-86
Ford Foundation, 81, 199-200, 203, 205, 215, 257, 261, 263, 265
Fourteenth Amendment, 146, 242, 243
Freedom rides, 171
Freedom-of-choice plans, 181
Fuller, Harry, 25, 27, 32

Gandhi, Mohandas K., 162, 164-65
Gardner, John W., 42
General Dynamics Corporation, 82, 255
General Electric Company, 72, 82, 255
General Foods Corporation, 82
General Mills Corporation, 77
General Motors Corporation, 255
Ginzberg, Eli, 82, 83
Goldwater, Barry, 103
Gordon, Kermit, 197

Goslin, Willard, 7-8, 9, 12, 13, 15
Government and Manpower, 85
Gray areas projects, 200
Great Cities School Improvement Studies, 218, 219
Groves, General L. R., 40
Guardians of American Education, 14

Hackett, David, 199
Hamilton, Alexander, 56
Harrington, Michael, 188-92, 195, 205
Harry Briggs, Jr. v. R. W. Elliot, 149
Harvard Club, 33
Harvard Cognition Project, 130-31
Harvard Educational Review, 241
Harvard University, 45, 77
Hayes, Carlton J. H., 31
Head Start Project, 197, 210, 211-12, 218, 221-23
Heller, Walter, 188, 192-93, 197-98, 205, 206
Henry Street settlement house, 200
Hess, Robert, 215
Hill, Lister, 103, 107
Hofstadter, Richard, 5
Houser, George, 162
Howard University, 213-14, 218
Humphrey, Hubert, 178-79, 185, 199, 207

Illinois Secondary School Curriculum Program, 20
Improving the Work Skills of the Nation, 85
Ineffective Soldier, The, 82
Information and Education Division (War Department), 63
Inhelder, Barbel, 133-34
Institute Rousseau of Geneva, 133
Integration, 105, 166; tokenism, 182-83
Interstate Commerce Commission, 172
IQ tests, 36, 43, 57, 220-21, 241; social-class bias of, 221

Jefferson, Thomas, 56
Jensen, Arthur, 241
Job Corps, 206, 207, 208
Johns Hopkins University, 238
Johns Manville Corporation, 77

Johnson, Lyndon B., 53, 66, 70, 72, 175–76, 183, 184, 192, 196–98, 204, 206, 213–14, 219, 223–25, 227–28, 232, 251
Jones & Laughlin Steel Corporation, 72
Junior High School Mathematics, 124

Katz, Michael, 87
Kennedy, John F., 103, 172–76, 188–89, 192, 196, 199
Kennedy, Robert F., 174, 199, 216, 217
Keppel, Francis, 216–17, 226–27
Keppel, Frederick P., 152
Kiesling, Herbert, 249
Kilpatrick, William Heard, 9, 11
King, Martin Luther, 162, 163–67, 169, 171–72, 173, 174–75, 257, 265
Koerner, James D., 30–32
Korean war, 41, 65

League of Nations, 64
Legal Services Project, 210
Lenin, Nikolai, 164
Lewis, Fulton, Jr., 14
Life, 35, 117
Life-adjustment education movement, 19–21
Little Rock crisis (1957), 158–60
Lost Divisions, The, 82
Loyalty oaths, 15
Lynchings, 143, 145, 161
Lynd, Albert, 23–25

McCarthy, Joseph, 5
Madison, James, 56
Magruder, Frank Abbott, 14
Manhattan project, 40, 255, 256
Mann, Horace, 17
Manpower channeling policies, 2, 3, 52–92, 93, 113, 186, 228, 259; National Manpower Council, 81–92; in the public schools, 56–59; Selective Service debates, 66–81; universal military training, 59–65
Manpower Policies for a Democratic Society, 81, 85
Manpower race, 7, 52, 53, 85–86, 89
Manpower shortage, 52, 53–56, 73; causes of, 54
March on Washington Movement, 142, 167, 172, 174, 175

Marland, Sidney P., 233–35, 242–43
Marshall, Thurgood, 170
Martin Luther King and the Montgomery Story, 171
Marx, Karl, 14, 164
Mason, William Smith, 31
Mass media, racial injustice and (1950s), 161–62
Massachusetts Institute of Technology, 111
Metropolitan Life Insurance, 13
Mills, C. Wright, 39
Minute Men, 3
Miseducation of American Teachers, The, 31
Mobilization for Youth, 200, 203
Monsanto Chemical Corporation, 72
Montgomery bus boycott, 165–67
Morse, Wayne, 79, 103
Mosteller, Frederick, 251
Moynihan, Daniel Patrick, 218, 251–54
Murrow, Edward R., 33
Muste, A. J., 162, 163
Myrdal, Gunnar, 149, 150, 152–53, 187, 188, 192, 196

National Academy of Sciences, 31, 80, 108, 128
National Assocation for the Advancement of Colored People (NAACP), 143, 158, 170, 173, 180, 260, 265; *Brown* case, 145–50
National Assocation of Manufacturers, 85
National Assocation of Secondary School Principals, 35
National Commission for the Defense of Democracy through Education, 3
National Committee for Children and Youth, 199
National Conference on Education and Cultural Deprivation, 218
National Council for American Education, 8–9
National curriculums, development of, 93–139; NDEA of 1958, 96–113; the new curriculum, 113–28; Woods Hole Conference on (1959), 128–39
National Defense Education Act of 1958 (NDEA), 53, 94, 96–113, 138,

177, 256, 259, 262, 264; additions by Congress to, 102; cold-war concerns and, 96–99; congressional hearings on, 103–13
National Defense Fellowship program, 100
National Defense Research Committee, 40
National Education Association (NEA), 3, 18, 44, 47, 58, 85, 103–5, 107, 108, 217–18, 260, 264–65
National Institute of Education, 253
National Institute for Mental Health, 200
National Manpower Council, 81–92, 96, 255, 263; Columbia University conferences, 84–86; reports of, 85–92; role of secondary school in, 86–89
National Merit Scholarships, 136
National Peace Foundation, 139, 263
National Science Board, 108
National Science Foundation, 40–41, 44, 52, 74–76, 77–78, 85, 93–94, 96, 98, 99, 108, 109, 111–12, 138, 177, 256, 259, 263, 265; congressional appropriations, 116; established, 94; new curriculum movement, 113–28; teacher-training activities (1956), 117–18
National Science Foundation Act of 1950, 76
National Science Reserve, 76
National Scientific Personnel Board, 72–73
National Security Resources Board, 53–54, 72, 85
National Service Corps, 205
National Training Security Corps, 66
National Youth Administration, 59, 197
Naval Research Advisory Committee, 113
Nazi party, 28, 112
New curriculum movement, 113–28; cold war and, 127; Physical Science Study Committee, 113–20; School Mathematics Study Group, 120–26
New math, 121
New York Times, 253
Newton, Sir Isaac, 109

Nixon, Richard, 166, 232–33, 236, 237, 242–46, 250–51, 253, 258
Nonviolent confrontation, doctrine of, 162–67
North American Airlines, 255
North Atlantic Treaty Organization (NATO), 41, 96
North Carolina A&T College, 171

Office of Defense Mobilization, 85
Office of Economic Opportunity, 206, 209–11, 251
Office of Scientific Research and Development, 40
Ohlin, Lloyd, 202–4, 206
Other America, The: Poverty in the United States, 188–89

Paine, Thomas, 13
Parks, Rosa, 165–66
Peenemünde rocket center, 112
Permanent Scientific and Scholarly Commission on Secondary Education, 25, 26
Physical Science Study Committee (PSSC), 94, 111, 113–20, 126, 128
Piaget, Jean, 129, 133
Plessy, Homer, 146
Plessy v. Ferguson, 149
Policy for Scientific and Professional Manpower, A, 85
Policy for Skilled Manpower, A, 85
Poverty: culture of, 187–98; Council of Economic Advisers on, 192–97; disadvantaged and, 211–23; Harrington on, 188–92; income level, 193; legislation for, 204–11, 223–29; unemployment and, 188–90, 193; youth and, 198–204
President's Advisory Commission, 61–65, 67
President's Committee on Civil Rights, 143
President's Committee on Juvenile Delinquency, 199, 200
President's Task Force on Manpower Legislation, 207
Princeton University, 77
Principia, 109
Private Wealth and Public Education, 243
Proceedings of a Conference on the Utilization of Scientific and Professional Manpower, 85

Process of Education, The, 109, 128
Program for National Security, A, 61–65
Progressive education, battle against, 7–12
Progressive Education Increases Juvenile Delinquency, 9
Prosser, Charles A., 18–19
Public Policies and Manpower Resources, 85

Quackery in the Public Schools, 23–24
Quotas, school segregation, 181–82, 183

RAND Corporation, 121
Randolph, A. Philip, 142, 167, 168–69
Rauschenbusch, Walter, 163–64
Record cards, 48
Redstone Arsenal, 112
Reserve Officers Training Corps (ROTC), 65, 69, 70, 71, 177
Reserve Specialist Training Corps, 72
Revere, Paul, 3
Richardson, Elliot, 247–49, 250
Rickover, Vice-Admiral Hyman G., 32–37, 107
Riessman, Frank, 218, 219–20
RockefellerFoundation,215
Rockefeller Institute of Medical Research, 108
Rodriguez v. *San Antonio Independent School District*, 245
Rohm & Haas Company, 72
Roosevelt, Franklin D., 5, 40, 55, 60–61, 141, 142
Rosenberg, Anna, 67, 70
Rousseau, Jean-Jacques, 14
Russell Sage Foundation, 215

Saenger, Gerhart, 149
Saturday Review of Literature, 9
Satyagraha, Gandhian technique of, 162
Scholastic Aptitude Test (SAT), 43
School busing issue, 232, 237; equality of opportunity and, 245–50; of parochial students, 224
School Mathematics Study Group (SMSG), 94, 95, 113, 120–26, 128, 132; congressional appropriations, 124; goal of, 121, 125–26

Schools: anticommunist crusade, 7–15; antiintellectualism in, 15–37; Conant's study, 37–51; criticism of, 1–51, 52, 93; manpower channeling in, 56–59; nineteenth century, 1–2, 17; Soviet Union, communism and, 4, 6, 7–15, 33, 34, 36, 37, 45, 46, 47, 50
Science—The Endless Frontier, 75
Scientific Committees of the Selective Service System, 80
Scientific Manpower Advisory Committee, 72–74, 76, 79
Scientific Monthly, 27
Segregation, 105, 141, 146–47, 166, 172, 232, 238
Select Committee on Postwar Military Policy of the Congress, 61
Selective Service Act, 31
Selective Service College Qualification Test, 80, 83–84
Selective Service System, 31, 40, 52, 56, 65, 85, 228, 230, 231, 256, 259, 262, 263; debate over, 66–81; deferment system, 69–70, 71; qualification tests, 23
Selective Training and Service Act of 1940, 55
Senior Opportunity Services Project, 210
Serrano v. *Priest*, 241–42
Shriver, Sargent, 204, 205–6, 211, 221, 222–23
Sit-ins, 145, 171, 175, 231
Slums and Suburbs, 214–15
Smith, Gerald L. K., 9
Smith, H. Alexander, 107
Smith, Mortimer, 26, 27–30, 32
Smith College, 45
Social Frontier, 11
Social Security Administration, 193
Socialism, 12
Society of Business Magazine Editors, 33
Sons of the American Revolution, 9, 14
South Pacific, 159
Southern Christian Leadership Conference (SCLC), 162, 166–67, 171, 173, 260
Sputnik I, 38, 96, 97, 105, 116, 118
Standard Oil Company (New Jersey), 82, 255

States' Rights party, 145
Stevenson, Adlai, 5
Strategic Air Command, 97
Student Deferment and National Manpower Policy, 81
Student deferment system, 83
Student Non-Violent Coordinating Committee (SNCC), 162, 171–72, 173, 260
Study of American Intelligence, A, 43
Swann v. *Charlotte-Mecklenburg Board of Education,* 245–50

Teachers College (Columbia University), 11, 24
Teller, Edward, 112–13
Textbook market, 94–95, 125–26, 260; communism and, 13–14, 15
Thomas, Charles A., 72
Thomas-Hill-Taft Bill of 1948, 104
Thoreau, Henry David, 163
Thurmond, Strom, 103
Till, Emmett, 158
Time, 5, 35, 117
Title VI (Civil Rights Act of 1964), 176–85, 223
To Secure These Rights, 143
Totalitarianism, 14, 28, 50, 141, 164
Truman, Harry, 55–56, 61, 67, 68, 76, 104, 143, 145, 146, 209
Trytten, M. H., 31, 80–81, 108
Trytten plan, 31, 80–81, 108

Unemployment, 199; during the 1930s, 59; poverty and, 198–204
Union of Soviet Socialist Republics (USSR), 1, 7, 96, 101, 113, 135, 227, 255; criticism of schools in U.S. and, 4, 6, 7–15, 33, 34, 36, 37, 45, 46, 47, 50; Five Year Plan, 85–86; manpower race, 52, 53, 85–86, 89
U.S. Constitution, 55, 146, 148, 242
U.S. Department of Defense, 66–71, 85, 177
U.S. Department of Health, Education, and Welfare, 99–102, 180, 218, 225–26, 247, 250
U.S. Department of Justice, 169
U.S. Department of Labor, 205
U.S. Office of Education, 20, 101–2, 179–82, 183–84, 215, 233, 242, 248, 261, 266
U.S. Public Health Service, 67

U.S. Rubber Corporation, 255
U.S. Supreme Court, 55, 165, 166, 167, 180–81, 224, 237, 242, 244–45; *Brown* case, 145–50; civil rights rulings, 141, 145–60
U.S. War Department, 59, 60, 63
Universal military training, 41, 55–56; advisory commission recommendations, 61–65; citizenship program, 63; FDR on, 60–61; manpower channeling and, 59–65; Selective Service debate, 66–81; Truman on, 61
Universal Military Training and Service Act of 1951, 66, 256
University of California, 77
University of Chicago, 77, 215
University of Illinois, 20, 22, 27, 122, 132, 135
University of Illinois Committee on School Mathematics (UICSM), 121–22, 128
University of Maryland Mathematics Project, 122–23
University of South Carolina, 72
Upward Bound Project, 210
Urban and Rural Community Action Programs, 206, 209

Vaughan, Herbert E., 122
Veterans Administration (VA), 67
Vietnam war, 183, 231, 232
Vigilante groups, 4
Vocational education, 19, 48, 208–9, 212
Vocational guidance counseling, 2, 56–57, 215, 232
Volunteers in Service to America (VISTA), 205
V-2 rocket, 34, 112

War of 1812, 255
War on Poverty, 3, 53, 186–229, 237, 251, 257, 263
Warren, Earl, 148
Watts Riot, 232
Wayne State University, 45
Westinghouse Science Talent Search Award Ceremony, 33
Whaley, R. M., 108, 109, 128
White Citizens Councils, 157
Who Controls American Education? : A Guide for Laymen, 31–32
Who's Who, 13

Williams College, 71
Willis, Benjamin C., 172, 183–84
Wilson, Charles, 255
Womanpower, 85, 89–90
Woods Hole Conference (1959), 128–139
Work in the Lives of Married Women, 85
Work-Training Programs, 208
World War I, 34, 43, 57
World War II, 3, 5, 10, 34, 39, 54, 55, 65, 139, 141, 255

Yale University, 121

Yearbook of the American Association of School Administrators, 29
Youth Conservation Corps, 197, 206–7
Youth Employment Bill, 199
Youth Movement of the Methodist Church, 162
Youth Programs (Economic Opportunity Act of 1964), 206–9

Zacharias, Jerrold, 114, 116
Zoll, Allen, 8, 9, 14